Theresa,

SMYRNA SPOTLIGHTS

JOURNEY THROUGH LOCAL SMYRNA

BRITTANY SCARLETT STEVENS

Enjoy the journey!

Copyright © 2021 by Brittany Scarlett Stevens

All rights reserved.

No part of this book may be reproduced in any form or by any electronic or mechanical means, including information storage and retrieval systems, without written permission from the author, except for the use of brief quotations in a book review.

Edited by Zach Bohannon and Jennifer Collins

Author photo by Barbara Potter Photography

CONTENTS

Foreword	vii
Introduction	ix
Raborn Insurance	1
Jo's Custom Cakes And Catering	8
Biscuit Media Group	14
Bella Vista Coffee Shop	23
Red Wagon Nursery	32
Vanessa Haley, Makeup Artist/Aesthetician	38
The Casual Pint	43
Dow Smith Company, Inc.	52
Breaking Bread	61
Buckle And Hide Leather	69
Bob's Barbecue	80
Nesting Project	86
Tom's Florist	96
Walden Pumpkin Farm	103
Racquel Peebles, Attorney At Law	108
Custom Cup Sleeves	118
The Salt Barn	127
Game Galaxy Arcade	134
Sarah's Clean Team	140
The Remington Room	146
Front Street Sign Company	151
Courtnie R. Dunn, Author	163
Dr. Automotive	171
Affi Pest & Wildlife	177
Wilson's Photography	Bridal Country	184
Legacy Wine & Spirits	192
Cloud 9 Mobile Grooming	198
Janarty's Homemade Ice Cream	206
Stevens Law, PLLC	215
Smyrna Ready Mix	221
The Social Nutrition	228

Faded University	237
Marty Luffman, State Farm Insurance	243
Barbara Potter Photography	251
Designs By Sylvanye	259
Carpe Cafe & Carpe Artista	269
Glam House	Glam House Skin	279
Gil's Ace Hardware	283
Azteca Bakery And Eatery	294
Ginger Farms	299
Tony's Shoe Repair	304
Steve John's Appliance & Parts	309
Crimson Security Service	314
Family And Cosmetic Dentistry Of Smyrna	321
Smyrna Printing & Design	325
Zach Bohannon, Author	333
How To Support Local	339
Acknowledgments	343
About the Author	347

For Smyrna, and my beloved family.

FOREWORD

By Mary Esther Reed, Smyrna Mayor
 The Learning Circle, Owner

Welcome to the Town of Smyrna. I'm Mary Esther Reed and it is my privilege to serve as the Mayor of this great community. I have lived here my entire life and have watched our community grow from 4,500 residents to over 50,000. Being Mayor is a part-time position in Smyrna; my full-time job is as a small business owner.

I believe every business is a key contributor to a healthy local economy, but small businesses are the backbone of communities across this country. Smyrna is a vibrant, growing community, but remains a small Town at heart. As Mayor, it is important to me that our Town leadership promotes and supports local businesses to foster connectivity and strengthen relationships here in Smyrna.

Small, locally owned businesses are unique and bring character to our community. But they are so much more. I believe that the foundation of a strong community is neighbor helping neighbor, and small businesses are an essential component of this foundation. These entrepreneurs are the ones who support local events, local schools, local non-profits and foster new and old traditions that create and maintain our small-Town charm. Small business owners have planted roots in Smyrna, weaving themselves into the fabric of our community, making residents and visitors feel welcome. My hope is that our current residents and those moving to our Town choose to plant their roots here because they feel connected and want to be a part of our wonderful community. I invite each of you to the Town of Smyrna so you can see what a vibrant community we have planted and continue to grow.

INTRODUCTION

I am what you would call a born and bred local, having had the incredible fortune of living my entire life in Smyrna, Tennessee. I grew up here, eventually co-founding a law practice with my brother, Robert, and have been very involved in my church and the community, as well as in the nonprofit space, for as long as I can remember. To put it simply, Smyrna is my home. This community has been so wonderful to myself and my family. I've also enjoyed having a front row seat to the innovation driving the exponential growth taking place in our town, thanks in large part to many of the individuals featured throughout this book.

My intention and overall purpose for this book is to educate and inspire each of us to be more intentional with our spending habits and to support our local businesses as much as possible, all in order to preserve our small (but growing!) town's uniqueness.

As of this publication, I am Court Clerk for the Town of Smyrna. I was first elected in 2016 and have proudly held the seat ever since. That said, I never set out to run for public office. Prior to my current role, I enjoyed my (very) private citizen status as a practicing attorney. However, when there came an immediate need for someone to fill the seat due to a sudden vacancy, I said a prayer, took a leap of faith, and stepped up to serve my community. Serving in this capacity has been the highest honor of my professional career to date, and I will always be grateful to my constituents for giving me this amazing opportunity. My elected position has provided me a platform I may not have otherwise had, and I strive to use my platform in a positive manner that inspires, uplifts, and empowers others. Also, I hope to encourage others to give back and support our local community as much as possible: to shop local, buy local, eat local, play local... you get the idea. There are many social benefits to supporting small and local businesses—and I promise you'll learn about them throughout this book. Namely, our small businesses give back to the community and fuel our local economy. They flavor our community and serve as the fabric of our small town's story. These are the businesses that step up to sponsor our Little League teams and show up to support our local nonprofits. In fact, through the "Clerks for Coats" coat drive, several of the small businesses spotlighted throughout this book have helped the Smyrna Court Clerk's Office collect nearly 1,000 winter clothing donations over the last four years, all for children in our very own community.

I could go on and on about the value of these businesses and their stories, but that's what this book is about: I'll let these inspiring business owners share their unique stories all in their own words.

Why publish this book to showcase some of our small businesses, and why now? As much as these businesses have helped our community, we all know they've recently needed our support more than ever. The COVID-19 pandemic tragically shattered many small and local businesses, and it did so on a global scale. Smyrna's economy was no exception. So although I've done my best to use my platform to promote the importance of supporting local businesses over the years, I knew I had to do more when our businesses took a hit. I genuinely *wanted* to do more. When thinking about how to accomplish something for our town, I came back to the fact that I identify as a lifelong learner and voracious reader, reading between 50-100 books each year—primarily nonfiction books on law, business development, and personal development. The concept of writing a book to spotlight some of our amazing local business leaders came from marrying my immense love for reading and my dream of someday publishing my own book. Hence, *Smyrna Spotlights: Journey Through Local Smyrna* was born.

There are so many fabulous small businesses right here in Smyrna. I proudly call many of the individuals featured throughout this book my dear friends. They are entrepreneurs, innovators, path-breaking pioneers, and idealists who've been bold enough to manifest the American Dream of launching an independent business and executing their vision to make their community, and indeed the world, a better place. Their stories are powerful, and will transform your beliefs on what it takes to own and operate a small business in the post-COVID-19 world.

Smyrna Spotlights is a celebration of our small businesses in Smyrna: a celebration of community cultivation, the resiliency to persist when times get tough, an unwavering dedication to our neighbors' life work and overall missions. It is a celebration of the journey inspiring millions in local communities all around the world via the movement to #SupportLocal, and so much more.

I hope you are just as inspired by our neighbors' incredible entrepreneurial journeys as I am. So, sit back, relax, grab a cup of coffee from one of our superb local cafes, and join me in this captivating journey through local Smyrna, spotlighting some of our town's locally owned small businesses. And when you're done reading, please be sure to support our local businesses and share their stories with your friends, families, and networks. We must all do our part to support our small businesses in order for them to survive.

Lastly, in wrapping up this introduction, I should mention that the net proceeds from this book will be donated to local nonprofits. Now, let's begin our journey....

-Brittany Scarlett Stevens

RABORN INSURANCE
AS TOLD BY BAKER RABORN

Website: www.Raborn.net
Email: baker@raborn.net
Phone: (615)-459-4145

Tell me about your (small) business.

Derek, Greg, and I all shared a room so that dad could start our agency in our third bedroom in 1973. At that time, dad worked for Travelers Insurance. The only other agent in town had just closed, so he decided to start his own agency.

We sell around 75% commercial, and the rest personal and life insurance. Dad retired about twenty years ago, and Derek, Wayne, and I have owned and operated the agency since then.

. . .

What is your favorite part about having a small business in Smyrna?

The community. When you have a business, it gives you the opportunity to get involved in helping your community in ways that might otherwise be complicated. All three of us are involved on many levels with different groups. Small business is very important to local organizations, and Smyrna still has that small town feel even with all the growth, which makes it extra special.

How did growing up in Smyrna shape you?

Back then, we were a small town. Everyone knew who you were and who your parents were. I remember saving my money and riding my bike to the Five and Dime for a toy and candy, or calling Mr. Mingle to ask permission to camp at the dam on his property when floating the creek. You always felt safe. My father used to volunteer us for stuff because he wanted to teach us to be volunteers, which is why I did the same with my kids. But for me, I feel like I grew up with Smyrna. The older I get, it seems the town has grown with me. Overall, the officials have managed it in a positive way.

What's the first thing you do every morning to start your day on the right foot?

Always coffee with Rhonda and the news, so we can talk about our day. We then will have a glass with a fresh lemon squeezed into water, have for many years and seems to work well.

. . .

What are you most excited about for your small business?

Right now, we are finally remodeling the inside. But as far as business goes, many people do not realize our capabilities. We are actually licensed in multiple states for commercial, and can do very large contractor bonds and liability all over. We have the companies, the name, the location, and everything they need to continue to build it. Derek, Wayne, and I took it beyond what my father ever expected, and I would love to see what the next generation could do.

What does a typical day look like for you?

There is no typical day, some are slow and easy, many are busy and stressful. Some days I sell policies, while other days I fight adjusters over claims. I think that is one thing that makes us different; we will actually get into the trenches with our clients and fight for them. We have, on many occasions, made adjusters change their minds, but even we cannot win them all. My biggest stress is knowing I am responsible for protecting someone's financial investments in their car, home, business, or life, and being afraid I missed something.

What element of your business do you take the most pride in?

Service. I tell people I am not in sales, I am in service. Anyone who knows me knows I don't sell, but if you have a problem, I enjoy helping. I believe if I were more of a salesman that I might make more money. But in a society of pushy sales, cold calls, and mass mailing, I think word-of-mouth based off good service really makes us different.

What has been your biggest business milestone to date that you are most proud of?

We will celebrate our fiftieth anniversary in 2023. I have been here thirty-three years so far, and thinking of us as still being a locally owned family business after fifty years is exciting.

What advice would you give to someone wanting to pursue a career in insurance?

Learn the products. I have had to tell some agents about the policy forms they sell. I cannot imagine how anyone could sell something they do not know in depth. Also take "Certified Insurance Counselor" (CIC). You will learn insurance in depth, how to read contracts, and how to help your clients with proper protection and claims. The industry always changes, educate yourself to keep up.

What has been the best piece of business advice you have ever received?

See people. If you are stuck away in an office you are not being seen. Volunteering is a great way to see people too, that way you get to help out, and others get to meet you in a positive way. Dad always said, "even if you are just going out to dinner you are still doing business."

Who has been the most influential person or mentor to you during your entrepreneurial journey and why?

My father, not only in business, but in life. I was blessed to be raised by a wonderful set of parents and Dad had a special insight not only into business, but people and life. He would give us his opinion and advice, and always had our backs. He gave us the freedom to try, and if we messed up, he would help. He was always our biggest cheerleader and pushed us to be better.

What have been some of your biggest business challenges you have faced and how have you overcome them?

I was at a corporate meeting fifteen years ago when the CEO of a major company said that since people now look at insurance as a commodity that the company would start treating it like one.

That is how our industry went away from service to pressure sales. We lost many clients who were just price shopping, to realizing insurance is a protective blanket over your properties, and not a commodity. We stayed the course. Many people who left eventually came back when they realized there really is something to having local customer service.

What does success mean to you?

Being able to sleep at night with a clear conscious, and pay my bills with enough to enjoy life and travel with Rhonda, and hopefully retire one day. We have a tight family we love spending time with, great friends, and our health, not much else in life I could wish for.

What do you enjoy doing in your spare time?

I am happiest when all my family is over, and we are having a big cookout on our patio. Rhonda's mother is one of eighteen, so she has a lot of family.

I am on the board for the Senior Activity Center, Shirley's Way TN, and the Smyrna Rotary Club board. My favorite event by far is the Wings of Freedom Rotary Fish Fry. I remember years ago my father saying, "I love a good party." I think of this every year when we fire up the fryers. It is really special not just for the fellowship, but the spirit of what it brings, and the support it gives the community. I work harder that day than any day of the year, and I love every second of it and the people I do it with.

. . .

How big of an impact has social media had on your small business?

We have always based our business on word-of-mouth. I have seen other businesses have great success with it, and one was hurt with a vicious targeted case that had people from around the country piling on falsely, so it can be a minefield.

What does supporting local mean to you?

Everything. I buy local first, and if something is not here, I look for US-owned businesses. We have to support our local businesses if we want them to support us.

Local matters. When I get new tires, I go to a locally owned place. When I need supplies, I try to go local. I will pay a little more to get something from Gil's Ace Hardware rather than a big box store, because Ace supports local charities. We often have people come by for sponsorships, but when we ask them who their insurance is with, they usually have someone online.

People need to understand that if you spend your money with a locally owned business, you will help support local organizations. Also, in our case, if you buy local, you will have a local agent who can explain policies and help you fight, if needed. A 1-800 number will not provide that level of customer service, nor sponsor much at the local level. So, when you go to a local business and ask for support for your kids, ask yourself: do you support local?

Ask any Little League team, or high school program if major online retailers support them. Did a big box build the playground? Did the out of state online insurance agency help with their fundraiser, or even care where Smyrna is? If people do not support local businesses, they will not have the community they want because big business does not care too much about how clean our streets are, or how good our ball fields look, or anything except more sales in a region.

.   .   .

Where do you see yourself and your small business 5-10 years from now?

In the next five years, I hope to have the next generation in training them. It will take at least another five years to get them up to speed, and probably ten years to take over. If we can get the right people we trust to protect our reputation and business, then I see the agency being stronger, and bigger than ever, and I hope to slow down some and enjoy more family time, and fish fries.

We've loved being a part of your journey. What's coming next that we can be a part of to support you?

Our fiftieth anniversary is in 2023. We look forward to it and hope to be stronger than ever then.

Is there anything else you would like people to know about you or your small business?

There is a huge difference in coverage. If all you do is look at price, you are missing the majority of the product, especially in property like homes. Everyone thinks the limits on the front tell everything, but in actuality, that is just one small part. The exclusions and endorsements are the real coverage and people who just look at price are missing the purpose of why they are buying insurance in the first place. Read the quotes, read the coverages, and ask questions.

A good agent will have a good general knowledge of all markets, not just the one they are selling. Never ever get it from a 1-800 number, because you will not be able to fight them on your own, that's when clients usually return.

Even if I do not have your insurance, if you have an insurance question I will discuss it and not pressure you for a quote. I believe the more everyone knows about insurance, the better it is for me, so I like to educate people. Insurance will affect you the rest of your life no matter what you do, so educate yourself.

JO'S CUSTOM CAKES AND CATERING
AS TOLD BY JO WEST

Website: www.JosCakesandCatering.com
Facebook: Jos Custom Cakes and Catering
Instagram: @Joscustomcakesandcatering
Phone: 615-459-9305

Tell me about your (small) business.

Jo's Custom Cakes and Catering opened June 13, 2003. We are a family-owned business located at 117 Spring Circle.

We provide all types of food services, including off-premises catering for any occasion. Our specialties are wedding and corporate events like Christmas parties, grand openings, customer appreciations, and milestone events. We can assist with all your food and beverage needs, as well as staffing, DJs, bartenders, rentals, and a complete line of desserts. We are known for our 3D sculpted cakes that look real dogs, characters from movies- you name it, we have probably made one! We are also known for our wedding cakes that taste as good as they look.

The most important thing you will receive from us is our service. We always try to go the extra mile for all our customers. There is no event too small for us. If it is important to you, it is important to us.

What inspired you start a custom cake and catering business?

I have always loved cooking and baking. I taught myself to bake when I was blessed with a brother at the age of fourteen. I just wanted to make birthday cakes for him. People would see my cakes and ask me to make one for them. At that time, I was an auto mechanic, working on cars in our family business. When it closed, I started working at Crosslin Supply, mixing paint (which is a lot like icing-you start with something white and make it a color). I started catering from my home, and in 1998, I decided to go to Culinary School to make sure I was doing everything right. I was accepted at the Opryland Hotel Culinary Institute and spent two years and nine months there, working in every restaurant and food division.

I earned an Associate's Degree in Applied Science with a concentration in Food Science from Vol State. Once I graduated, I assumed I could rent a kitchen, which turned out to be non-existent. My parents had a pole barn in their backyard, and after begging (pestering) the Town for months, they allowed me to build my commercial kitchen where the pole barn was. I am truly fortunate. I walk to work every day! We opened our doors in 2003, with my nephew's wedding the first job we did the first week we were open.

What is your favorite part about having a small business in Smyrna?

The people we meet. Smyrna is getting bigger, but it has not lost its small-town feel (yet!). Southern hospitality is what we base our business on! We treat people the way we want to be treated. We welcome any and everyone. Once you have done business with us, you are family. We love our customers!

What are you most excited about for your small business?

I am most excited with some changes that are coming soon. The business is growing, and we are always watching for new things to make it better!

What does a typical day look like for you?

A typical day usually starts at 7:00 a.m. I check emails, start the coffee, and check on what needs to be done for the day. We decorate, design, and "build" until 12:30 p.m. At 12:30 p.m., we watch (are addicted to) *The Bold and the Beautiful.* We watch while we eat lunch (sometimes). After lunch, back to work, answering phones, answering emails, making buttercream, baking cakes. My day usually ends around 9-10 p.m. I walk home and feed my cat, Blackie, and head to bed.

What is the biggest lesson you've learned in owning and operating a small business?

How much time you actually put into your business. It becomes your life.

·   ·   ·

Are there any favorite mantras you live your life by?

One of my favorite quotes is in a little book we received in Culinary School. "You will have plenty of time to sleep when you die."

What has been your biggest business milestone to date that you are most proud of?

Making a birthday cake for Tony Stewart (NASCAR driver) and seeing someone Tweet about eating it from the Charlotte Speedway! They liked it!

We have been commissioned to build and bake gingerbread houses for the MTSU president's mansion, often replicas of campus buildings since 2013. Also, in 2019, I created a gingerbread house replica of one of the most recognized iconic landmarks, the historic Rutherford County Courthouse. That went viral!

What have been some of your biggest business challenges you have faced and how have you overcome them?

Of course, 2020 has been our biggest challenge so far. Everything cancelled in March, April, and May, but thanks to some awesome customers, we pivoted to meals-to-go, and they ordered those- some every week! Thank you! Before that, the recession of 2008 was a real blow to our business. Before that, we mostly did corporate catering. We pivoted big time and tried to diversify to not have all our eggs in one basket!

What advice would you give to someone wanting to pursue a career similar to yours?

I always tell people wanting to get into either cake/bakery or catering to go work for someone else first. Learn as much as they can and then they will know if they want this to be their life.

What has been the best piece of business advice you have ever received?

It was from my dad, John Wright, Jr. When we had the auto repair shop, he always told me to treat people the way I wanted to be treated. Be honest and do the best I can. One of my favorite quotes was from Sylvia Weinstock- the Queen of cakes. "Wow costs money!"

Who has been the most influential person or mentor to you during your entrepreneurial journey and why?

My mother, Fran Wright. At eight-three, she is still working with me every day. I hope to be as active as she is when I am her age.

What do you enjoy doing in your spare time?

I love to paint (on canvas) and volunteer. I am a part of the Smyrna Citizens Police Academy Alumni Association and have been the recording secretary for years. I also volunteer with A Soldier's Child Foundation, teaching cake decorating classes and donating cakes for the local children's birthdays. I work with a 501C organization in Franklin called Brightstone. It is a school for disabled adults. I started with them in 2000, and after graduating from school, took over their Christmas Concert Catering. The first year we might have had fifty people. In 2019, the attendance was approximately eight hundred and fifty people. Our gift to them is a giant cake and all the catering for their Christmas program. Finally, I work with the Tony Stewart Foundation, which raises funds for disabled children, animals, and injured race car drivers. (Three of my favorite things... well, race car drivers, not the injured part!) We are members of SiMA (Smyrna Independent Merchant's Association) and the Chamber of Commerce. We also donate food to the Rotary Fish Fry.

How big of an impact has social media had on your small business?

Social media has had an amazing influence on our business. Facebook has given us a platform to show people our work and engage with them. We have followers all around the world now!

What does supporting local mean to you?

I have always believed in supporting local business. We will always have the national stores, but the local 'mom and pop' businesses are my favorite. If a local company supports me, I will support them. We learned at SiMA that 68% of each dollar spent at a local establishment stays in the community. That helps everyone! These local businesses are our neighbors, friends, and family.

Jo's Custom Cakes and Catering has won several prestigious awards voted on by the community, including several Best of Main Street Awards and several Ruthie's Awards for Favorite Catering. Where do you see yourself and your small business 5-10 years from now?

We are really hoping we can expand our building, as we are out of space.

Is there anything else you would like people to know about you or your small business?

One thing about us that I do not think most people realize is that we are a "one stop shop" for all your event needs. We supply awesome food, amazing desserts-not just cakes (we have a line of cheesecakes!), staffing, rentals, DJs, and almost anything else you need to create the perfect event! Wouldn't it be so much easier to have to deal with one company instead of five or six?

BISCUIT MEDIA GROUP
AS TOLD BY CHRIS HEISELMAN

Website: www.biscuitmediagroup.com
Facebook: Biscuit Media Group
Instagram: @biscuitmediagroup

Tell me about your (small) business.

Biscuit Media Group began as a boutique marketing and PR firm in Chicago in 1994. My wife, Lori Heiselman, began by offering a full range of publicity, including creating and executing publicity plans for clients, crafting news releases and building and maintaining relationships with various media outlets all over the country.

Initially, Biscuit's clientele focused mainly on bands and musicians in the faith-based market. Eventually, as the company became well-established, the scope of services grew to include media publicity for authors and feature films.

After relocating to the Nashville area, Lori and I met and eventually got married. At the time I was a director, writer, videographer and editor and had worked in the television industry for more than twenty years. I had recently relocated to Smyrna and started a new venture as a broadcasting instructor for Metro Nashville Public Schools.

During the course of many face-to-face meetings and dinners, we discovered that most clients were in need of video services to varying degrees. Authors wanted video book trailers, testimonials or just explainer videos for their websites and social media.

The 2010s were truly a golden age for harnessing the power contained in a short marketing video. Social media platforms like Facebook and Twitter were still relatively new, and local businesses were discovering that they didn't need huge advertising budgets or promotional campaigns to compete with national brands. Biscuit Media Group made the easy decision to expand and offer video production to its list of media and publicity services. Marketing videos for area artists like authors Kinda Wilson and Dr. Pete Sulack soon followed, as well as various other artists such as radio host Carmen Laberge.

The use of traditional PR methods combined with new media strategies has been a recipe for success for Biscuit, not only for high-profile clients like The Pilgrim's Progress movie and musicians like Plumb, authors such as Dr. David Chadwick, but also for local businesses who are eager to leverage publicity and video marketing to their advantage. Consistently ranked as one of the top PR firms in the

Nashville area speaks to the attention to detail and the attitude that no client is too big or too small for Biscuit Media Group to represent.

Why publicity? What inspired you to start a public relations firm?

In Biscuit's infancy, Lori identified a lack of media exposure for independent projects. Artists were searching for a unique approach that relied more on personal touch and fresh strategies than cookie-cutter methodology.

You have worked with many celebrated artists, filmmakers, authors, and musicians in the world of faith-friendly and family-friendly entertainment and landed major appearances for clients on various news outlets and radio shows. What types of PR methods and strategies do you employ to land such impressive press coverage?

First and foremost, establishing and fostering mutually beneficial relationships with media outlets is a hallmark of Biscuit Media. This network allows us to relate the story-within-the-story and really solidify our reputation as a trusted and reputable publicity machine. Additionally, when a client signs on with Biscuit, they know they won't get lost in the shuffle of myriad artists or projects. Limiting our clientele allows us to focus on tailoring PR needs to the specific project and communicate effectively with all stakeholders.

How does it make you feel watching your clients interact with fans, signing autographs, and snapping selfies at book signings?

Biscuit Media Group is fortunate to be able to support and work for only the projects we truly believe in. This selectiveness makes it especially gratifying to see artists succeed and also humbling to see them interact with fans at various events. We know that we had at least a small part in their hearing about the new album, or reading about the latest movie. Being able to connect clients and fans is a large reason we do what we do.

Why is video content so important for brands and (small) businesses when it comes to marketing their message?

In today's world, being able to get your message to someone with video is paramount. Market research on the effectiveness of videos in advertising compared to text-only appeals is continually updated, and the numbers keep showing dramatic results that point to one irrefutable fact: in order to more successfully market your product or service, you need video support on your social media or website. This is especially beneficial for small businesses who no longer have to rely on local TV or radio stations to produce and air their advertising. Typically, those campaigns, although effective, are costly to create and put into a rotation for the duration of the contract. Technology has advanced to the point where a mom and pop business can create a video, put it on their Facebook page, and create meaningful engagement at a nominal cost.

At Biscuit, we not only write, shoot, direct and edit our own videos, we also utilize our background in education to inform clients about how to use best practices to their advantage when it comes to marketing. That way, they can make informed decisions  about what they *want* when it comes to a project, instead of taking our word for what they *need*. Being able to provide this understanding and empower them to feel confident they're making a wise investment makes for a symbiotic relationship and a less-stressful experience.

. . .

What is your favorite part about having a small business in Smyrna?

No one is a stranger. Working with other small businesses toward a common goal is how communities are forged. We are fortunate to be able to meet up with clients at places like Carpe Cafe or The Casual Pint and create working partnerships in truly organic ways. As a small business ourselves, we feel like helping entrepreneurs succeed is a major part of our mission.

What brought you to Smyrna?

When we began looking for the ideal location for Biscuit, Smyrna really hit all the criteria. Although Nashville and other larger cities are attractive in their own right, we loved the opportunity we had to really get involved with the town and the people. Groups like SiMA and the Rotary Club are great for networking and building relationships, and events like Depot Days and the Farmers Market are perfect for seeing and making friends. It really doesn't take long to feel like the people in Smyrna are part of your family.

What does a typical day look like for you?

A typical day goes through several stages, with few exceptions. I review emails in the morning, create a to-do list, consult with current clients and then begin or resume content creation. At the end of the day, I send emails updating progress with respect to the current projects.

What is the biggest lesson you've learned in owning and operating a small business?

The biggest lesson we've learned is that what is profitable is not always profitable. A client or project may offer a large paycheck, but that's not what makes the best fit for us. We have to believe in a project before we invest our time and efforts. Having faith in a project keeps us secure in the knowledge that we're giving the client our best, and that we are maintaining the highest standards of quality. That's how we build our reputation.

Is there a favorite mantra you live by?

I could, and probably should rotate mantras in and out of my life on a regular basis, but the one that has been with me since childhood is, "Strive for perfection, but accept excellence". In most of life's endeavors, the textbook definition of perfection is unattainable, but that should not discourage us from trying to achieve it.

How have you grown your small business from an idea to where it is now?

Biscuit's evolution sprang from a simple idea to work in concert promotion into an all-purpose PR firm by continuously being open to new ideas and being in the habit of saying "yes."

What are your daily habits that you live by that have set you and your small business up for success?

Since our days at Biscuit are so different all the time, our habitual practices have to be general in nature. First and foremost, we communicate. We know clients and would-be clients are usually waiting on products and services from us, and we like to keep them informed of our progress. We feel like this is a basic courtesy, but it serves a dual purpose of keeping us motivated to achieve results.

Expressing gratitude is something we began incorporating as a habit into our daily routine a few years ago, and it never fails to pay dividends. We're grateful for everything we have, and the people we're fortunate enough to work with. Developing and nurturing this habit has opened up a whole new dynamic to the culture of our company, and the positivity is contagious.

What has been your biggest business milestone to date that you are most proud of?

We measure our successes on a project-by-project basis, so milestones, at least in the traditional sense, are more difficult to track. Longevity in a competitive industry is something we're proud of, so that thirty year benchmark will be pretty special!

What have been some of your biggest business challenges you have faced and how have you overcome them?

Our standards are very high for our company and the projects we choose, so our biggest challenges come from having to politely turn down a client or discontinue a working relationship when something arises that crosses the line with those standards. Business ethics is something we take seriously, and our corporate identity is unapologetically rooted in our moral code.

What advice would you give to someone wanting to pursue a career similar to yours?

Build and continue to develop relationships. Relationships translate to reputations. By fostering positive relationships, you discover that doors open up to you that might not have even been present before. In reality, this is just an essential practice in any business, but it bears repeating to anyone who endeavors to work in PR.

What 1-3 books have impacted your life the most and why?

We are both avid readers, so books have had a major impact on our lives and careers. The Bible, *A Man Called Ove* and *The Alchemist* are just a few that speak to our hearts in how to approach life and business.

How has failure or apparent failure set you up for future success?

Entrepreneurs tend to look at failures in such a negative light. Learning opportunities are found in every setback, which means we get better every time we fail. I'm a more effective communicator than I was last week simply because I said something negatively, then learned how to say it positively.

Who has been the most influential person or mentor to you during your entrepreneurial journey and why?

Penny Hunter has been a major influence in Lori's career because she's an example of making wise decisions and always choosing projects that serve a greater good. She puts people before projects and leads with grace and humility. Not only does she gracefully display these extraordinary qualities, but she often does so while being the only woman in the room.

What do you enjoy doing in your spare time?

We like to spend time with our dogs, travel and attend sporting events. We both have hearts for service and place particular emphasis on community, so we like to volunteer with local events and organizations whenever we can. Lori has been an emcee at Depot Days for a music stage, and also served on the Smyrna Arts Commission. I have served as a board member for The Senior Activity Center of Smyrna, and created testimonial videos for SiMA. Biscuit Media Group has proudly sponsored the annual Spaghetti Dinner fundraiser for the Senior Activity Center for several years.

What does success mean to you?

The idea of "success" is a social construct, but I feel we get the most out of life when we are able to spend a great deal of time with family and friends, give back to the community and laugh often.

Where do you see yourself and your small business 5-10 years from now?

We hope to continue to build relationships and show steady growth for the next ten years by building our clientele and representing projects that speak to us. We also want to be mentors and guides for young people who decide to enter the world of media and public relations.

How big of an impact has social media had on your small business?

Most of our recognition is generated from clients who are grateful and appreciate the work we've done for them. These posts on social media create engagement from others and help us leverage our networking skills to generate more business opportunities that might not otherwise exist.

What does supporting local mean to you?

To us, supporting local means shopping at local businesses, eating at local restaurants, helping entrepreneurs succeed and giving our time to community events. Besides the obvious economic benefit of keeping more dollars in the community, supporting local businesses creates family-to-family relationships. There is a mutual trust that exists within these relationships because these businesses are owned by our neighbors, and they have an investment in the well-being of the community.

BELLA VISTA COFFEE SHOP
AS TOLD BY DANIELA REINA

Website: www.bellavista.menufy.com
Facebook: Bella Vista Coffee Shop
Instagram: @bellavistacoffeeshop

Tell me about your (small) business.

We are a barista coffee shop, with a good environment, great food, music, video games, and more. Our menu items are handmade fresh every day. Our coffee beans are South American. It's a mix of Colombian, Costa Rica, Bolivia, and Venezuela, all mixed in one bag.

Because we are local, we choose other local companies, such as Frothy Monkey, to roast our beans.

Every bag is freshly roasted. We slice all the meats, the cheeses, we create all the sauces. The Green Sauce is our most popular sauce. Our plantain chips offer a little bit of South American culture. Everything has the Latin touch, which I think is a big part of our success—the extra  flavor we can offer to Smyrna. We create everything in-house. All of our crew is trained to be baristas, bakers, and panini masters. We are proud because everyone has been trained to be unique.

We have four unique freak shakes as well as seasonal coffee drinks. Some drinks like the Dolce Coco started as a seasonal drink but became so popular that we had to put it on the main menu.

We have empanadas on the weekends because I had to bring some of my culture to my business. My goal is to eventually serve them every day.

Our homemade sauces became so popular that I had to sell bottles. The green sauce is a Venezuelan recipe that comes from my city. We use that sauce with everything. We put it on the side with our plantain chips, which are also made fresh. Every single sauce is freshly made in house- no preservatives. Some of our paninis come with a secret sauce. For example, the Say Cheese comes with a pink sauce, which is really popular. We incorporate a a lot of our culture and mix it with Italian and American culture and create fantastic combination of flavors. We try to create a perfect balance between coffee and flavor.

We built this place from the ground up. I am so proud of this business. I know how much time and effort is involved in starting a business. Everything in this space has a meaning. Bella is a vibe. We have people that stay all day because they feel so relaxed and work all day. To me, it's really important to be an immigrant and have people from other cultures.

My cousin, Jimmy, started here as a barista and is now the assistant manager. Jimmy went to school in Venezuela to become a barista (he was also trained as a lawyer back home). He moved here with me. This is a family-owned business. We are so proud of what we have built. We love our customers and consider them family, regardless of where they come from. Our door is open to everyone.

What inspired you to open a coffee shop?
One day, my fiancé asked what would be my dream job? I wanted something that would remind me of home, and having a coffee shop because we are well known for our coffee. We started doing coffee research and I saw an opportunity to buy a store in Nolensville.

It was tiny, and not in the best location. I realized I wanted to offer more to the customer than just a product. I wanted to offer a community.

I sold that place the very next day because I knew the concept I wanted wouldn't work. I started looking again. I'd only lived in Smyrna for six months, but I loved it. I think Smyrna is a diamond in the rough. It has a little bit of everything and is growing really fast. There is so much potential. Even though there is a Starbucks on the corner, we knew this was the place to be.

What is your favorite part about having a small business in Smyrna?

The people are so open to try new stuff. It's a pleasure any time they walk in especially when they don't know we are here and think we are a hidden gem. I'm going to do everything to get them back.

It makes me so proud when I see someone from the local community in my coffee shop. One of the Thunderbirds came in after the Air Show and it was an honor. I have a bestselling author who comes in. I love seeing people coming in and building community. It is an honor for me to see cops walking into the shop, paramedics, and nurses. I've had people come in, crying because they had a bad day, and I may be the only person they get to talk to that day. Customers know when they walk in, they will be greeted with a smile, and it will be genuine.

What brought you to Smyrna?

I'm originally from Venezuela. I have been here a little over six years. Unfortunately, I had to leave everything behind due to some things going on in the country and start all over again. I came here with $200 in my pocket. No family, no friends, nothing.

When I first moved to America, I lived in Florida for six months. I had some friends in Nashville and moved there. It wasn't easy. Being away from my family was very hard. I began working at a warehouse in Smyrna for the first few years and would drive around town to see what was new. It was a hard job, but I did whatever I had to do to start in this country. I have always been a foodie and a fan of local businesses, even back in Venezuela.

If you were born in this amazing country, you are blessed and you have all the opportunities. I am so blessed to live here. I respect the rule of law. This is home. I embrace everything about this culture. I want to be a part of this culture and learn everything about American history, American culture, and American food. It's an honor to me.

What makes the dining experience at Bella Vista so unique and special?

You will see me, the owner, working with my bare hands and taking care of customers. The ambiance we create, the lights, the music, the comfort you feel when you walk in— that's the experience I was trying to bring when I was building everything. Most of what we used to create this space was left behind by the previous occupant. For example, we used leftover paint from the mural to paint the floors. I love walking to the tables and thanking people for coming and asking how their experience has been.

What advice would you give to someone wanting to pursue a career similar to yours?

Some young customers want to have their own coffee shops. I encourage them that they can become the best barista in the world. This can be a career if you want. You can learn about business. I have two degrees back home—one in Mass Communication and another in Culinary Skills. I didn't know anything about business until I had my own. I didn't know how to manage people or run a business. It's a learning process. For example, when I opened, I didn't know anything about coffee so I had to go to school again and learn how to become a barista and learned about coffee from our roasters. I'm never going to stop learning. I try to be an example to the kids.

What has been your biggest business milestone to date that you are most proud of?

So far, to receive acknowledgement from the community. To hear people say my coffee shop looks like something they would see in Nashville. There are so many amazing businesses here. To hear people say, "you are doing a great job," or, "do you have any other businesses or locations?" Or, when customers say, "thank you." The opportunity to have my mom here and for her to see what I have overcome. I have a twin sister in Argentina, she's never seen my business. They see it on social media and are so proud.

We also just celebrated our second anniversary. Every year we will celebrate and make it bigger. We always try to do stuff for the community like giveaways. We just want to make our community a part of it.

What have been some of your biggest business challenges you have faced and how have you overcome them?

COVID-19. I'm blessed because I was able to keep my business open thanks to my customers. Some people drove over forty-five minutes and would tell me this is their favorite coffee shop. They want us to survive. There are no words. I'm really happy.

Bella Vista has won several prestigious awards voted on by the community, including Firefly Awards for Best New Business, Best Social Media and Best Customer Service. Where do you see yourself and your small business 5-10 years from now?

I'm really proud when our customers appreciate the effort. Being an immigrant, that really matters to me. It makes all the effort, energy, and stress worth it. When we get that kind of recognition, we are doing something right.

We are going to expand our kitchen to make it more functional. We are going to have a bigger kitchen, more menu options, build a new coffee bar that will be bigger. We will have two espresso machines so we can offer even more drinks. We also want to include more art and merchandise.

Bella will expand and have multiple locations around Rutherford County. I'm not going to stop until I make it happen.

What is your favorite go-to meal from Bella Vista?

I'm a classic person, so the Do Not Share panini is a must. It has the perfect balance between healthy and flavorful. It melts in your mouth.

I'm simple when it comes to coffee because I like to taste the coffee beans. I love Cuban coffee. It's the perfect balance between coffee, creaminess and sweet. It's a classic combination, but out of this world. I try to offer this to all customers because they won't find it anywhere. So far, the ones who have tried it have ordered it again. I also love our banana bread. It's one of our signature hand-crafted desserts. It's a must and goes great with coffee.

. . .

How big of an impact has social media had on your small business?

It helps my business a lot when people share our posts or leave reviews because when people are visiting, they drive all the way to Bella because they saw a review on Google, Yelp, or Facebook. I'm very appreciative when someone takes the time to engage with our posts or write a review. It makes a huge difference.

What does supporting local mean to you?

Supporting local is creating an impact into the community and helping their business stay open. I'm going to always choose a local restaurant or business.

When you buy something from us, you are supporting local. My coffee is from a local business. My food is from a local business, so it's like a ripple effect when people support local. Sometimes, local is not always cheaper, but we provide premium quality. As business owners, we create that mindset and explain to our customers the difference between a chain from a local business. We are seeing younger customers choose local more and more.

We support each other as business owners. I love going to The Social Nutrition and Janarty's. Janelle and Marty come here once a week. They are amazing.

Are there any other ways people can support your small business?

We have gift cards, stickers, and campfire mugs.

You can order online through Uber Eats, Doordash, and Menufy, and even have it delivered to you locally. Also, we sell our signature sauces and special whole bean coffee bags. You can have the best coffee beans from Latin America in the comfort of your home.

· · ·

Is there anything else you would like people to know about you or your small business?

We have an open mic for anyone who wants to perform—musicians, comedians and trivia nights. Our logo represents our tri-star for the state of Tennessee because deep inside my heart, I'm a Smyrnain.

I'm blessed this county received me with open arms. It's an honor.

RED WAGON NURSERY

AS TOLD BY BRIAN & MICHELLE HYTRY (HUSBAND AND WIFE) AND DAN & ANGELA HYTRY (HUSBAND AND WIFE)

Website: www.redwagonnursery.com
Instagram: @redwagonnursery
Facebook: Red Wagon Nursery

Tell me about your (small) business.

Red Wagon Nursery is a friendly, local, and family-owned garden center. We offer healthy and beautiful trees, plants, and shrubs. We also carry perennials, annuals, organic soil amendments, bagged mulch, planters, and pots. Stop by on any given day and you will find brothers, Brian and Dan, manning the ship. If you visit us on weekends, you are likely run into the rest of the family—wives, children, grandparents, and maybe even a dog or two.

We have humble beginnings rooted in a passion for plants, hard work, and achieving the "American Dream." As teenagers, both Brian and Dan worked selling Christmas trees for a family friend in the busy city of San Francisco. To escape the hustle and bustle and unite family, everyone eventually moved to Middle Tennessee.

After years of working with plants and landscaping, the early childhood passion to be around plants and trees was reignited and the work to establish Red Wagon Nursery began. So, while our history as a company is a new one, our love and knowledge of the industry spans decades.

Why plants? What inspired you to open a nursery?

We have a sign in the garden center that displays a great quote from Aubrey Hepburn: "To plant a garden is to believe in tomorrow." There's a lot of truth in that. It's definitely a fun business because we get to help people make their homes more beautiful.

What is your favorite part about having a small business in Smyrna?

We have really gotten to know so many folks through this business and feel so honored to have landed in Smyrna. This town has an immense tight-knit community feel to it. We are proud members of SiMA, who drives an ongoing public education campaign to inform customers fully about the benefits of doing business locally. Every week, customers tell us that they're so glad we are here and they are so glad to shop local.

. . .

What are you most excited about for your small business?

Growing and evolving. It's amazing how far we have come in just four short years. It's so rewarding being able to bring our ideas to full fruition. Every comment customers make we take into consideration and try to create a place that folks love to visit. We are so excited about the future and how we can better serve Smyrna!

What's the first thing you do every morning to start your day on the right foot?

Each of us have variations to our morning routines, but we are all early risers. I personally have found lots of benefit in heading to the gym first thing and getting in a few minutes of reading. It seems to set the day up for success. Did I mention coffee?

What does a typical day look like for you?

Everyday flies by and is always a bit different, which is a good thing. For the most part, we are making plant orders, unloading trucks, making deliveries, watering and tending to plants, and our favorite—helping customers.

What is the biggest lesson you've learned in owning and operating a small business?

We are all responsible for our own successes and failures. While there are lots of variables in economics, demographics, and even something as unpredictable as the weather—it's the things you do *daily* to grow and improve your business that really move the ball forward.

Are there any favorite quotes that inspire you?

"Achievement happens when we pursue and attain what we want.

Success comes when we are in clear pursuit of why we want it." – Simon Sinek

"Get after it." –Jocko Willink

"You can't build a reputation on what you are going to do." –Henry Ford

How have you grown your small business from an idea to where it is now?

Like most things, little by little. It can be overwhelming to take on a giant project. The first couple of years were probably the most challenging because everything was new. We were setting procedures and processes in place and simply  figuring out what worked and what didn't. It's important to be able to adjust when something doesn't work. Each year we have learned more. It's ever evolving.

What has been your biggest business milestone to date that you are most proud of?

Year over year growth and each year having more of a presence in the community.

What have been some of your biggest business challenges you have faced and how have you overcome them?

Finding ways to organically grow to let the community know that our garden center exists in Smyrna. It still amazes us how many times folks come in and say they didn't know we were here!

. . .

What advice would you give to someone wanting to pursue a career similar to yours?

Do what you love; love what you do.

What has been the best piece of business advice you have ever received?

Always strive for the "why."

What are some of the biggest lessons you've learned in owning a small business?

Don't be stagnate, always look for ways to grow your business.

What 1-3 books have impacted your life the most and why?

Good to Great by Jim Collins, *Extreme Ownership* by Jocko Willink, and *Indistractable* by Nir Eyal.

Who has been the most influential person or mentor to you during your entrepreneurial journey and why?

No one person has been an influence. We have relied on past careers that have helped formulate our entrepreneurial careers.

What does success mean to you?

Success has very different meanings. Our success is having a good quality garden center in the Smyrna community. It's also waking up looking forward to going to "work."

. . .

Where do you see yourself and your small business 5-10 years from now?

We see ourselves enjoying continued growth, and maintaining a quality garden center for many years to come.

Why is supporting local businesses so important?

There is an unspoken kinship between business owners. We understand each other's struggles and triumphs. We all support each other. It helps build a strong community.

VANESSA HALEY, MAKEUP ARTIST/AESTHETICIAN
AS TOLD BY VANESSA HALEY

Website: www.vanessahaleymua.com
Facebook: Vanessa Hayley- Makeup Artist/Aesthetician
Instagram: @vanessahaleymua | @lovesmyrnatn

Why beauty and skincare?

I've always loved makeup and working for Clinique as a regional makeup artist developed my love of skincare. Gaining my aesthetics license also gave an added layer of flexibility to my schedule while my son was still in school.

What is your favorite part about having a small business in Smyrna?

Working with friends and neighbors. Also, the convenience of being close is immeasurable.

What brought you to Smyrna?

My husband, Jeremy, grew up in Smyrna. After we married in 1992, we rented a duplex off Almaville Road owned by his parents for a few years while saving up for our first home. Having grown up in Nashville, it was quite the culture shock, but when it came time to purchase, making Smyrna home just made the most sense.

What do you love most about makeup?

Helping ladies of every age see the beauty of their natural features. Every face is different, and every face is beautiful.

Why should people invest in an aesthetician for their skin?

Aestheticians are able to manipulate the epidermal layers of skin with different types of exfoliation to minimize basic aging concerns (wrinkles, dark spots, etc.) before they become too deep and require harsh treatments by a doctor. We will also set you up with the correct at home skin care regimen to further your improvement.

Which element of your job do you most enjoy?

Hearing the joy in a client's voice when that 'horrible dark spot' is no longer visible, or when she's been wearing the same makeup look for years and sees her new look for the first time.

Also, I love getting notes from my brides saying how beautiful they felt on their wedding day.

What's your favorite makeup product or brand and why?

As most professional makeup artists ("MUA") will agree, I don't have one favorite brand. At any given moment there are eight to ten different brands in my professional (and personal) makeup kit. Those are generally chosen based on product durability, saturation of colors, blend ability, and how it shows on camera.

. . .

You also get to collaborate with other local small business owners in the creative space, including local photographers, to provide professional makeup for weddings, senior photos, and other special milestone occasions. Do you have any favorite photoshoot memories?

My absolute favorite memory is from a shoot with my best friend and her motorcycle. Oftentimes the photographer will have several ideas for the MUA to create at different times in the shoot. After a few lip and hair changes, the photographer said, "Okay, oil her up." We exchanged questioned looks, then proceeded to change her into less fabric and I covered her with baby oil from head to toe. Almost twenty years later, we still laugh about that day!

Another great memory was when Carla (Carla Lynn Photography) sent me to do makeup for Erin Oprea. She's a friend, and a personal trainer. I knew that they had a shoot later that day, but I didn't know what for until in the middle of makeup when I kept hearing her refer to 'Carrie's wardrobe.' Then Carrie called to make some adjustments, and it dawned on me that this was Carrie Underwood's personal trainer. Without me asking too many questions, she did confirm who the shoot was with. When I left, I called Carla screaming into the phone! Afterwards, I discovered she had already signed a non-disclosure agreement with Carrie's team and Glamour Magazine, so she couldn't tell me what it was for. That ended up being my first national print work.

What have been some of your biggest business challenges you have faced and how have you overcome them?

Finding people to work and partner with that have the same values, work ethic, and love for people.

What do you enjoy doing in your spare time?

Do small business owners have spare time? I do schedule time each week to work with the SiMA team as a Community Liaison. We utilize social media and local gatherings to boost knowledge of local business and encourage shopping local.

SiMA (Smyrna Independent Merchants Association) is a group of individuals and business owners that have a common goal to promote local commerce. We encourage everyone to "Think Locally" when shopping for goods and services. When you shop at a local independently owned business, 68% of every dollar gets reinvested in the community. Local chains, 43% reinvested; online, 0% reinvested.

We also organize and direct the annual Depot Days Celebration, and try to help other community organizations with their events and fundraisers. These events allow opportunities for small businesses to get their products and services in front of thousands of people in one place.

What does supporting local mean to you?

I always encourage shopping local at our small businesses in Smyrna first, chain retail in Smyrna second, then county options, then state options. Unless it's a local business's website, always choose online last.

Sixty-eight percent of every dollar spent in a locally owned business gets recirculated back into the local economy. Our way of life and local economy depend on the health of our small mom and pop businesses.

How big of an impact has social media had on your small business?

Social media has been a game changer for the beauty industry! While much of my business is driven by word-of-mouth, which I am so thankful for, adding social media has opened an advertising avenue fulfilling the visual aspect needed to really show my work as an artist. It also allows clients and friends to share my work while telling all their friends that I'm talented and trustworthy.

. . .

We've loved being a part of your journey. What's coming next that we can be a part of to support you?

Not sure what's next, but I pray daily for God's direction, discernment, and that little nudge when it's needed.

THE CASUAL PINT
AS TOLD BY CHRISTOPHER NORRIS

Website: smyrna.thecasualpint.com
Facebook: Casual Pint Smyrna
Instagram: @casualpintsmyrna
Phone: (615) 462-7421

Tell me about your (small) business.

Casual Pint is a craft beer bar. We have thirty-two drafts and about two-hundred and fifty bottled and canned beers to offer for both on-premise and off-premise consumption. We also serve a full menu of tasty comfort foods to enjoy with your beer, cider, wine, or other beverage. In the store and online you can find Casual Pint Smyrna growlers, insulated pints, and other merchandise for sale as well.

We opened our doors in December of 2017, and just celebrated our third anniversary. Granted the third year didn't go as expected, but it was still a great accomplishment to get to the three-year mark.

We have weekly events, such as trivia and poker nights, as well as other special events like tap features from various breweries or our recent Beer Madness brewery tournament. An additional service that we offer is our beer truck, or Mobile Pint. The Mobile Pint has six taps on the side, and is available to rent for events like weddings or family reunions. You can also usually find the Mobile Pint at many of the Smyrna festivals. If you don't need an entire truck, but you need a keg for your kegorator for an event, we can order one for you. We just need about a week's notice. Even if we don't have something in stock, we can see if it's available to order.

What is your favorite part about having a small business in Smyrna?

When I was looking to open Casual Pint, I was new to the Nashville area. Smyrna seemed a promising option since there was no craft beer spot in the area. Plus, I grew up in a small town and it's always fun when I can find a great place somewhere away from all the other areas that everyone else goes. So, the idea of opening a store someplace that wasn't yet the go-to hangout, appealed to me. There's always a risk to that, since smaller communities mean fewer potential customers, of course. But with how things were growing in Nashville and Murfreesboro, with Smyrna about halfway between, there seemed ample opportunity for growth.

I end up spending most of my time in the store, so I don't get out as much as I'd like, but I still get to meet lots of great people. We try to keep a feeling of family in the store. When you come in, you feel welcomed, and not just by the staff, but by other customers as well.

What is your favorite beer you currently offer?

Owning a craft beer bar, this is not a fair question. Sticking with what is on tap right now, I'd probably go with an Oskar Blues G'Knight. But if you asked me later, I might say Printshop Baker Creek or Saugatuck Double Dipped Neapolitan. My favorite beer is always what sounds best at the moment.

What is your go-to meal order?

Food is a little easier to choose since I'm the one that made the menu. If I had a go-to meal, it'd be a German Brat with potato salad and something like an amber ale or maybe a bit darker like a brown. Hofbrau Dunkel is on regularly, so I'd probably go with that. One thing to note, our menu does offer pairing suggestions for what type of beer (light, malty, hoppy, dark, fruity) might go best with the item you ordered. Our beer cheese is made in-house, so if you want something quick, you can't go wrong with the pretzels and beer cheese.

What are you most excited about for your small business?

I just like seeing the growing community that has been built within The Casual Pint. I'm happier about that than anything else. Sure, the point of a business is to make money, but the point of a local establishment is to be a hangout. A place that locals want to go and the place they want to bring their friends, family, and visitors to. I want to keep that going.

. . .

What does a typical day look like for you?

I don't really have a "typical" day. Some days are more focused on inventory and ordering, some on business tasks, some on planning future events, etc. It all depends on what needs to be done. Each day is different in the store too. Tuesdays  are poker night. Wednesdays are trivia night. Fridays and Saturdays are generally busier, of course. And I may have to spend some time behind the bar or in the kitchen. Plus, brewery or distributor reps stop in from time to time to bring sample beers or to check on how things are going, and if they can help sell their beer or setup an event. I also want to spend some time talking with customers, visiting with regulars, and hopefully finding some first-time or second-time customers that decide they want to make Casual Pint a regular spot, too.

Are there any favorite mantras you live your life by?

One of my favorite quotes came from a friend in college. We were playing video games. I was frustrated and trying like crazy to get back into the game. He said, "the key is not to want it," and that's something that's stuck with me. What it means to me is that sometimes we can get so caught up in what we *want* to happen that we don't focus on what we are actually doing. In the instance of the game, it was maybe wanting the next piece to be the perfect piece, and when it wasn't, just throwing the unwanted piece away, which then led to further difficulty. Or, maybe you're playing sports and you're down, and you really want to win the game, but you focus on winning instead of playing to the best of your ability. You may *want* to win, but if that just makes you crazy, you're probably not going to be able to figure out how to get the win. Same thing with business. You may *want* a full house every day. But that's not going to happen tomorrow. That may be the goal, but what you need to focus on is what is going right and keep that going. And find out what is not going right and fix it.

What has been your biggest business milestone to date that you are most proud of?

I think the growth from year one to year two is the thing I'm most proud of. We had a 32% growth in year two. That was a great feeling to see that change from where things were at the start to where they were looking to head. Of course, year three (2020) ended up being an unexpected challenge, but that change from the first to second year, which was representative of the support from the community, helped carry things through 2020 and hopefully will put things back on the path to further growth.

What have been some of your biggest business challenges you have faced and how have you overcome them?

The biggest challenges have been "learning on the go." There's not necessarily a "how to" manual for opening a new business. Especially if it's something different. Granted, opening a tap room or bar isn't necessarily a unique event. But opening it in a particular area may be unique. Sometimes the hardest part is just finding the right place to start or the right person to talk to. Once you get that, then you can start creating a plan for what you need to get done.

What advice would you give to someone wanting to pursue a career similar to yours?

Expect things to cost more than you think. Or expect that there will be costs that you can't anticipate and try to build that into your plan. And if you can, take it slow, don't necessarily commit to everything you may want to do all at once. Once you find a few strategies that are working, build those into a plan. You'll need to spend money on marketing, but more spending isn't necessarily equivalent to more business. Make sure you are doing what you can to get the word out before you open though, but don't be surprised when that initial interest fades. Sometimes, it's just a matter of getting the word out to the local community and often the best way for that to happen is via word-of-mouth and that takes time.

How has failure or apparent failure set you up for future success?

I didn't really know what beer was going to be popular when I first opened the doors. I knew what beer I liked, but that doesn't mean that's the beer the community is going to go for. So, initially, I had a different idea of what beer I was going to have on tap. I had to adjust that for what was actually selling. I had to figure out what my customers were looking for. I ended up spending a good deal more in the first year on the draft selection than I needed to. Note that each community is different, so even if a beer or type of beer sells well across town that doesn't mean it will sell everywhere.

Where do you see yourself and your small business 5-10 years from now?

I hope that the Casual Pint is still a great local hangout, and all our regulars are still regulars. And every time you come in, someone knows you and is happy to see you.

What does success mean to you?

It means finding a place you are content.

What do you enjoy doing in your spare time?

I enjoy going to breweries. My wife and I are always looking for breweries to visit while we're traveling or on vacation. Or a taproom like Casual Pint that features a selection of local breweries. Some place we might be able to try something new and get a feel for the locale. Aside from that, I do enjoy spending time with my kids. My son just started tee-ball. It's been fun watching my daughter do everything from gymnastics, theater, cooking to dance.

From a business standpoint, I like having an opportunity to get out in the community, too. We take the beer truck to local events such as Simply Smyrna, Depot Days, and the Rotary Fish Fry. It's great to be able to sponsor or support those events and it's also a good opportunity to get our name out to the community. Plus, all last summer we were able to operate the truck like a "beer ice cream truck." We drove around neighborhoods delivering beer door-to-door. It was a lot of fun and great to see the neighbors come out excited to see us. It was a highlight during a trying time.

How big of an impact has social media had on your small business?

Having followers posting about you or interacting with your posts is great. Not only does it give you a feeling of accomplishment or that you're on the right track when fans want to talk about whatever you're talking about, but it's great when they  help spread the word, too. Anytime a follower interacts with your posts or reposts or even just brings up your business, it's an opportunity to reach another potential fan. And really, I think it works better when it goes from person to person rather than business to "internet". But when your friend mentions something specifically or says they like something specifically, you are more likely to take note.

What does supporting local mean to you?

Supporting local means having both regular local businesses that you go to and trying new local businesses from time to time, too. And when you do, if you like it, let other people know.

Supporting local businesses means more opportunity for more local businesses. Sure, Target and Walmart are easy. It's one stop and done. But sometimes you want something a bit more unique and that's not going to be at someplace that you find in "every town America." After all, when you travel, do you want to go to only places that you can find at home? No, or I don't anyway. I want to go to someplace unique to that town or someplace that offers something unique to that town or area. But, unless your business is in an area that is primarily supported by tourists, such as Broadway in Nashville, local businesses can't rely on out-of-town customers only. So, if the locals don't shop local, then all those small businesses can't make it.

Are there any other ways people can support your small business?

People can support Casual Pint, and craft beer in general, by visiting local breweries, pubs, bars and tap rooms and trying something new. If you like something on tap, see if you can get some to go, either in a growler or package. Buying growlers and other merchandise is great too. You get something to use and it's extra advertising for the business. If you're wearing a shirt with your favorite brewery on it, someone else may notice and wonder where that place is. And if you have a growler to fill up, it's also a reminder that you want to go back and get some more delicious beer to enjoy.

Casual Pint makes supporting local easy too. We're a local business that supports other local, small businesses. We bring in beer from lots of microbrews (small businesses themselves) all to one place, but we also try to have special focus on the local breweries. In addition to the beer, we have events that feature other local businesses. Once a month we have Yoga with Akiko, who is a local yoga instructor. We host a weekly poker event with Steel Wheel Poker League on Tuesday nights. We feature a podcast that is recorded on-site. Zac Johnson records his podcast, Pour Choice of Words, in our store on a semi-weekly basis. Same with @localbrewdude. He comes in, tries beers Casual Pint, and talks about them on social media.

We've loved being a part of your journey. What's coming next that we can be a part of to support you?

2020 was a struggle, and it was hard to really predict or plan for anything in the future. We've started to see a positive trend, and now are looking to plan more events. Look for us at events over the summer as well. If you see that Casual Pint beer truck is going to be out, come out and find us. Also, be on the lookout for our next round of the Mug Club. It comes around once a year and is your opportunity to get 20 oz of beer at the 16 oz price in your own mug for the entire year!

Is there anything else you would like people to know about you or your small business?

Being part of the Smyrna community has been a great opportunity. It's been a pleasure getting to know people as they've come in and become regulars. And it's been fun watching strangers become friends. It's always great to hear customers tell you that they like coming in because everyone makes them feel welcome. I wouldn't have it any other way. It keeps me coming back, too.

DOW SMITH COMPANY, INC.
AS TOLD BY DOW SMITH

Website: www.dowsmith.com
Facebook: Dow Smith Company, Inc.
Instagram: @dowsmithcompany

Tell me about your (small) business.

We are a design build company who glorifies Christ, honors family, and pursues excellence. We work throughout Middle Tennessee designing and building mid-sized commercial buildings and tenant build-out, specifically churches or healthcare providers not attached to a hospital, or businesses with ten to fifty employees, including banks and retail spaces. We handle anything from renovations to ground up construction.

We partner with our clients to be a trusted advisor and simplify every step of the construction process. Our goal is to help our clients get the best construction value for their investment.

We have twenty employees. Eight of us are in the office, and the other twelve are out in the field serving as superintendents, carpenters, and our foremen.

In 2022, Dow Smith Company will celebrate thirty years.

What inspired you to start a design build company?

I feel like I was called to go into construction when I was in high school. I started my own business in 1992 when I was working with my father. I loved working with my father, but wanted to start my own company. One of my first projects was for Smyrna/Rutherford County Airport Authority when the Smyrna Airport got its own identity and charter. I renovated Building 661 for Colonel Fitzhugh and John Black. That was one of my first projects, and one reason why Smyrna is so dear to me.

What is your favorite part about having a small business in Smyrna?

One is geography. My office is one mile from my home. It was a great blessing to have breakfast with my boys and help them get ready for school when they were growing up, while being able to get to work on time. It is so nice not having to fight Nashville traffic. I love the vibe here in Smyrna. I love our diversity. I love the culture of what Smyrna is.

What brought you to Smyrna?

I married Cindy Taliaferro Smith in 1989. She was born and

raised here. When she graduated from pharmacy school in Memphis, we wanted to come back to Middle Tennessee. We lived in her grandparents' house up on Hilltop. I was glad to come to Smyrna with her.

What is the process when someone comes to you and wants to build or renovate a commercial office or building?

There are four steps. The first is vision collection. That involves putting together the team, which includes an architect, designer, engineer, and other construction people. We need to hear from the doctor or the church as far as what is their vision and how they serve their patients or their members.

The second part will be the design phase, and really that is broken into three components. Basically, that involves designing a building that can meet their needs as they can afford. Also, getting the permits from Town Hall. We bring in licensed designers and we facilitate that design to get through all the requirements. The third is the construction or renovation. A large portion of the finances is required here. Then, the fourth part is post-construction where the client moves in and occupies the building.

What advice would you give business owners that are looking to build or renovate?

I would use the same criteria you would use to pick your doctor, lawyer, or accountant. Who can give the best end product and save you money for the whole journey? A key part is making sure that you have your team assembled early. Your banker needs to be on board early with your designer as well as with your construction provider.

. . .

What have been some of your most memorable jobs?

There are two that come to mind. The Smyrna Bowling Center was a big milestone project for us. We worked with Roy Baudoin in 1996, in the early days of the business. It was a big job and very high-profile, a key part of our history. One of our most visible jobs is Woodfin's Funeral Home in 2000.

What has been your most challenging job to date?

In 2006, we did some construction work at the Smyrna Church of Christ. We connected and made two buildings, the school and the church auditorium, function as one building. We detached the building from the original structure. It was extremely challenging because the floor levels were different. We did some major structural changes in keeping the church and school in operation at the same time. We worked on the master plan for about six or eight months. It took a little less than a year to do that project. We love additions and renovations as much as new construction.

What makes the experience of working with Dow Smith Company so unique and special?

A lot of people want to trade for somebody with a briefcase. They think if someone is from Nashville or some big city, he's going to be better than somebody around here. In my case and in my industry, that is totally not true. In order for us to deliver a product, I don't care who you are, but you have to have local subcontractors. Someone from out of county may not be able to use these local subcontractors.

Another thing with us being local is we know and have a healthy working relationship with local vendors. We know the people in Planning & Zoning and Codes. We know the standards, what they're looking for, and what to expect. Because of that, we can get to the review process much faster. We can answer their questions on the initial application before they ask. If you want to build in Rutherford

County, especially in Smyrna, you need someone local. You will save time and money.

We also prefer to use local service vendors. Our electrician that we use is based here in Smyrna. Our heating and air is all Rutherford County. Our main plumber is Sadler Brothers Plumbing. They have a great service division.

What is it like to attend your clients' groundbreaking ceremonies and ribbon cuttings?

We love ribbon cutting ceremonies because the job is done and our clients can move in. Groundbreaking ceremonies are the time we have to really produce. We have a sense of business. The groundbreaking for us is not a celebration. It is for the client and it should be, because once the client gets to the groundbreaking ceremony their hard work is over. We like to celebrate that moment with them. The groundbreaking is our huddle time. When you're in the huddle, you don't celebrate. You think about the plan that you have to execute. The groundbreaking is like the touchdown dance. We have scored. We're in. We can celebrate at the ribbon cutting ceremony.

Tell me about your new podcast.

It is called From the Ground Up. We have already recorded four episodes. It's been a lot of fun, and I've learned a lot doing it. We're still learning how to do it, but it's a great venue to tell our story. We want to tell who we are, what we do, and how we do it. But more importantly, we want to hear other people's stories. Also, we want to spread the word of what all happens here in our community.

Dow Smith Company places a huge emphasis on company culture and has won Best Christian Workplace Institute (BCWI) since 2016. Why is company culture so important to your business?

Company culture is very important to us. Patrick Lencioni once said, "Culture will eat strategy for breakfast." I really found that to be true because you can have the best strategy and you can even have the best roster, but if you have a culture that is toxic, it's not going to be successful. The BCWI certification is a credit to all of us, and we all make this a great place to work. I'm really grateful to my team. Adding a Life Coach and Chaplain has been one of our best decisions. It's made us better people and a better company.

What is the biggest lesson you've learned in owning and operating a small business?

Where there is structure, there is freedom. To me that means when we understand what we're to do, what our role is, and what others' roles are, what's in bounds, what's out of bounds, and what the rules are. I try to apply that here in our office for how we communicate. Where there's no structure, there's chaos.

What have been some of your biggest business challenges you have faced and how have you overcome them?

COVID-19 has been the biggest challenge that I've experienced as a business owner. It has shaken us, it has chiseled us, and we have really grown from it. The last three quarters of 2020 into the first quarter 2021 were definitely the most challenging and we learned the most. Work had to stop for us in the summer of 2020. A lot of projects that restarted once it was ok to restart had to pivot as far as what they wanted to build and many changed their timing. Things for us really started picking up in the fourth quarter of 2020, but everything has changed since then. I also learned I can work from home almost as effectively as I can from the office. We've learned a lot, we've changed, and we've had to adjust, but we are better for it.

. . .

Do you ever stop to think that you are in some ways building a legacy in Smyrna since many of these structures you have built will last for years to come?

Honestly, I haven't really thought about it as a legacy, but it's a good point because I do notice the services I have used in my house. Sometimes, I think about how Jerry Davis poured the concrete. These buildings that stay- it very much does leave a legacy of the one who installed that particular structure. There is some bittersweetness as I drive through town and reflect. I am grateful for what we built.

Where do you see yourself and your small business 5-10 years from now?

We have a lot of exciting projects in the pipeline in the very early design phase. I'm very excited about our future.

What 1-3 books have impacted your life the most and why?

The Bible is where the transformation happens.

Leading with the Limp very much impacted me and talked about how we really need to acknowledge and even embrace our brokenness. Awareness brings immediate improvement.

What do you enjoy doing in your spare time?

I've been in Rotary since 1994. I really enjoy that time and the friendships. I'm really proud of the Fish Fry and the amount of money we have raised and poured back into the community.

When I'm not working, my favorite thing to do is sit on my back porch with Cindy and my boys. I enjoy smoking ribs or shoulder. During the fall on Friday nights, you'll see me at Smyrna High. I'm the end zone camera coach. I love supporting Smyrna High football and all their after school activities.

I was a member of the Public Building Authority ("PBA") for

many years when it was put together. I really enjoyed my time being on the PBA.

How big of an impact has social media had on your small business?

It's very important. One thing I recently learned is that the majority of our web traffic is generated through social media. SEO (Search Engine Optimization) is so important. Social media is essentially today's Yellow Pages.

I have more of an appreciation for how important social media is and the fact that it's not going away. It's growing and is going to continue to change. A lot of supporting other businesses is through social media. Google reviews and our online reviews are really big for our vendors. It's very important for our local vendors to see online reviews because often they make decisions based on what they read and learn from online reviews. It is social proof. It is very important to give reviews for local businesses. It moves the needle forward for them.

What does supporting local mean to you?

I try to be intentional about buying gas and groceries here in Smyrna. If we can keep our sales tax dollars here, it really does make a big difference. Of course, it is important to support local businesses by eating at local restaurants, things like that. For example, I get my dry cleaning done at Smyrna Cleaners with Mr. Kim. I love visiting Mr. Kim. I shop a lot at Gil's Ace Hardware. I enjoy the culture and the people there. Supporting local means buying and doing as much business in the city limits of Smyrna, and specifically the locally owned businesses. These business owners live and work here in Smyrna and it is important to support them and their businesses.

We're all in this together. My office is in downtown Smyrna. If my neighbors succeed, the value of their property is going to go up. The value of my property goes up, and they are just going to help me. I do believe a rising tide lifts all boats and as my neighbor does better so will I.

Are there any other ways people can support your small business?

We've got more of a service that ends up being a product. We can run some preliminary numbers and provide preliminary drawings to determine whether or not a project should move forward. We offer that as a supplemental service. So, if you are considering building and/or renovating, we can give you some good data to help you make that decision. We do a lot of due diligence work.

Is there anything else you would like people to know about you or your small business?

Smyrna is growing. With growth means changes. I know traffic is going to be a necessary evil. As we grow, there are going to be major inconveniences. But the benefits far outweigh that. In my opinion, one of the main ones being your home will be worth more when more people come here. We're going to have more job opportunities in Smyrna. I highly recommend if you can live and work in Smyrna to do so. Your life will be immensely blessed.

BREAKING BREAD
AS TOLD BY ANDREA CORKE

Facebook: Breaking Bread

Tell me about your (small) business.
　　I started my business out of my home in 1988. I celebrated twenty years in business at this location May 17, 2021.

We are open Monday – Friday 10:30 a.m. to 4:00 p.m. We also have gift certificates, take-out and catering services.

What inspired you to open a homestyle meat and three luncheonette complete with red-and-white checkered tablecloths in the historic Train Depot District?

I started making homestyle meals at a young age. I was on my own at sixteen and, by the age of eighteen, I had to learn to take care of myself and my eldest son. I did not have the money to go out to eat at all. I needed to make sure that we were fed, so I would cook our meals. Then it grew to feeding my family and the neighborhood. The food developed over time and more and more people were served. I did not know at the time that my cooking would turn into my ministry. Moreover, my job in the aerospace industry was continuing to layoff periodically and cooking was my way of surviving.

In reference to the red and white tablecloths- the look is mistakenly thought to be related to a "country-kitchen." However, the red and white tablecloths are a representation of this being a Christian restaurant that is covered in the blood of Jesus.

What is your favorite part about having a small business in Smyrna?

Being able to employ the people who work with me and giving back to the community. I also love being able to offer meals to my seniors. Because so many times the seniors are overlooked, I want them to know that they are loved and cared for.

What brought you to Smyrna?

I was not originally from Smyrna. My mother's job brought me here. However, within three to six months she left and went back to Memphis, but I stayed, and God took care of me.

You have the words "Faith, Joy, Hope, Love" in white lettering, as well as Bible verses painted along the walls, and a prayer request list patrons often fill up. Why is faith so important to your business?

The name Breaking Bread came from the Bible. "And they devoted themselves to the apostle's teaching and to fellowship to the breaking of bread and to prayer" (Acts 2:42). Faith is something that you cannot see, and I was being led by the Spirit to act in faith when I started the restaurant. One day I was driving past the street and I saw a 'for rent' sign. I was led by the Spirit to call the number and the rest grew from there. I know that my life is an example of following God's plan of serving and praying for His people.

What makes the dining experience at Breaking Bread so unique and special?

We play Christian music, and we were doing so before it became acceptable to do so. I also provide a unique experience to customers by being able to see God's Word all around the restaurant which is intended to bless and strengthen those who walk through our doors. People are being fed the Word in their spirits and food to their bodies.

What is your favorite go-to meal from Breaking Bread?

I am focused on eating green vegetables, specifically I eat green beans or collard/turnip greens daily.

. . .

What does a typical day look like for you?

A typical day is twelve hours or more. I come to the restaurant and prepare the food around 6:00 a.m. We are open from 10:30 a.m. to 4:00 p.m., and I am actively involved in serving customers. I also deliver meals to two daycares, and one after-school program every day. After my deliveries, I come back and close the restaurant with my staff. Then I prep for the next day.

Are there any favorite mantras you live your life by?

"Do unto others as you would have them do unto you."

What has been your biggest business milestone to date that you are most proud of?

The ability to purchase all new equipment. When I first started, everything was used. I have been able to upgrade everything over time to what I want it to be. I am continuing to improve on the remodeling of my kitchen, and I know that it is a work in progress that I continue to watch grow.

What have been some of your biggest business challenges you have faced and how have you overcome them?

When the parking lot across the street was being built. During this time, Lancaster Christian Academy and Blessed Beginnings Daycare hired me to prepare cafeteria lunches for their whole schools. These assignments lasted as long as the construction on the parking lot, nearly two years. These contracts blessed me.

What are some of the biggest lessons you've learned in owning a small business?

The biggest lessons include: don't move too fast when you need to make a business decision. It is important to be mindful and take a moment to pray, process and get clarity. Understand what it is you are getting into. Also, pay your bills, and pay your employees a salary that they can live on. Let your employees know that they are valuable to the business. It takes a team to make a business come together.

What advice would you give to someone wanting to pursue a career similar to yours?

Make sure that this is something that they were called to do. This is not an easy business to pursue. The overhead is very high, and it requires processes that need to be followed. I am definitely in my purpose. Many people can cook, but if you don't understand the daily operations of the business, it won't be sustainable. You have to be willing to eat, sleep, and breathe this. You cannot just be willing to "own" the business. You have to be willing to work it. That means washing dishes, going to the grocery store, taking out the trash, being the plumber, etc.

What has been the best piece of business advice you have ever received?

I received a quote from Apostle Amos Howard, who said, "make a plan and stay the course." I am doing just that.

What 1-3 books have impacted your life the most and why?

The Bible, this is my roadmap for life.

Battlefield of the Mind by Joyce Meyer. This helped me to better understand to watch how I think.

Seeking His Face by Charles Stanley. This book changed my daily walk with God because it was a daily devotional that took Biblical principles and put them in everyday life.

· · ·

How has failure or apparent failure set you up for future success?

My failure was when I wasn't taking care of my finances, and everything seemed to come in on me. Once I understood the importance of managing my financial situation and applied God's principles everything turned around, and I have continued to improve.

Who has been the most influential person or mentor to you during your entrepreneurial journey and why?

Some of the persons who have provided me counsel and advisement on this journey that have had an everlasting impact on my life include Apostle Amos and Yolanda Howard who taught me about excellence as you serve and financial management. Also, Carolyn Peebles (Focus Class) who helped me understand better the importance of structure and order.

In 2017, *The Murfreesboro Post* named you a Remarkable Rutherford Woman for the incredible impact you and your business have had on the local community.

You have used your platform as a business owner to elevate your employees, often fellow church members. You also donated meals to federal employees affected by the government shutdown in 2019. Why is giving back to the community so important to you?

I was very humbled by the honor. I am just about my Father's business. I am being used by God to bless others through this business and that is what it is all about. You can never lose in giving.

. . .

Breaking Bread has won several prestigious awards voted on by the community, including Taste of Smyrna's Best Entrée as well as a Firefly for Best Restaurant. Where do you see yourself and your small business 5-10 years from now?

In five to ten years, I would like to be able to have people in place to work the daily business, and I can work the back office and continue to cater private events.

What does success mean to you?

Success to me is not so much the money but being able to provide steady employment for others and create a good life for myself and be able to sew into other ministries and charities through my business.

What do you enjoy doing in your spare time?

I like to do outreach when I am not at the restaurant. On the first Saturday of each month the restaurant and a team of volunteers serve meals to all five senior living complexes in Smyrna. I like pampering time, attending movies, and going out to eat at fine dining restaurants. I also love to shop.

How big of an impact has social media had on your small business?

People have been able to learn about my business not only by word-of-mouth but social media has allowed me to be in the presence of people that may not otherwise know about my business.

What does supporting local mean to you?

Supporting local means being a patron to other local businesses. It is important because supporting one another helps and uplifts those business owners and helps them to support their families.

. . .

We've loved being a part of your journey. What's coming next that we can be a part of to support you?

Breaking Bread will continue to keep its doors open to the community and provide outreach. Your patronage helps us to continue to do so.

BUCKLE AND HIDE LEATHER
AS TOLD BY STEVE JOHNSON

Website: www.bucklehideleather.com
Facebook: Buckle and Hide Leather
Instagram: @buckleandhide
YouTube: buckleandhideleatherllc

Tell me about your (small) business.
 We sell our own belts, wallets, and accessories, as well as quality leather items and apparel which are all made outside of our store.
 The business started in my garage and built slowly from there.

We have been in business as a retail shop since 2013, but we were at the Nashville Flea Market and online before then. We also provide patch sewing and sew small leather goods at the shop. I am in the shop full-time, and my wife helps as needed. We also have a few employees that help keep the shop going.

What inspired you to open a business offering handmade leather goods as well as patch sewing services?

While in my teens, I was inspired by the leather shops of the Smoky Mountains area. I have done this type of work most of my life. The patch sewing was something we fell into quite by accident when a customer early in the opening of the shop saw the machines and asked if we could sew patches. During those very lean days, that idea took root and has been a great addition to the shop. We feel like it provides a wonderful opportunity for outreach and often provides that "barbershop" type feel while customers are having their patches sewn and communicating with each other.

What is your favorite part about having a small business in Smyrna?

Operating a business is a lot of hours and hard work, but when someone compliments your shop and says they are glad you're there, it means a lot. I've always been a self-starter and not a good fit for a cubicle. I have made many friends in this area and am proud to call Smyrna my home. I appreciate the small town feel of the area and strive to shop at other small businesses in the area as well.

What brought you to Smyrna?

I am originally from Ohio. I moved here in 2001 to pursue a drumming career, which I continued for about fifteen years. I met my wife, Sharon, here thirteen years ago as I was going between drumming and operating my leather business online and at the flea market. We opened the shop in 2013, and the drumming became too much to handle with my days at the shop, so I retired from that and started doing the leatherwork full time.

My wife grew up in La Vergne and graduated from Smyrna High School. Both of her children also graduated from Smyrna. I was able to attend many of the events with them and that helped introduce me to more of the community as well, since my music often took me out of town.

What is the process for making and customizing leather belts?

The items we make start with the leather hide. There are two main types we use: vegetable tanned leather and chrome tanned leather. Vegetable tanning uses tree bark and other natural processes and can take up to six weeks to tan. This type of leather may be embossed, stained, molded, etc. Items that need to be personalized with names, initials, or designs stamped into the surface start with this type of leather. We also make other items from chrome tanned leather. This type of tanning is done with chromium and is mostly used on leather apparel, furniture leathers, etc. This type of tanning takes only one to two days. The leather that is chrome tanned cannot be embossed like the vegetable tanned leather but is very durable. We will let the customer know if the item that they choose is from a type of leather that cannot be embossed.

To make our belts, we start with the hide and cut it into strips. One end then gets thinned a bit so that it can be folded over to hold the buckle, which we typically snap in place. We typically have the belts ready to this point when the customer comes into the shop. If the customer just wants a name embossed into the leather, and staff members are available, they may watch while it is being done. Many of the belts can be sized to fit while the customer waits and watches, but some special orders may take up to several weeks. We stock hundreds of belts that are ready to wear, but personalized items typically have to be ordered and shipped or picked up later. We don't advertise repairs, but occasionally are able to accommodate minor repairs.

Tell me about your patch sewing services.

We sew on patches that are brought in as well as patches for sale in the store. These are typically sewn onto leather vests, but can also be sewn onto caps, jackets, denim jackets, shirts, bags, and backpacks. We frequently have a variety of customers from motorcycle clubs and groups as well as individuals. We offer it done while you wait, which everyone loves. There is a fee for sewing on the individual patches which varies depending on the size and location of the patch. We even have a machine that we can use to sew your patches over pockets and keep the pockets open. Our busiest day is typically Saturday, so if you need a complete patch transfer, it would be better to come one day during the week.

What are you most excited about for your small business?

Our customers. We have a lot of repeat business, and our customer base continues to grow and broaden. That doesn't happen overnight, and you have to be able to hold on for that to happen. We are so excited to have repeat customers and patrons who come in saying they were referred by a friend or by someone else. Thank you, patrons!

What is the first thing you do every morning to start your day on the right foot?

I try really hard to spend one to two hours daily early before opening the shop studying the Bible. This part of the day is very important to me. I think about it for the rest of the day. "Finally, brothers, whatever is true, whatever is noble, whatever is right, whatever is pure, whatever is lovely, whatever is admirable-if anything is excellent or praiseworthy-think about such things" (Philippians 4:8).

How have you grown your small business from an idea to where it is now?

Back in my younger days, a wise business man told me, "Don't grow too fast." That has led me to grow slowly this time from my garage to now having the shop. I used my past experiences in leather making and business to have a store where people can come to buy handmade as well as quality sourced leather goods. My wife and I both have brought sewing skills to the mix, making the patch sewing as well as sewing of small leather goods a continued daily process.

What are your daily habits or systems that you live by that have set you and your small business up for success?

We try our best to treat everyone fairly, again that goes back to the Golden Rule. We try to let others know what sets us apart-quality leather goods that you can touch and feel. We strive to have a family atmosphere as well. We constantly work to provide more educational materials about leather goods and how to select and care for them, etc.

What has been your biggest business milestone to date that you are most proud of?

Twelve years ago, I was operating this business out of my garage and the trunk of my car, selling at flea markets, craft shows, and on the internet. Now, looking at where we are after eight years of business as a retail store, it is a humbling experience. On our first day of opening the shop, we looked like a flea market booth in a building. We have worked hard to gradually make these changes.

. . .

What have been some of your biggest business challenges you have faced and how have you overcome them?

Some of our biggest challenges were during the startup years. We juggled having the flea market booth and extra jobs for saving cash to invest in tools and fixtures to have a setup to sell products. The first year was tough in the first version of the retail shop. My wife and I would set up the booth at the flea market. She would then work at the shop, and I would work at the flea market over the weekend. We basically had to have two setups, one for each place to keep from tearing down the shop to take it to the flea market.

What advice would you give to someone wanting to pursue a career similar to yours?

Start small (proof of concept). Be patient. Be unique. Don't borrow money to start. Save your startup cash and turn it back into the business to keep you going until you feel like it is running. No debt at all if possible. I listen to Dave Ramsey and watch a lot of Shark Tank and The Profit.

What has been the best piece of business advice you have ever received?

As I said, I was told not to "grow too fast." I also read the book, *More Than A Hobby* by David Green. One thing that really impacted me in that book was to move out seasonal and non-selling items quickly as they cost much more money sitting on the shelf.

What are some of the biggest lessons you've learned in owning a small business?

I've been told I'm conservative in making quick decisions, particularly with money. Also, you have to pay attention to local and national trends before making big decisions. If I had to choose the biggest lesson I've learned, it would be watching cash flow.

Being a business owner sometimes seems like playing Whack-a-Mole. Whenever one thing gets done, something else always pops up. You truly have to almost be a jack-of-all-trades, and yet sometimes feel like a master of none. There is always so much to be done, not just making leather goods, there is paperwork, payroll, purchasing, cleaning and janitorial work, social media and marketing, website maintenance, and more! You have to learn to accept help from others when possible or seek others that can help with the jobs that you cannot quite get a handle on completing.

What 1-3 books have impacted your life the most and why?

The Bible; *Financial Peace and The Total Money Makeover* by Dave Ramsey, and *The E-Myth* by Michael Gerber. The Bible helps keep me from focusing on worldly things. The Dave Ramsey books have helped me to focus on being debt-free. The book by Michael Gerber is great for improving production and technical implementation in business.

How has failure or apparent failure set you up for future success?

When I was in my mid-twenties, I started up three mall leather/Western stores and fell into debt after I purchased items following a trend, which ended, plunging me into extreme debt and bankruptcy. I had to close all of those stores, and I lost everything I had built. That was an extremely difficult lesson, which taught me to follow the previous advice I was given of, "Don't try to grow too fast." When I had the idea to build this store, I decided that no matter how long it took, I would build it up gradually and not go into debt. This has been something that some of my vendors have been extremely cooperative in helping me to purchase smaller quantities of items at a time. I learned a great deal from that experience.

Who has been the most influential person or mentor to you during your entrepreneurial journey and why?

My parents were "pickers," I guess. They taught me that if you sold $100 worth then you have to keep $50 to buy something to make another $50. You can't just blow the $100 or you will have nothing to use to make the next $50. It's a snowball effect. In other words, you have to be disciplined with your money and make it work for you. They used to take me to the flea market weekly while I was growing up. My dad would also repair, buy, and sell bicycles. My mom would sell socks and aprons. I sold leather items. We would all go as a family and I loved helping to sell stuff. My brother hated it!

Where do you see yourself and your small business 5-10 years from now?

I would love to be able to equalize home and work life, where I would not be at the shop routinely six days a week. I would love for the business to continue in the same location.

What does success mean to you?

Success means the freedom to make my own decisions, I like being my own boss.

What do you enjoy doing in your spare time?

I like to watch old Westerns, music documentaries, cat videos, and work on projects around the house. Sharon loves to sew, try new recipes, and read books of all kinds constantly. The most important things to us are Jesus first, family second; everything else follows those first two. It's difficult for us to do many events outside the shop. We try to participate in events that celebrate our Veterans, to show our appreciation for their sacrifice and service.

How big of an impact has social media had on your small business?

We are extremely grateful for reviews. We have had customers come to the store saying they saw our Google reviews and that gave them the encouragement needed to visit the shop when traveling.

We have grown our digital presence over the lifespan of the shop, which has been very difficult. In the past, Sharon kept up with our social media presence during her time off (she works full time as a nurse and works in the shop, as needed). Now, we have an employee who is instrumental in helping boost our online presence. We are continually trying to improve our presence digitally. It is so crowded online! We have had our own YouTube Channel for some time. The goal this year is to work on improving product descriptions through using video and to make educational/informational videos for that channel.

What does supporting local mean to you?

Supporting local now means more than it ever has, with the digital age making everything accessible at your fingertips. You're supporting your neighbors and your local economy when you shop local. The taxes we pay help pay for the local infrastructure (roads, water system, city workers, security, and emergency personnel) and that is so important.

Are there any other ways people can support your small business?

Most everything today, no matter the item, can be purchased and shipped to your door from the "big" websites. Specifically for leather though, you cannot feel, smell, and try on that item. I hear over and over about failed attempts at buying leather vests online before the customer finds us. Many times, the customer is able to walk out with an item they are able to physically try on and touch when they come into the shop. We carry sizes to fit most. They can typically wear it out the same day. That is a huge selling point for our customers to come into the shop. That's even better than overnight shipping.

You can't ship the experience or the relationship, or seeing the belt being made, or having your favorite patch sewn on while you wait, the interaction of being served in person cannot be done online. We do have a website with an ever-improving selection from our shop, but it's mostly our smaller items, not leather apparel due to shipping costs and correct fitting. It is too costly for returns and exchanges on large items.

Please support your local stores by purchasing from them and not using them to try on your items and then purchase the item online from one of the "big" websites. Your local shop owner has gone to a great deal of trouble to find products that are well liked in this area and that will help boost the local economy.

We've loved being a part of your journey. What's coming next that we can be a part of to support you?

We are always trying to improve our shop but, hopefully, we are going to add leather crafting kits and maybe a class to help make an item. It is our long-term goal to educate customers about leather and leather care. We want to continue to be an all-purpose and family-oriented leather shop. We would love for you to keep up with us on social media and feel free to come in or message us with ideas for topics for leather-related educational videos.

Is there anything else you would like people to know about you or your small business?

I'm just a normal guy that has been able to do something I like, but it's been a long road to get where we are. It's our goal to be the best leather shop we can be: period.

BOB'S BARBECUE
AS TOLD BY JEFF LANNING

Website: www.bobs-barbecue-barbecue-restaurant.business.site
Facebook: Bob's Barbecue

Tell me about your (small) business.

We opened Bob's Barbecue in 1988. I was twenty-three years old.

From day one, we've sold pulled pork, turkey, ribs, and wings, the basics. We've never tried to have a huge menu. We do the basic barbecue picnic type foods, and we do it well. We added loaded barbecue baked potatoes. It's been a staple menu item. We've kept our menu pretty simple and it's worked well over the years.

We do a lot of catering. We can accommodate small and large groups. We cater holidays, parties, church groups, sporting events—we can do it all.

What is your favorite part about having a small business in Smyrna?

The most rewarding part is being able to see people come in where we've sponsored ball teams and finding their pictures on the wall and show their kids. That's been one of the cool parts about being here so long is when people can still find themselves after so many years. My dad and I started coaching in 1988. We have pictures in here from 1988.

What brought you to Smyrna?

My uncle and cousin own some barbecue franchises. I started working for my uncle in 1985. In 1988, we decided to put a place here in Smyrna. Jeff's Barbecue did not have a very good ring to it, so we went with Bob's Barbecue. My dad is Bob. He helped me get started. Around this time, Nissan was getting started so we felt like Smyrna was a good spot.

My dad didn't want to name it Bob's. He tried to come up with a zillion other ideas. I said, "No, we're going to name it Bob's Barbecue." I get called Bob *all* the time. If I'm called Bob, then it's from work or somebody in Smyrna.

Bob didn't really work here, just when we needed help. He was a pharmacist. He wanted it to do well since his name was on it. Bob was originally from Lawrenceburg before moving to La Vergne.

. . .

How has the small business landscape changed since you first opened in 1988?

It was a lot different back then. We had some small restaurant chains, places like Shoney's, Captain D's and Wendy's. We also had the Catfish House. There was no liquor by the drink. Big chains really didn't look to come here. We were the barbecue place in Smyrna. Luckily, we did it well enough to keep people coming back.

We did have a Bob's in Murfreesboro and a couple of other locations. None have been as successful as Smyrna.

I'm at a point now where I'm hiring kids of employees. It's really special to have them come back. Their parents want their kids to work at Bob's and learn how to work.

We recently had one little girl's mom post a picture of her, "First day at Bob's." People commented, "That was my first job." We have been here that long that we see neat things like that.

What are some of the biggest lessons you've learned in owning a small business?

Not to dwell on the daily things. You have to look at things over a length of time. You will have good days and bad. You always show up the next day and go back to work.

What has been your biggest business milestone to date that you are most proud of?

Being in business this long is a milestone. Somebody once said, you've been in business for over thirty years, you must be really good. I'm just really stubborn. You get up and work as hard as you can in hopes that people show up hungry and ready to eat.

We've been fortunate that we've been in a town where people have embraced us. The Lord's blessed us with people coming and being hungry.

.   .   .

What have been some of your biggest business challenges you have faced and how have you overcome them?

We had a fire ten years ago. I was on the way here and the building was on fire. I got a phone call from my (local) insurance agent. He told me, "You have insurance. It's ok, you don't have to worry." He stood in my parking lot and waited for me to arrive. We had to close the restaurant for six months. The fire caused a lot of damage and we even lost some of our prized photo plaques.

The boy who caused the fire admitted he burned the place down. He wrote a college paper about it. His teacher couldn't believe he got to keep his job. He was a good kid, he just messed up. Now, he eats free whenever he wants.

It was a trying time. I wasn't ready to go out of business. I wondered if people would come back. At that time, we had a restaurant in La Vergne. That helped out a lot so that we could still operate. I hoped our customers would come back, they did. We were so grateful, and still are.

Who has been the most influential person or mentor to you during your entrepreneurial journey and why?

I remember the first day I opened in January of 1988. There was three inches of snow on the ground. I have learned that barbecue isn't sold much when it's snowing. We were standing around waiting for customers. Mr. 'Coon' Victory's family owned Crosslin Supply across the street, and he wanted to feed his employees. As time goes on, the more that's meant to me for him to come out on our first day.

Crosslin had a customer appreciation day throughout the years, and we always provided the food. We had fun joking and giving Mr. Victory a hard time. That's what you do, you support the guy across the street. I didn't know anyone at that point. It meant a lot having someone that was always there when I was overwhelmed. On hard days, I would look across the street, and Mr. Victory's truck was always there. I thought, "well, he does it every day, I need to do it every day, too." Looking back, I remember how much it meant but now it means even more now.

I couldn't say anything nice enough for all Mr. Victory did for me over the years. He was a mentor without being one. I went over one day when my son, Brett, was little. We were looking for sponsors for his team. Coon said to send Brett. It's his sponsorship. I learned that from Coon, and I've remembered that over the years. I do that now when teams come to Bob's.

I once had two middle school football players come in looking for sponsors. I wrote a note to the coach and said I'd feed the team before a game and signed my name and number. I told the coach I wanted those boys to be recognized for getting the meal. They did what they were supposed to do. I fed this team one game a year for years. I ran into those same boys later on. They said the coach told the team they got the barbecue, and they were so excited.

What does supporting local mean to you?

When we first opened, Crosslin Supply was across the street. You could go in and see the owner. You walked in Sub Station II and you and would see Miss Alice and Dan. That to me was supporting local. You supported the people that were right there and they supported you. My buddy Robert Buck owns Buck's Jewelry. He recently asked me when Bob's opened. I told him I opened before he did. We didn't even think about going anywhere else to start a business. That to me is supporting local.

I have fond memories of swapping with other small businesses anytime one of us would run out of things like cups or straws. I used to always swap with Miss Alice, or Karin's Kustard. Paul Plunkett, my friend who owns the Smyrna Skate Center, and I have swapped for years. We'd swap birthdays and skating parties. We'd feed his church youth group. But you have to be willing to be a friend to have a friend.

It's so hard to own and operate a business. Now, everybody else has moved in. Smyrna is no longer the a small town. It still boils down to being a community town, but you have to work at it. If we're not careful, all of the sudden we don't have places like LubeShop or Buck's Jewelry. If you don't support them, the next thing we know, we will have a bunch of corporations. If they don't see a dollar they will pull out. Small business owners like me have been here for years. We have our homes here, our kids grew up, our grandkids live here now. You want to stay in your town. You're very invested. You have pride in it. My grandkids go to school here and I coach them. It's full circle.

Sometimes it's more convenient to go to the big places. They provide jobs, which is nice, but we need people to support the 'little guys' and their small businesses.

What do you enjoy doing in your spare time?

I've coached baseball and all different sports. I coached at Riverdale for twenty years. I did it up until my grandson turned five. I wasn't at his practice one day and he called me to ask why. I told him I had to be at high school practice. I told the high school I was done that day, and that I'd be coaching my grandson. I don't miss any of his practices now. You want to be involved, especially if they want you around.

How big of an impact has social media had on your small business?

I love it when employees say, "You've got to read this post or review." Or, like the mom who posted about her daughter coming to work for her first day of her first job at Bob's. Bob's was her mom's first job. Those are the things that mean a lot. It means something when someone posts reviews and food photos and says how much they enjoyed our food. We just try to put good food on every plate and be the best we can be. We love when someone posts about us because we've had an impact.

NESTING PROJECT
AS TOLD BY CORINNE MORSE

Website: www.nestingproject.com
Facebook: Nesting Project LLC
Instagram: @Nesting_Project

Tell me about your (small) business.
    We are a "Life Event" design and print company that specializes in DTG (direct to garment) printing, invitations, embroidery, and

screen printing. A nest is an ever-changing safe place. It's a home made from twigs, yarn, mud, and more. Our goal is to add the extra things in life to make the nest more livable, more comfortable, and more meaningful.

A life event is any moment in your life that you'd like to take a little extra time to enjoy, to remember, to stamp forever on your memory and simply celebrate. It could be a new baby, a birthday, a graduation, a wedding, a new house, an heirloom, or even a goodbye.

Over our eleven years in business, we've launched numerous products that have sometimes surprised us by the overwhelming interest. That's been so exciting.

About five years in, we created a set of sibling shirts that went viral and had us working all hours of the day for months and really helped springboard our growth. You may have seen them on Facebook. There are many copies of it today around the internet. As they say, "Imitation is a sign of flattery," and that's how we chose to look at it. We had no idea at first what caused a sudden surge in the orders, but with a little detective work, we found the online source as a radio station post within a few hours. We went from receiving a good handful of online orders per day to receiving over one hundred every day of just this one product. Over the years, we've sold over five thousand sets of these shirts around the world, and it all started with a gift to a friend and her children. That's the best part of the story.

The shirts read:
    "I'm the Oldest, I Make the Rules."
    "I'm in the Middle, I'm the Reason We Have Rules."
    "I'm the Youngest, The Rules Don't Apply to Me."

A lot of families have that one 'special' recipe that has been passed down for generations, and often brings back sweet and sentimental memories of lost loved ones, especially around the holidays. Nesting Project can actually take a family's handwritten recipe and put it on a tea towel (or pillow) in order to honor their

precious loved one and keep their memory alive. How does it make you feel knowing your business plays a special role in preserving, cherishing, and continuing family memories and traditions?

We adore our recipe tea towels. If you have one of those family favorite recipes handed down for generations written by your grandmother or grandfather, we take the recipe and print it in the original handwriting onto tea towels to share with loved ones without the worry of preserving the recipe. It's meant to get some splatters and splashes on it. That's what we call love. The towels are washable and extremely affordable for such a sentimental tear-jerking gift.

Oh, I love weddings. My favorite collection of items is, of course, within our wedding category. We have funny and bright bachelorette and bachelor party shirts, and coozies to start the events, but more importantly, we have entire paper suites to help set the mood for the event. Illustrations are a Nesting Project staple. We design classic and simple invitations, but our illustrations really created a wedding niche for us. It all started with the Rocky Mountains and the Boetcher Mansion where a bride was having a fall wedding. Now, we have over two hundred mountain locales illustrated and numerous countrysides and cities. A bride can submit a photo of her exact venue or view from the venue and we will illustrate it to create an entire suite of wedding paper products from Save the Dates to invitations, from cork coaster favors to programs, from seating charts to thank you cards, and so much more. We strive to provide our brides and their families with budget-friendly, but high-quality unique products. Many of our families will return for anniversary posters of the illustrations or wall art to adorn their new homes.

In every instance, when we have something custom, you work directly with a designer. Each customer is given up to four rounds of changes on proofs to ensure that the final product is exactly what they were searching for. We try to leave no stone unturned, and make sure that our customers experience a boutique experience, whether they want our full creative help, or, if they want it to be super simple and hands-off. That's the beauty of having a small staff of nine people who dedicate every day to making someone else's life extra special without the headache of having to try to "nail it" the Pinterest DIY way.

What is your favorite part about having a small business in Smyrna?

I initially looked at a building on Front Street that has since become an antique store. In August of 2018, my mom and my brother (a real estate mogul in Oklahoma) were visiting and I decided to take them one Saturday to look at the prospective building. The owner did not show up and we left deflated. That night, my mom, determined to help me, found the cutest little building just around the corner while scouring the internet for possibilities. In person it was even cuter and bigger than I thought. By Wednesday, my husband and I made an offer on the building. The current occupants didn't want to close shop until the following December, which could not have been better timing for us. We had to get through the upcoming holiday season in place before we could move. After a few renovations, it would be our new home in January 2019.

Tom's Florist had been in that very location for over a decade, and we were about to start our second decade. It seemed like fate. The transition was easier than we thought and when people asked where we were located, it was so fun to watch their eyes light up when I would say, "Do you know where Tom's Florist was? That's it, that's Nesting Project now." Nine out of ten people knew where I was talking about, and that really helped us get a foothold quickly. I still use that as a marker. It puts a smile on my face now when I overhear people saying, "You know where Nesting Project is on the corner of Hazelwood and Enon Springs?" I get a little giddy.

What brought you to Smyrna?

I have absolutely loved our journey to Smyrna. We started in our homes in Nashville and Franklin. When I moved to Nolensville, we decided to open our first retail location. It grew quickly thanks to some online viral sales, and we quickly outgrew our space. We had our retail location at one end of Nolensville and our production building at the other end. Luckily, that was still only a five-minute drive. It was hard though to run things back and forth, as we did not allow customers in our production facility. With the booming real estate market, we were desperate to find a location where we could move everything back into one building. After exhausting every possible location in the existing store's area, we finally decided to "look around", and I couldn't be happier that we did.

What does a typical day look like for you?

What does typical mean? (Laughs.) In small business, I don't feel like there is a typical. I wear fifteen different hats at any given time so my day changes to be whatever my staff or our clients need. I could be the day's designer, gopher, the programmer, the shipper, the printer, or the admin. I was blessed with extra energy without any need for caffeine or coffee so unless it's 7:00 a.m., the only constant for a "typical" day is a pair of comfy "running" shoes.

What are your daily habits or systems that you live by that have set you and your small business up for success?

You must make time for yourself and your family. My daily workout is my time to nourish and feed my body, to detach from work. I work all day and all night while I'm sleeping. Date nights with my husband at least twice a month. Game nights or dance parties with my kids.

What has been your biggest business milestone to date that you are most proud of?

I had a business partner and wasn't sure how we were going to transition through her exit and then the pandemic hit. I would say my biggest milestone is keeping my entire staff through the pandemic.

What have been some of your biggest business challenges you have faced and how have you overcome them?

The pandemic was the hardest. Life events all but stopped occurring. Everything we built our products around for ten years stopped and I had eight employees I needed to keep paying. We had to pivot hard, and we had to pivot weekly. It was exhausting but so worth it when we kept the doors open.

We created funny shirt sayings for dealing with the pandemic and our families. We converted our shop to a mask making facility and produced over ten thousand masks in an effort to be part of the solution of getting us all back to normal life. That is a major part of our mission: to be a part of the community, to give back and to be an inspiration in helping cultivate and explore the creative world of art.

Most of our business is still online. We have seven different Etsy shops. I know that sounds like a lot, but each shop is like a department in a larger department store to help with SEO on Etsy. One shop focuses solely on one of our trademark brands, Last Bash In Nash. Another focuses solely on embroidery, etc.

I would say that at least 80% of our business had been online until the pandemic, and then during some months it was 80% local. During Christmas we seemed to shift back to mostly online as the world continued to stay locked down. The trend has been similar this year as well, but there are certain months of the year that our local clientele surges.

We really love to help with fundraising for local groups so they can create a sense of community around a certain person or subject while earning some fundraising dollars. That's the beauty of DTG printing. There are no setup fees or out of pocket expenses to create the fundraiser and the percentage of each sale that goes back to the person or organization increases as the quantity increases. So, sometimes those local or in-person numbers can be skewed since much of the revenue goes back to the groups.

What is the biggest lesson you've learned in owning and operating a small business?

Process. You have to figure out your process for consistency and expectation and you have to be willing to change your processes often as technology and staff changes.

Are there any favorite mantras you live your life by?

"Educate and be the change." "Leap, the net will appear." "Eat dessert first, life is uncertain." "When today gets you down, start again tomorrow."

What advice would you give to someone wanting to pursue a career similar to yours?

Educate yourself but don't let analysis paralysis hold you back. You must jump at some point.

What has been the best piece of business advice you have ever received?

You must learn to own your business and not let your business own you. Honestly, I'm still struggling with this one.

How has failure or apparent failure set you up for future success?

For me, failure is a relative term. I don't believe in failure, per se. I think failure is simply an opportunity to reflect and to learn how to get back up, to pivot. The only true failure is if it ends a life. Other than that, it's simply a road bump that allows us to either crank up the speed, slow down or make a turn.

. . .

Who has been the most influential person or mentor to you during your entrepreneurial journey and why?

My brother. He was on his own entrepreneurial journey and just like we did when we were younger, he would pose questions to me about what I ultimately wanted from this venture. Did I want time, did I want money, did I just want to make a difference? Instead of telling me I had to do something one way or another, he simply made me search for my own answers.

What does success mean to you?

Another relative term. For me, it means happiness. Do I make enough to pay my bills? Do I have enough time to spend with my children? Do I laugh and love my friends and neighbors? Have I given back enough of myself to make a difference? That's it.

Where do you see yourself and your small business 5-10 years from now?

I would like to eventually give my business to my staff. They are the blood, sweat and tears of our every day, and I want to build up enough to give them a little slice of ownership. They work with that sense every day, and I'd like to be able to actually reward them for their ethic.

What do you enjoy doing in your spare time?

I sit on three boards, the Nolensville Farmers Market, Round Up for Nolensville, and Carpe Artista. I am the chair for the Broken Wheel Music Festival in Nolensville each fall. I still play music and write songs. I dance with a company of women (jazz, modern, ballet, etc.). I work out every day to clear my mind.

. . .

How big of an impact has social media had on your small business?

Recommendations and referrals are our life blood. The viral hits and the trends we become a part of are integral to keeping my local staff in their seats.

What does supporting local mean to you?

Without sounding silly, I can only say, it means everything to me. Small business is the backbone of American society. My parents were teachers and my husband's parents worked their whole lives for one or maybe two large corporations. Small business, though not for the faint of heart, is the American Dream in my book. If you work hard, open your mind to all the possibilities, there are endless roads in front of you. They may not be lucrative roads, but if you are searching for more than money, they can stretch and work your brain and body in ways you never imagined. Of course, you have to make enough to live on, but I moved here originally for music. Although I had a pretty solid career in the industry, when it was time to move on and I'd been my own boss my whole life, it made the most sense to continue down that path and to nurture the arts.

Why is supporting local businesses so important?

I was a Political Science major at Stanford University in California. All of my friends are big wigs at huge dot coms in Silicon Valley or doctors, etc. I love politics and I hate them. The place we can all make the biggest impact is in our local economies and communities. We will be hard pressed to make national changes from our homes or small businesses, but putting our money back into our communities and volunteering our time in our communities brings life, love, happiness, and support to our friends and neighbors while fostering a circle of life we want to be a part of.

. . .

Is there anything else you would like people to know about you or your small business?

Because we have so many products for weddings, people often ask us if we do event planning, to which I always answer, "No, but I have a list of local, amazing planners if you'd like me to share." For us, it's about community and network. We try to stick to what we do best and build up those who do things better.

TOM'S FLORIST
AS TOLD BY BUNNY KEMP

Website: www.tomsfloristsmyrna.com
Facebook: Tom's Florist
Instagram: @tomsfloristsmyrna

Tell me about your (small) business.

We deliver fresh, beautiful flowers every weekday to Smyrna, Murfreesboro, La Vergne, Antioch and Nashville. We love to make one-of-a-kind fresh flower bouquets and arrangements as gifts for any occasion, from birthdays to anniversaries. We also make fresh flower arrangements for funerals and sympathy gifts. We make corsages and boutonnieres for proms and other formal occasions. We also feature live plants and planted arrangements, fruit and snack gift baskets, chocolates, teddy bears, balloons and Marie Tilley's handcrafted gift cards for all your gifting needs.

Orders can be placed 24/7 on our website. You can order in person during store hours or over the phone by talking to one of our friendly staff members who will do their best to guide you through the process to ensure you get the perfect gift or floral arrangement. We have been at our current location for over two years, and our floral designers have over eighteen years of combined experience.

What inspired you to open a floral arrangement and gift shop?

I retired after working for Walgreens for twenty-five years. I always thought about having a shop of my own. The opportunity arose to buy AAA and Tom's Florist. I had connections to both businesses and knew the owners. I worked with the owner of Tom's Florist thirty years previously. The opportunity was too good to pass up, and here I am! I love having a business with no corporate rules where I can take care of my people and make our customers happy too.

What is your favorite part about having a small business in Smyrna?

I enjoy that I am still able to take care of some of my former customers from Walgreens, albeit in a different capacity. I love that there is still a sense of community even as the population of the area grows. And I love being only five minutes away from home.

. . .

What are you most excited about for your small business?

I am really looking forward to getting our business more well known in the local area so that customers can order directly with us and get more for their money. We currently receive a lot of our orders through a wire service, which means a percentage of the money goes to a large corporation.

What does a typical day look like for you?

We open at 8:00 a.m. The first job of the day is to write up the orders that have come in overnight. While I do that, another staff member fills buckets with water and flower food and gets ready for the daily delivery of fresh flowers. Our floral designers start creating our beautiful arrangements at 8:30 a.m. and aim to have all that day's orders made by mid-day. As soon as the fresh flowers are delivered to us, we condition them (cut them and remove some leaves), and then put them in the fridge which helps to keep them fresher longer. The deliveries start leaving the shop at 10.30 a.m., and we finish delivering by 7:00 p.m. each evening. We have some great, friendly delivery drivers, including my husband! The afternoons are for filing, starting the following day's orders, replenishing the shelves of vases and bowls and for cleaning. So much cleaning!

How have you grown your small business from an idea to where it is now?

Hard work, creativity and dedication. I feel the biggest influence on growing my business has been having a staff which really cares about their work. We take pride in our creations and serving our community in whatever their floral needs are.

. . .

What are some of the biggest lessons you've learned in owning a small business?

Keep your employees happy. Don't hesitate to get in there and help out. A happy team is living the dream! Also, I hadn't previously realized how hard it would be to make a profit as a member of a wire service. They can be challenging to work with, and although we get a large portion of our work through them, trying to balance profit with customer satisfaction can be hard when you are working on a set design. That is why we will always recommend a designer's choice arrangement over a set design. We encourage people to call local businesses rather than ordering through the online wire service. We really just want to do the best possible for our customers!

What has been your biggest business milestone to date that you are most proud of?

I am very proud that since I took on the business we have been continually growing and we have taken the growth in our stride. We are so grateful to our loyal customers who come back time and time again.

What have been some of your biggest business challenges you have faced and how have you overcome them?

The first year in the business was a big learning curve for me. I had to quickly learn which flowers we would need, especially for peaks. Trying to estimate red rose sales for Valentine's Day so that we would have enough stock to service our customers without having excess. After a couple of years, we now have a good system in place, but it definitely took us making mistakes to learn.

. . .

What has been the best piece of business advice you have ever received?

Have a good balance between work and family. Always stop to smell the roses!

Who has been the most influential person or mentor to you during your entrepreneurial journey and why?

Misty, our flower wholesaler representative. She has been invaluable helping me with flower orders, guiding me to know what is available, what is excellent quality, and how much I might need. We speak nearly every day, and she has been a guiding light.

Where do you see yourself and your small business 5-10 years from now?

I hope that within five years my business will have flourished, so that when I start thinking about retiring (permanently this time), the next owner will have a blooming business to run, and I will have pride to know that I was a vital part of a florist that has been in business in Smyrna for over fifty years.

What does success mean to you?

For me, success is running my business the way I want. Having a thriving business where I can look after my employees, and also have time for me, separate from the business. And most importantly, we consider it a success when we bring a smile to the faces of our customers.

What do you enjoy doing in your spare time?

My husband and I enjoy taking the dog camping, and enjoying

the beauty of nature. We have previously enjoyed volunteering for Food for Families and I was a volunteer at Smyrna Senior Activity Center. We also love to attend our church activities.

As a business, we enjoyed taking part in Depot Days. We also had a float at the Smyrna Christmas Parade which was so much fun, we handed out roses and it was amazing to be so involved with the community.

How big of an impact has social media had on your small business?

We love sharing our work on Facebook and Instagram. We find it a great tool for showing potential customers what we could create for them. We would really love to grow this further to really involve more of the community in what we do day-to-day. We love to hear your feedback. It's great to know when we've done a wonderful job, but we also want to know where we can improve so we can serve our customers better.

What does supporting local mean to you?

Supporting local means servicing our community, using businesses run by locals, businesses that produce or grow local products. If our local businesses do well, our community does well. Supporting local businesses keeps our community connected, while helping others strive for their success.

We've loved being a part of your journey. What's coming next that we can be a part of to support you?

A florist isn't just for Valentine's Day and Mother's Day. We can create arrangements for any occasion, a table centerpiece for Thanksgiving or Christmas; a bouquet to congratulate your graduate, a small gift to say, "I'm thinking of you", a corsage for prom, roses to get you out of the doghouse, balloons to celebrate a birthday, or we can help you create a suitable funeral or sympathy arrangement to celebrate the life of a loved one.

Is there anything else you would like people to know about you or your small business?

People can support local florists by ordering directly from them. Look online to find a florist local to the person you want to send flowers to, and then call the florist directly rather than using a go-between company. Florists do usually have their own websites, but oftentimes, you will get an even better service if you speak to the florist directly. You can ask which flowers are fresh, if they have any particularly lovely roses in store that day, or ask them for any lovely containers they could put an arrangement in. Trust the expertise of your local florist. You will always get a better value arrangement and they will always appreciate your support of their business.

We truly love our jobs and knowing that our creation will put a smile on the face of the recipient. We really are so lucky to do this work and be a part of this community. Thank you to every one of you who let us create something for you!

WALDEN PUMPKIN FARM
AS TOLD BY HEATHER WALDEN

Website: www.waldenpumpkinfarm.com
Facebook: Walden Pumpkin Farm-Smyrna
Instagram: @Walden_pumpkin_farm

Tell me about your (small) business.

We purchased Walden Farm in 1986. It is nestled between the rolling hills of Rutherford and Williamson Counties. This two hundred sixty-five-acre farm became the perfect place for the family to establish a homestead, and a place of serenity and harmony for the family to live and grow. Three generations of Waldens live on the farm.

In 1999, the next chapter unfolded. A few rows of pumpkins were planted in the garden just for fun. We had no idea we'd be picking close to five hundred pumpkins at harvest time. What were we going to do with all those pumpkins? Not knowing the answer, we picked them all and piled them up against the barn. The answer soon came as people pulled into the farm to inquire about buying a pumpkin. The idea was planted, and we knew the interest was definitely there. After much thought and planning, the family decided to grow more pumpkins and open the farm for the community to enjoy.

In the fall of 2000, Walden Farm opened to a wonderful reception from the public. School tours were booked, and the open fields were soon filled with cars. The community welcomed our family-oriented farm where kids and adults were alike in their curiosity about life on the farm.

From May through October the work doesn't stop. We each have an important role in operating the farm and making a wonderful experience for the public. We have approximately eighty seasonal workers, including twenty-two family members. We also have weekend/weekday workers and tour guides. It is a fun and rewarding time for each of us.

Walden Farm is open from late September through October 31st each year. As the heat of summer is lulling into the crisp coolness of autumn, people from all over Middle Tennessee come to enjoy picking out that perfect pumpkin or just rocking on the barn porch. We are so fulfilled by smiling faces and those who truly enjoy the farm.

Hayrides, farm animals, hay and corn mazes, Tennessee Slip 'n' Slide, delicious food and treats are just some of what the farm offers. We sell a large variety of pumpkins, gourds, mums, Indian corn, cornstalks, and straw bales. The Country Store sells a complete selection of fall decorating items, delicious jams, jellies, and our own local honey. We have amazing fall wreaths for your front door and beautiful centerpieces for your fall  party or Thanksgiving table. We have local jams, jellies, and you'll want to try the honey from our bees here on the farm. We also have farm toys, gift items and Halloween items such as carving kits and trick or treat bags. Come hungry, because we have a large food menu including BBQ, hamburgers, hot dogs, fresh cut ribbon fries, pumpkin fudge, funnel cakes and much more! You'll want to grab a cup of hot spiced cider while you're here.

What is your favorite part about having a small business in Smyrna?

We love seeing familiar faces from year to year, and always enjoy meeting new ones! Many families have made coming to Walden Farm one of their family traditions and we are so blessed and honored by that.

What are some of the biggest lessons you've learned in owning a small business?

Everything does not have to happen all at once. Let things progress as your business grows.

For our business, it's not just about a customer buying a pumpkin. It's about creating an experience for getting that perfect pumpkin that people want to enjoy year after year. Make people happy and they will come back!

What have been some of your biggest business challenges you have faced and how have you overcome them?

We have some "growing pains" each year. As the community grows, so does our crowd. We work hard to make sure that people are happy and comfortable when they are here. We are able to spread activities out or move things around. Some of this is going to happen regardless, so we make the best of it.

What advice would you give to someone wanting to pursue a career similar to yours?

Start small. Keep things simple and only spend what you can at the time. This business, like most, takes time to build.

Who has been the most influential person or mentor to you during your entrepreneurial journey and why?

When we decided to grow pumpkins, we reached out to the Gentry family in Franklin. They have an agritourism business like ours. At the time, we didn't know where to begin or what to do. The Gentrys were very gracious and shared some tips and tricks with us to help us get started.

What do you enjoy doing in your spare time?

We are all involved in local churches in the area. We enjoy camping. Some of us fish and hunt, while others enjoy the quiet moments to sit on the porch with a good book.

What does supporting local mean to you?

Supporting local is very important to us and every small business in this community. We know people can buy a pumpkin at a grocery store, but we have created an experience here at Walden Farm for people to enjoy. When people buy pumpkins or other items from us, it allows us to keep sharing our farm with you.

Is there anything else you would like people to know about you or your small business?

This year marks our twenty-first year in business. We are excited to see more people this year. Start a new tradition for your family by visiting Walden Pumpkin Farm!

RACQUEL PEEBLES, ATTORNEY AT LAW
AS TOLD BY RACQUEL PEEBLES

Website: www.peeblesfirm.com
Facebook: Racquel Peebles, Attorney-at-Law
Instagram: @racquel.peebles
Email: racquel@peeblesfirm.com
Phone: 615.751.6115

Tell me about your (small) business.

I primarily practice in corporate and business law, wills, probate and estates, and adoption law, with some work in real estate law. I have been a practicing attorney for twenty-five years. I graduated from Emory University School of Law in 1996. I practiced for seven years in Atlanta before moving back home in 2003 where I have been practicing since.

What inspired you to become an attorney?

My family says that I said I wanted to be an attorney when I was five, and I never changed my mind. I believe that sometimes we are led in our spirits to walk a certain path because of the value that it brings to the world although we don't always understand at the time. However, I went through law school with helping my community as my goal. I graduated from Smyrna High in 1989, and I went to Memphis State University and graduated with a degree in Political Science in 1993. Then directly to law school.

What is your favorite part about having a small business in Smyrna?

Helping people. I like being a resource for my community. I know that Smyrna is a special place and being the first lawyer of color to open an office here has been extremely special to me. Being a native has also given me the opportunity to provide quality legal services to my family, friends, and neighbors. People trust me and I don't take that lightly.

How did your childhood in Smyrna shape you?

Being born and raised in Smyrna has shaped everything about me. My family goes back at least six generations. I grew up in Hilltop around my whole family. My ancestors bought the land where my grandmother's home is located in 1907. I was raised in my grandmother's home. There were always friends and neighbors at our house. I learned a sense of community, and I also learned about taking care of my neighbor.

Two important principles I learned were (1) to have a strong work ethic and (2) to be an individual. My family has always been supportive on this journey. I know what it means to work hard, and I didn't mind doing so. So, when I decided to move back to Smyrna and open my own law practice, I wasn't swayed by the obstacles that I would face.

What are you most excited about for your small business?

I am excited to be transitioning my practice. I have practiced in the same location for thirteen years, but recently re-located to 511 Enon Springs Road, East. However, I will continue to provide the same services to assist clients with their legal needs.

How have you grown your small business from an idea to where it is now?

I closed my practice in Roswell, Georgia and moved back to Smyrna when I was four months pregnant with my daughter. I knew I wanted to raise my family and practice law in Smyrna, and it was time to come home. I knew it was God's purpose for my life. When I moved home, I started building my law practice taking cases for my family and friends. I also taught classes in the evening with the University of Phoenix-Nashville Campus for four years.

My business has grown as the result of hard work, professionalism, self-analysis, a supportive clientele, and God's grace. As a business owner, self-motivation is critical. My practice has always been unconventional. I am not in the office 9-5, but I still work twelve to fourteen hours most days. As a sole practitioner, I have to be the lawyer performing all of the legal work, and also the accountant, marketing manager, office manager, receptionist, HR manager, IT specialist, etc. It has required a lot of long hours learning and working the administrative side of running a business as well as time to learn and grow my craft as laws change and evolve.

I've learned that being a service business requires personal involvement which allows for unique perspective. I have to be resourceful and willing to be flexible.

I have had great mentors and business colleagues that have been guides throughout my career. This has helped me tailor my business practices and build a business that has lasted twenty years. Also, client referrals are a large part of how I grow and sustain my business. I am appreciative of every mention and every card given out.

What does a typical day look like for you?

There are no two days that look the same. I may be in court, meetings with clients, or researching and drafting legal documents. I work with clients by the method that is easier for them. I speak with clients by phone, email or in-person and try to meet at times convenient for the parties involved. In addition, I participate in meetings, workshops, and scheduled events involving the Town.

What is the biggest lesson you've learned in owning and operating a small business?

Know your worth. My job encompasses twenty-five years of experience, legal research, understanding of statutes and case law. My knowledge is the foundation of my legal practice, and how I apply it is the value that I bring to my clients. Many people contact me and want me to tell them how to do something, but every case has its own nuances that people do not realize can change the outcome of their specific case. Knowing how to interpret the facts is the value of my knowledge. And because of this knowledge I have clients across the state from all walks of life.

. . .

What are your daily habits or systems that you live by that have set you and your small business up for success?

1) I try to treat clients like I would want to be treated. I want to be professional. I explain legal issues in plain language so that clients can be vested in the process as well as the outcomes of their cases. Most times clients appreciate it, but there are others who do not care and just want the result in their favor, and I try to understand both perspectives.

2) I keep my calendar updated, and I am constantly checking to make sure that I am keeping all of my appointments, meetings and hearings scheduled, and I make sure to have time for case preparation.

3) Also, I try to be present with my family when we are together. I let them know that they matter, and nothing is more important.

Are there any favorite mantras you live your life by?

My motto has been the same since I started my business, and I still believe in it. It appears on my letterhead: "Dedicated to providing sound legal counsel in the stewardship of life and business."™

What has been your biggest business milestone to date that you are most proud of?

My biggest business milestone is twofold. First, I have been able to practice law as a solo practitioner for twenty years and second, while being a business owner, I have raised two beautiful, intelligent, Christ-centered children with a sense of self and who understand the importance of family and community.

I am amazed at God's goodness, and how He has blessed me. I also had a strong support system from my family and friends that continues to this day.

In the midst of this journey, I went through a divorce and had to continue to work to take care of my family. I could not have done all of the things without them helping me.

I have also received a few accolades during my career-ones I didn't expect. In 2009, I was named as an honoree for Murfreesboro Magazine Women in Business. In 2013, I was honored by Venus Chapter #61 Order of the Eastern Star for Service to Family, Church and Community. In 2017, I was presented with the Legacy of Honor in Government at Smyrna by the AAHS of Rutherford County. I feel blessed to be acknowledged by my community.

What have been some of your biggest business challenges you have faced and how have you overcome them?

Balancing work and personal. I would say that I have yet to master the balance. The goal in this season of my life is to become more balanced in my personal life.

What advice would you give to someone wanting to pursue a career similar to yours?

Find individuals in different stages of their career who are willing to talk to you and give you real life truths about the practice of law so that you can learn from their knowledge and experience and make informed decisions. My career was not traditional. I have had to balance multiple roles. Having individuals to walk with you on your journey is invaluable.

What has been the best piece of business advice you have ever received?

The biggest investment I can make in my business is investing in myself. It is important to be mindful of taking care of yourself because no one can do this for you. It is imperative to remember to take time to invest in yourself, both, personally and professionally.

. . .

What are some of the biggest lessons you've learned in owning a small business?

1) Being a business owner is not a passive experience. It requires focus, diligence, and vulnerability. I don't know everything, and I have to be willing to ask for help and delegate when necessary; otherwise, do the work. 2) When I remember that my business is my ministry it helps me keep the daily activities in proper perspective. Being an attorney does not define me. It is a mechanism to serve and help others. 3) If I don't manage my business, my business will manage me. 4) Working for myself does not lessen the pressure of a daily grind. It actually adds to the pressure to perform. I cannot afford to be mediocre. I have multiple bosses because I have multiple clients. The goal is to have repeat clients who value my work and want me handling their cases. 5) Not every prospect that I meet with is intended to become a client. Sometimes it is not about the money, but it can be about peace of mind or time investment. I need to listen to my gut-it doesn't mislead.

How has failure or apparent failure set you up for future success?

What I have come to know through the challenges is that failure requires reflection and analysis. Failure highlights parts of my thought process that may need to be changed. Failure reveals flaws, but flaws don't have to be bad. Flaws can be positive if you learn from them and turn them into a strength. It is all in your perspective. Most of all, failure makes me work harder. I am often underestimated by those around me, and I am not expected to succeed. Consequently, I operate differently than most people. They all have an impact in one way or another.

Who has been the most influential person or mentor to you during your entrepreneurial journey and why?

I can't say that I have had one influence. Multiple individuals have influenced my entrepreneurial journey through the years- family, neighbors, other mothers, community leaders, attorneys, church members and ministers, business owners, and my children. If we are paying attention, God places people all along our paths that guide, influence and direct us.

Do you have any favorite memories with, or lessons learned from Ms. Imogene Bolin?

Imogen Bolin has been a mentor, a friend, and my family. We have practiced together for fifteen years. We started our journey as colleagues in 2005. She is a wise, caring, influential attorney and community leader. She also has a story for every occasion. She is a trailblazer for women in the law and served as the first Town Judge for Smyrna. Ms. Bolin understands how history factors into law and political arenas and knows how important this information can be to resolving an issue.

Ms. Bolin has always been active in the community. She saw a need and asked the attorneys in the building to create a way to address it. For more than ten years, the Attorneys at the Victory House have held a Christmas Open House where we accepted monetary donations and unwrapped toys to distribute to children in the Rutherford County foster system through CASA (Court Appointed Special Advocates). Each year, it has grown. We did not have the Open House in 2020 because of the pandemic, but we collected more than $11,000 in donations. There have been some devoted contributors, and we are honored that they contribute each year to this great cause.

What 1-3 books have impacted your life the most and why

The Bible; *Ethical Ambition* by Derrick Bell; *Humility, True Greatness* by C.J. Mahaney

These books help me to have a perspective that keeps me grounded and focus on what is important.

Where do you see yourself and your small business 5-10 years from now?

This last year has changed how many businesses operate. The practice of law was not immune from the world experiencing a pandemic. I hope to be able to integrate the practice of law with technology in a manner that adds value to my clients.

What do you enjoy doing in your spare time?

I do not have a lot of spare time. I am a single mom with two teenage kids. I also serve as a councilwoman for Smyrna. Some of the activities that we participate in include events with the Senior Activity Center, Rotary Fish Fry, CDC Alert Back to School Event, and Smyrna and Linebaugh Library events. I try to spend any time that I have doing things that my kids like to do. My son likes gymnastics and roller skating, and my daughter loves all things crafty and fashion-related. I also have family members who participate in school sports and I like to support them. I also like to cook for my family and friends.

What does supporting local mean to you?

Supporting local means eating, shopping, and patronizing businesses around the Town of Smyrna as much as we can. Small businesses are the cornerstone of our local economy, and the lifeblood of our community. We live in such a blessed place, and we are prospering in a great way. We as citizens need to be intentional about the support that we give to our fellow business owners. It is necessary and essential to our town continuing to prosper and sustain itself. Local businesses are operated by our friends and neighbors, and our patronage helps to feed our families, grow our communities, and build the local tax base.

Is there anything else you would like people to know about you or your small business?

I am the first person of color and the first woman of color to have a law practice in Smyrna.

I would like to express my appreciation for the support that all of the community has shown to me. Smyrna is a great place to live, work and play, and I am glad to be a part of this community, and I look forward to many more years of providing legal services.

CUSTOM CUP SLEEVES
AS TOLD BY J. SCOTT LAW

Website: www.customcupsleeves.com
Facebook: Custom Cup Sleeves
Instagram: @ccsleeves
Twitter: @ccsleeves

Tell me about your (small) business.

We provide custom printed cup sleeves for a personal touch to any occasion where hot or cold beverages are served in paper or plastic cups. We also provide plain paper hot cups and plastic cups as an ancillary product for folks that may not have access to these complimentary products in small quantities.

What inspired you to start a business offering custom printed cup sleeves?

The specific business of customized cup sleeves was more of a "God Thing." After being in corporate America over the course of almost thirty years, it was time to do something different. I had a desire to start a business for probably the last ten years of my time in telecom. I took a voluntary incentive plan and retired from AT&T in 1998 with the intent to leave the industry, but was lured back by Bellsouth for the last and best ten years of my career. I even prayed that God would take the desire to start a business away from me if it wasn't His will, but when AT&T bought out Bellsouth in 2006, I knew it was time to make a move. Because I was nowhere near retirement age, I still needed a source of income. I spent the last two years at AT&T looking earnestly for a business to start. I wanted something that would enable me to work on my timeframe, day or night, something that did not require a store front where I would have to be there from 8:00 a.m.-5:00 p.m., and something that was relocatable in case I decided to move (which I did in 2017).

In my search, I ran across a coffee supply business in New York that had been getting numerous requests for customized coffee sleeves in small quantities. Up to this point, I did not even know the industry term for the cardboard around your coffee cup was called a "coffee sleeve." I love coffee, so this intrigued me. In researching, I found out that it was very difficult to purchase custom coffee sleeves in smaller quantities as the industry standard is a minimum of forty cases with a four to six week turn-around for custom printing. This is over fifty thousand sleeves on a 3'x 4' pallet 4' high. This is about the size of most small coffee shops' entire storage room and at a couple of thousand dollars, this was out of reach for shops just starting out, not to mention they couldn't wait four to six weeks for them to arrive, and since the coffee supply business wasn't interested in the printing business, they wanted to sell the idea they had been playing with. I negotiated the purchase of that idea along with a small commercial printer and a few boxes of sleeves, then in June of 2008, I retired from AT&T for the second time, and Custom Cup Sleeves was born.

I set up shop in our home office with a computer, the printer, and a toll-free telephone number. We launched our website on August 1, 2008. One of the agreements with the coffee supply shop was for them to add a link from their website to ours for a period of a year and that was really our only method of advertising. Over the course of the next two years, I sought to learn how to create graphics, upgraded the equipment, improved the process to make it more efficient and moved from my office to the garage. Also, during this time the business had grown to the point I could hire someone to print, and later, a person to answer the phone. This person, Richelle Davis, is still with us today and the heart and soul of our business. As we continued to slowly grow, we moved out of our garage into some storage units (which is an interesting story for another time), and finally into the office/warehouse where we are located today.

What is your favorite part about having a small business in Smyrna?

While our business is literally world-wide, we ship to every state in the U.S. and have shipped to every continent except Antarctica, and although Smyrna has exploded in size over the last ten years, it still has a small town feel we wanted for our business.

. . .

Smyrna Spotlights

What brought you to Smyrna?

My family and I moved to Smyrna in 1990. After growing up in Maryville, TN, my wife and I moved to Middle Tennessee after a five-year period in Florida, just before our first child was born in 1986. We settled in Smyrna after being drawn here by the abundance of parks, recreation, and the feel of community.

What are you most excited about for your small business?

The potential for growth. We have several thousand customers, and while custom printed sleeves will remain our primary service, there are many options to expand our sales of other products to a customer base that has grown to know and trust our commitment to quality and customer service.

What's the first thing you do every morning to start your day on the right foot?

There is a quote from U.S. Navy Admiral William McRaven, "If you want to change the world, start off by making your bed." The thought is if you accomplish one small thing each morning, such as making your bed, it will set the tone to accomplish larger tasks, and even if you have a bad day, when you get home, you can look at the bed you made and take pride in at least one thing you did and have hope that tomorrow will be a better day. While I am not especially fond of bed making, my wife really likes this quote and reinforces it for me when I complain about making the bed!

What does a typical day look like for you?

We put together orders that we receive overnight via email or our website, take additional orders during the day and get those orders printed and shipped. Our objective is to ship orders the day after we receive them, which we almost always achieve, so while our task is simple, the execution of that task can be very complex with too many variables to plan for.

What is the biggest lesson you've learned in owning and operating a small business?

The fact that I knew nothing about owning and operating a business! Clients in my market segment at AT&T had to bill at least a million dollars in telecom and part of my job was negotiating contracts for these customers, so I thought I knew business. I knew nothing about bookkeeping, credit card processing, website development or maintenance, or all the taxes associated with owning a small business, especially the taxes. When we started hiring employees there were more taxes to learn, all the things that were behind the scenes in my corporate America job.

Are there any favorite mantras you live your life by?

I have always tried to live by what is commonly known as "the Golden Rule." To paraphrase Jesus' words in Matthew 7:12, "Treat others the way you want to be treated." It's just that simple, something I think we, as a society, would do well to remember.

What are your daily habits or systems that you live by that have set you and your small business up for success?

I firmly believe that if you treat everyone with respect and do what you say you are going to do, you will be successful in any business. Our policy is that the customer will be satisfied, period. If you are not happy with the product you receive, we will re-print it, return your money, or both.

What has been your biggest business milestone to date that you are most proud of?

Probably hitting our ten-year mark. Having survived and even thrived over this period is very satisfying.

What have been some of your biggest business challenges you have faced and how have you overcome them?

Knowing how fast or even if you want to grow your business beyond a certain point. Bigger isn't always better. Servicing our customers and keeping good employees are more important than just growing the business. But if we get those two things right, the business will grow on its own.

What advice would you give to someone wanting to pursue a career similar to yours?

I think you can pick any service-oriented business and simply do what you say you are going to do, show up when you say you will, charge a fair price and you will be successful. Folks will appreciate that, which will result in word-of-mouth that will easily grow your business. There are just too many businesses that are looking for the big payday and neglect showing up or calling back on the smaller jobs. That kind of word-of-mouth will sink a business. It's a sad statement, but these days you can be outstanding by just doing the minimum, common sense, and common decency requirements.

What has been the best piece of business advice you have ever received?

"Under promise and over deliver." Don't make promises you aren't sure you can keep and always do more than is expected.

. . .

What are some of the biggest lessons you've learned in owning a small business?

Don't assume you know everything about running a small business just because you own one. Be open and willing to seek and accept advice. There is always something to learn.

What 1-3 books have impacted your life the most and why?

I am a big believer in reading and have tried to instill in my children that "readers are leaders." I am also a Christian, so the Bible has always been the book that I have strived to use, although not always successfully, as the guide to living a life of meaning. Also, *Blue Like Jazz* by Donald Miller, and *A Life Well Lived* by Tommy Nelson are other books that have spoken to me at various times in my life.

Who has been the most influential person or mentor to you during your entrepreneurial journey and why?

I must give a huge amount of credit to a man named Tom Hyde. Tom was one of the smartest men I have ever had the pleasure of knowing. He was a businessman in Murfreesboro, whose primary business was recruiting employee candidates with a focus on Japanese/English bilingual skills. He also had businesses in real estate and financial services. I was introduced to him at a Christmas party and, for whatever reason, Tom took an interest in our business and shared his experience and ideas along with tools he had developed in building his businesses to help us achieve the growth we have experienced. Tom had the vision that it could grow to what it is today. Sadly, Tom was taken from us by cancer in 2018.

Where do you see yourself and your small business 5-10 years from now?

That's a tough question. I am blessed that we have been in business for going on thirteen years and don't think about not having the business; but realistically something will likely come along in the next ten years that could take the place of a paper coffee sleeve and make our business less relative. In the meantime, I think we should try to expand our product offerings to our customer base in case that should happen.

What does success mean to you?

Success to me is having the freedom of time. Time to do the things you want to do and enjoy the people you love and who love you.

How big of an impact has social media had on your small business?

We like to give "shout-outs" to our customers by posting pictures of our sleeves with their logos and encourage them to share their pictures as well. We enjoy seeing the creative ways and places customers display their sleeves.

What does supporting local mean to you?

Seeking out small, locally owned businesses rather than always going to the chain stores. My wife jokes on vacation that every restaurant I pick must have someone's name on the sign. There is probably some truth to that. I do try to go out of my way to support local businesses.

I believe small businesses are the backbone of America, and the heart of a lot of small towns. These businesses typically employ local folks who also live in the area and customers become friends and neighbors. This fosters a culture and community that larger chain stores, who are beholden to their stockholders, can never do.

. . .

Are there any other ways people can support your small business?

We have a unique product in custom printed cup sleeves that doesn't necessarily appeal to the masses. Our target customers are "Mom and Pop" coffee shops, churches, schools, etc. Places where coffee is served to lots of folks. With that said, we also do smaller "combo-packs" of cups and lids along with custom sleeves that may interest folks that are planning weddings, business and networking events, retirement parties, etc.

Is there anything else you would like people to know about you or your small business?

I would be remiss if I did not brag about our employees. We are very fortunate to have the greatest group of folks, that have become more like family than employees. Richelle, Lisa, CJ, Conner, Ronnie, Miller, and Glenn each take pride in their work. They know their expectations and meet them every day, and I think we have the best customer service to be found, period. I can't say enough good things about this group. Without question, they make our business what it is.

THE SALT BARN
AS TOLD BY JODI CROSSNOE

Website: www.TheSaltBarnUS.com
Facebook: The Salt Barn US
Instagram: @TheSaltBarnUS

Tell me about your (small) business.

The Salt Barn is a holistic day spa. We opened our doors in July 2018, offering an amazing salt cave, float tank, detox foot baths, and an infrared sauna. In March 2020, we were able to expand into the suite next to us. In June 2020, we began offering massage therapy and esthetics, and also added another float tank and another infrared sauna. Along with our services, we also have a wide variety of gift items in our retail area including several shapes and sizes of Himalayan salt lamps and decorative salt warmers, Himalayan salt massage stones, CBD oils, doTERRA essential oils, beauty products by KPS and doTERRA, essential oil diffusers and much more. We also make many of our products that we sell in our retail area. Those products include salt scrubs, bath salts, body butters, Himalayan salt jewelry, lip scrubs, cuticle oils, Macrame/Himalayan salt pieces and more.

What inspired you to get into the wellness industry, and specifically open a salt cave?

I am a breast cancer survivor and a true believer that holistic treatments truly work. While going through chemotherapy, radiation therapy, and multiple surgeries for many months and feeling and seeing how it was affecting my body and my mind, I began researching what I could do to rid my body of all the toxins that I was being subjected to. I sort of stumbled onto the benefits of halotherapy (salt therapy) and ionic detox foot baths and float therapy. I wanted to try out these therapies but unfortunately there wasn't any place local that had anything like that. I didn't give it a whole lot of thought at the time and simply moved on. I was working a full-time job as an accountant. When I decided to quit my job in early 2018, I knew I couldn't just be a stay-at-home mom. I took a few months off, and it was at that point I realized what I wanted to do... open my very own salt cave!

What are you most excited about for your small business?

I am most excited about my small business continuing to grow and offer more services. I love meeting new people and helping them live a healthier life.

How has being a cancer survivor inspired your entrepreneurial journey?

Being a cancer survivor has changed me a lot. It has changed my outlook on everything, really. I am more thankful for the amazing and wonderful things in my life. My kids, my family, my health, and of course, my business and all the blessings it has brought me. I don't take one thing for granted. When you go through something like cancer, it really makes you step back and realize how quickly things can change and makes you appreciate your family and friends and the moments that you have with them. I love this community, and love helping others. I feel like The Salt Barn is my way of doing that, which is why I give free salt cave sessions to all cancer patients and survivors.

I would tell anyone impacted by cancer to keep dreaming and keep looking forward and to stay positive. Anything is possible. Do what makes you happy and surround yourself with positive and happy people.

Out of all of the services The Salt Barn provides, what is your favorite and why?

My favorite service is the salt cave because it is so very relaxing, and there's nothing quite like it.

·   ·   ·

What's the first thing you do every morning to start your day on the right foot?

Think about the day ahead of me and picture myself happy, smiling and enjoying every minute of it!

What is the biggest lesson you've learned in owning and operating a small business?

Listen to your customers, listen to your employees, and listen to your heart.

Are there any favorite mantras you live your life by?

Stay positive and good things and good people will be drawn to you.

What have been some of your biggest business challenges you have faced and how have you overcome them?

The biggest challenge we have faced has definitely been COVID-19. Having to close our business for several months was very stressful, but something positive did come out of it. We were able to use that time to expand our business into the suite next to us and grow our business by offering more services.

What advice would you give to someone wanting to pursue a career similar to yours?

Do lots of research, and be 100% sure that this is what you want to do because, it is a lot of work.

·   ·   ·

What has been the best piece of business advice you have ever received?

Don't be afraid to ask for help when you need it.

What 1-3 books have impacted your life the most and why?

How to Win Friends and Influence People by Dale Carnegie. This book taught me how to communicate well with others.

How has failure or apparent failure set you up for future success?

I don't like to lose or fail at anything. I've always had a competitive nature. When something doesn't go the way I want it to, that just fuels my fire and makes me work harder to achieve the results I want.

Who has been the most influential person or mentor to you during your entrepreneurial journey and why?

My mom. It may sound crazy to say that since she passed away in 2013, five years before I even started this business, but it's true. I think of my mom every single day. I'm always asking myself, "what would my mom have done in this situation?" or, "what would mom think about this?" I know she's watching over me and guiding me in all that I do and that makes me want to succeed even more.

Where do you see yourself and your small business 5-10 years from now?

I would love to see The Salt Barn located on a piece of land that we own in a "barn-shaped" building that we own with a few more locations in the southeast.

What does success mean to you?

Doing what you love and earning an honest living while doing it!

. . .

What do you enjoy doing in your spare time?

I love going to antique stores, flea markets, auctions and garage sales with my husband and mother-in-law, refinishing antique furniture, boating, or riding jet skis, driving and going to car shows in my antique cars ('48 Chevy truck/'51 Mercury/ '55 Chevy), gardening and working in my yard, riding my bicycle, and I even took a quilting class earlier this year!

How big of an impact has social media had on your small business?

I believe having great customer feedback and so many positive reviews makes a huge impact on our business. We've had people come to The Salt Barn from all over the U.S. and many of them say it is because of all the positive reviews we have!

What does supporting local mean to you?

It means shopping and buying locally at small businesses to help keep them in business. It keeps our economy strong, provides local jobs and supports local families.

Think locally owned small businesses when looking for a gift or an experience for someone. We have lots of things to choose from like salt lamps, jewelry, salt scrubs and essential oils but you can also just get a gift certificate that can be used for services or for items in our gift shop.

. . .

We've loved being a part of your journey. What's coming next that we can be a part of to support you?

Memberships, ice water therapy, Yoga classes, lash extensions, make-and-take classes...

Is there anything else you would like people to know about you or your small business?

A lot of the antiques and decorations in The Salt Barn belonged to my parents and are from their log home property in southern Illinois. Seeing those items everyday reminds me of them and keeps their memory alive.

GAME GALAXY ARCADE
AS TOLD BY JASON WILSON

Photos courtesy of Barbara Potter Photography

Facebook: Game Galaxy Arcade
Instagram: @Gamegalaxysmyrna

Tell me about your (small) business.
   Game Galaxy is one of the largest traditional arcades in the country with around four hundred and fifty physical games including

one hundred fifty-five pinball machines. I am the only owner. We have been open for thirteen years. We offer affordable free play for $12 all day per person, or $10 all day for each person for a family of four or more. We hold pinball and fighting game tournaments as well as have a classic game store for purchases of older favorites like the NES, N64, PlayStation, and many others! We also repair arcade and pinball machines from 1978 and up. Game Galaxy is located at the center of Smyrna's downtown historic district (across the railroad tracks).

In many ways, Game Galaxy is a hands-on museum of video game history. Your front room covers all nine generations of home gaming consoles, with the retro systems like Atari 2600 and Nintendo 64 even hooked-up to CRT televisions. And your arcade features everything from original Williams and Bally pinball machines to classic games such as Ms. Pac-Man, a collection of Nintendo VS. cabinets, and the Mortal Kombat series. When (and why) did you start collecting all these systems and machines?

The Middle Tennessee area really didn't have any affordable places for kids and families to enjoy. The country had just started a recession and I figured there was an opportunity for cheap, affordable family entertainment. Plus, I needed a place to store my arcade games, which were starting to grow exponentially at the time. Free storage and people get to play the games sounded like a win/win. I had always wanted to open an arcade since I was very little and grew up an arcade rat, so this just seemed like the natural thing to do.

Game Galaxy is the largest arcade in Tennessee with over ten thousand arcade, pinball machines, and console (video) games. What are some of your most popular games?

Most of the Mortal Kombat and Street Fighter games are played frequently but our rhythm section including Jubeat and Sound Voltex are extremely popular and amongst the only places to play in the South. We have some rare laser games like Cliff Hanger and Firefox available to play as well as Tattoo Assassins, a canceled fighting game from Data East in the nineties. Eventually, we will put Punky Doodle on the floor, an unreleased Sunsoft arcade game that no one has that legend has given the creator of Pokemon his initial idea based on the characters in Punky Doodle.

Your arcade attracts dedicated gamers of all ages. How does it make you feel watching multiple-generations of gamers playing together and experiencing both the classic arcade cabinets as well as the newer console games that are more popular with the younger generations?

We hear a lot of the time how excited customers are coming here from all over the country to play their favorite game(s) they only saw at a 7-11 when they were a kid back in the day. The idea was in case kids were not as into the arcade and pinball machines Fortnite and other modern games awaited them in the console area. I always enjoy knowing kids can grow up like I did with this experience, as it was the most important aspect of creating me as a person, being able to enjoy video games in a social environment.

In addition to featuring an array of arcade games for gamers to play, you also buy and sell both retro and contemporary video game consoles, games, and accessories. What can players expect when shopping for and trading games at Game Galaxy?

We pay more than anyone in the area for most items in cash and offer very good trade credit.

Our game store selection is not large, but it is well stocked. We are always interested in purchasing large collections and have purchased a complete NES collection from a customer just in the last three years as an example of our buying power in order to bring in rare stuff for customers to purchase.

We do rent pinball and arcade machines monthly and for special events like weddings and corporate retreats, etc. We only repair arcade and pinball machines and occasionally will repair a console system or two.

Esports has exploded in popularity over the last decade, and Game Galaxy hosts tournaments that attract gamers from all over the state. What are some of your most popular tournament games, and how can players sign up to compete?

Most of the time we do Street Fighter V and Tekken 7. Our fight nights are Tuesdays after 6:00 p.m. and Saturdays after 1:00 p.m. Tournaments are currently announced on our Facebook page, which will always have updates to what games will be played.

What is your favorite part about having a small business in Smyrna?

The large amount of families that come in and enjoy the cheap entertainment. People are very friendly and it is our favorite city (I do reside here) for our locations past and present.

What brought you to Smyrna?

My spouse got a job in Murfreesboro (her hometown) working for the State. I had a great position as a Product Manager for a software peripheral company but with her doctorate and cost of living being significantly lower, it made a lot of sense to move out this way. That was back in 2007.

What has been your biggest business milestone to date that you are most proud of?

Thirteen years in business and counting. One fellow colleague gave us six months when we first opened in Smyrna. A lot of that kind of negativity without knowing the type of business we have and what we do drives us to succeed even more.

What are some of the biggest lessons you've learned in owning a small business?

Not having a partner allows less issues when it comes to decision-making and financial strongholds when one person has the funding and the other does not. I've lost one store based on the complexities of a business partnership and will not go that route again.

Smyrna Spotlights

. . .

What have been some of your biggest business challenges you have faced and how have you overcome them?

Moving large amounts of machines from locations closing in very finite amounts of time. A lot of perseverance and luck and help from our amazing crew from many years together have kept us afloat and very well grounded in times of stress.

How big of an impact has social media had on your small business?

I'll be the first to admit we are the absolute worst at marketing. We have $0 budget for it, so shockingly we have survived all these years on word-of-mouth. We have a Facebook page. That is about it!

What does supporting local mean to you?

Supporting family-owned businesses where your purchase goes directly to help them and not a mystery corporate CEO. Everything we get in goes back to the store for customers to enjoy. Pinball machines aren't cheap these days!

It gives Smyrna a great identity. With more and more places succumbing to corporations moving in you need eclectic businesses to show that they/we are willing to invest in the community. We are a dying breed and it becomes harder and harder to open new businesses these days. The litany of places that have come and gone here in the past decade is astounding.

We've loved being a part of your journey. What's coming next that we can be a part of to support you?

Smyrna keeps us very busy! It is like three stores in one! We don't have any definitive plans for expansion again but never say never!

SARAH'S CLEAN TEAM

AS TOLD BY SARAH FRANCIS

Website: www.sarahscleanteam.com
Facebook: sarahfrancis8896

Tell me about your (small) business.

We are a growing house cleaning business that has been around since 2003. I cleaned as a solo cleaner for fifteen years, then decided to hire. I currently have two cleaning techs, whose assigned clients love them! Sarah's Clean Team offers weekly, bi-weekly, monthly, move ins and outs, deep cleans, and even one-time house cleaning. We love animals, and love it when there are pets in the home. Your pets will get lots of attention. We use non-toxic cleaning supplies for you, your family, and pets' protection, as well as ours.

Also, we have teamed up with a non-profit called Cleaning for a Reason, issuing free cleaning for cancer patients all over the country. Cleaning for a Reason has done fifty thousand cleanings to date.

What inspired you to build a business around cleaning?

My aunt cleaned houses for some of her friends from church, and she would take me with her and show me how to clean. She was a great inspiration. I worked in an office for years but wasn't fulfilled. I loved to clean and should have started earlier. It was scary starting my business from the trunk of my car, but it has been the most rewarding job I could ever have.

What is your favorite part about having a small business in Smyrna?

The up-and-coming-ness of Smyrna. There are more and more people coming to Smyrna, the new neighborhoods, the new schools, I like the growth that Smyrna is showing with more creativity and beauty to this once very small town.

What are you most excited about for your small business?

Our growth! I am hiring women who are wanting financial as well as personal growth. I'm excited about giving women a job that will help them to be able to reach their goals and be there for their families in the evening.

What's the first thing you do every morning to start your day on the right foot?

I drink my coffee and love on my dog, Bear! She is my best friend, and if we don't get our morning time, we just don't have a good day.

What is the biggest lesson you've learned in owning and operating a small business?

I cannot remain an introvert! I have to show people that even though I am quiet and a behind-the-scenes type, I still love people and want to make connections.

Are there any favorite mantras you live your life by?

"A goal without a plan is just a wish."

How have you grown your small business from an idea to where it is now?

Keeping my focus and moving forward. Anyone with a business knows that there are days that you want to give up. Keeping my goals and planning when things weren't going as planned has been the way I have grown this business, and stayed with it for eighteen years.

What are your daily habits or systems that you live by that have set you and your small business up for success?

Keeping up with my important emails, discarding the rest. Second, checking in with the people on my team, making sure everything is good and there are no questions. Last, I would say, would be to make a short list of things to accomplish for the day.

What has been your biggest business milestone to date that you are most proud of?

Every time I have a client who is so thankful for our help with their home, it is the highlight of my day! That is why I do this. Now that I'm hiring cleaning techs, when they tell me that they love their job, that is what this is all about! Sarah's Clean Team is about having a heart for others in need, or, just making someone's life better and happier.

What advice would you give to someone wanting to pursue a career similar to yours?

Make sure that you're in shape! Seriously, I would say that this a rewarding job. You are helping busy folks, in this very fast-paced world that need help keeping their home healthy for their family.

What has been the best piece of business advice you have ever received?

Lift as you rise. We all want to make money and have the American Dream, and we can't do it by ourselves. When you have a small business, you have others that work with you. Be sure that the ones that are working with you are cared for and well compensated.

What 1-3 books have impacted your life the most and why?

Three Feet from Gold by Sharon Lechter. This book was so inspirational is the times that weren't the brightest in my working journey. It has pushed me when I needed it. *Traction* by Gino Wickman. This book was just plain entrepreneur education, a must read to get organized. *Get Out of Your Head* by Jennie Allen. This book is just a good unwinder when things get knotted.

. . .

How has failure or apparent failure set you up for future success?

Some of my failures were really bad, and I thought I wouldn't get out of them. But I learned to pick myself and find the other things that went wrong to keep it from happening again.

Who has been the most influential person or mentor to you during your entrepreneurial journey and why?

My uncle, Curtis. He is a genius of a business man, has "paid stupid tax," (his words), and loves talking numbers and business! I love that.

What do you enjoy doing in your spare time?

Watching my daughter, Molly, play softball and volleyball. I enjoy participating in Depot Days. We have sponsored events at Lancaster Christian Academy, where my daughter goes to school. We are a sponsor for Smyrna Fastpitch League and partner with Cleaning for a Reason.

How big of an impact has social media had on your small business?

The impact has been so instrumental in gaining new clients! I have clients who give five-star reviews, recommend us to others who are searching for a cleaning company, and share photos with their friends. I have had such a tremendous outpouring of love from my wonderful, happy clients, new people who call me bring up our positive reviews.

. . .

What does supporting local mean to you?

Supporting local to me means keeping your neighbor moving forward and up. Lift your neighbor and help your community while building support for a friend.

Also, helping your neighbor achieve their goals, build their dreams, and all the while giving their employees jobs. Small business owners are hard workers who deserve support, because you can always count on the fact that they are helping others behind the scenes.

THE REMINGTON ROOM
AS TOLD BY BECKY LANHAM

Website: www.theremingtonroom.com
Facebook: The Remington Room
Instagram: @theremingtonroom

Tell me about your (small) business.
My husband, Steve, and I opened The Remington Room in the fall of 2018. The venue offers event space for celebrations of up to one

hundred guests. We've hosted weddings, birthday parties, anniversary celebrations, graduation parties and more since our inception.

The namesake of our venue is our dog Sir Remington Beauregard, AKA Remy. He can usually be found giving tours to prospective clients and has often been requested to attend events in his tuxedo. Brides dig Remy. He has quite a collection of photos with brides over the years.

What is your favorite part about having a small business in Smyrna?
I love the small town feel that Smyrna has while still offering the amenities and comforts of a larger community.

What inspired you to get into the event space industry?
We actually fell into the industry by accident. We opened our first venue, The Warehouse in Murfreesboro, as a ballroom dance studio and someone asked to rent the space for a wedding. We quickly saw the potential that our space had and decided to give it a try.

What are you most excited about for your small business?
I'm excited to watch the continued growth of our venue as Smyrna grows. People will always want to celebrate their special occasions in life, and we are happy to be here to help them.

What does a typical day look like for you?
My days never look the same. They are always a mixture of checking emails, answering texts, writing contracts, cleaning toilets, meeting prospective clients to view the venue, etc.

What is the biggest lesson you've learned in owning and operating a small business?

Not to take anything or anyone too seriously. It's very easy to allow negative people or events to bring you down and slow your stride. I've come to accept that I must let things go and move on to the next project. There's no future in the past.

Are there any favorite mantras you live your life by?

"This Too Shall Pass." It took me a long time to really take this to heart, but I have recently accepted the fact that nothing is forever. We have to accept challenges and create a plan to move forward. The world doesn't stop when we do. There's no time to sit and wait.

What are your daily habits or systems that you live by that have set you and your small business up for success?

I never go to bed with anything in my inbox, if at all possible. I have to complete the tasks of the day to prevent procrastination.

What advice would you give to someone wanting to pursue a career similar to yours?

Go for it! There's never enough event space.

What has been the best piece of business advice you have ever received?

Location, Location, Location.

Smyrna Spotlights 149

· · ·

What are some of the biggest lessons you've learned in owning a small business?

I have learned that I don't always know as much as I think I do. Sometimes it's better to pay someone who is a specialist to perform certain jobs and try not to do everything myself.

Who has been the most influential person or mentor to you during your entrepreneurial journey and why?

My mother has always supported my entrepreneurial spirit since I was a little kid. From Kangaroo Krafts to BCK Pet Sitting, Mom was always there encouraging me. I remember her getting a phone call asking if BCK was bonded and insured. She replied, "They are ten-year olds." As an adult, she served as a sounding board and voice of reason in all of my endeavors. She passed away in November of 2020.

Where do you see yourself and your small business 5-10 years from now?

I hope that The Remington Room will continue to serve the community of Smyrna for years to come.

What does success mean to you?

To me, having success is being able to use my gifts and talents to enrich the lives of others.

What do you enjoy doing in your spare time?

I run the website www.volunteerrutherford.com for the community. I am also a twenty-five-year member of the Kiwanis Family of civic clubs. I also enjoy playing trivia and ballroom dancing.

· · ·

How big of an impact has social media had on your business?

Social media plays a large part in my business. With most people starting their searches on Facebook, it's important for me to keep fresh content and up-to-date information to get them connected.

What does supporting local mean to you?

Supporting local is the heart of any community. By supporting our friends and neighbors we can help ensure a stronger community from the inside out.

Supporting the local economy will create longevity for small business which is the backbone of any good community.

We've loved being a part of your journey. What's coming next that we can be a part of to support you?

I am always looking for ways to be able to serve more of Rutherford County. Who knows what will be in the pipeline next?

FRONT STREET SIGN COMPANY
AS TOLD BY JEREMY BYRD

Website: www.frontstreetsign.com
Facebook: Front Street Sign Company
Instagram: @frontstreetsign

Tell me about your business.

We are a one-stop custom sign shop specializing in vinyl graphics, indoor and outdoor signs (including electric signs), banners, graphic design services, awards, laser engraving, CNC routing, flatbed printing, embroidery, and much more. Front Street Sign Company is your source for all your marketing and branding needs. We make custom business cards, flyers, name tags for events, cups, shirts, hats, tablecloths, and tents. We can also engrave crystal or glass, and we cut our own acrylic. Whether you are looking for 1 or 100+ shirts, we can accommodate that need.

We also have professional videographers and photographers. We can photograph anything you want and turn it into a work of art, a decal, or whatever else you'd like.

Why signs? What inspired you to open a one-stop custom sign shop?

I'll start from the beginning. I lived on McNickle Drive and I came to the shop when I was twelve to get some decals for my bike because I was going to start a bicycle club.

In 1996, Jim Gammon offered me a job at Signs Now, which was in this same building. I worked here from age twelve to eighteen. He called me back when I was twenty-two. I worked at Signs Now part-time while also serving as a manager for UPS. I stayed with UPS for almost twenty years.

Jim called me back when I turned twenty-three, and wanted me to take over, but it just wasn't my time. I worked for Jim part-time, then my photography business started taking off. We were photographing fifty-two weddings a year. My wife and I had our first child and didn't want to be tied up on weekends photographing weddings. At this point, I was still at UPS. I felt like I was getting sucked into the corporate rat race, and I knew that wasn't what I wanted to do.

In 2016, Jim called again. He wanted me to buy both buildings. I told him that I didn't think I could afford to at that time. Turns out, I could afford both. I purchased both buildings, 100 Front Street (sign shop) and 103 Wright Street (attached garage/warehouse) for $198,000.00. He sold them to me, then he leased from me. At this point, I had no plans of being in the sign business at all, or so I thought.

He leased from me while he was trying to sell his franchise. The time came for his franchise to expire. We talked, and I felt led to do something. I prayed about it that night. The next morning, I made him an offer of $14,000.00 to buy the contents of the buildings, not an offer on the business.

I figured this was a good starting point, and he would either say yes or no. He said yes. I helped him load up all of his personal belongings. I came back inside and thought, "Well, now what?" At this point, I didn't know why I bought the contents, which included printers, a desk, and other equipment. I also got the welders and a plasma cutter. I figured I was just going to play in the warehouse since I'm a car guy.

I had spent $14,000 on the contents and $16,000 on the roofs. I felt like God was leading me to call somebody that I had photographed previously. He was working for a sign company when I photographed his wedding. I asked if he would be interested in going into business with me. I wanted somebody that could take care of my building while I played with cars in the warehouse. We came up with a deal for $30,000.

All I was trying to do was recapture my initial investment. I broke even. One hour before we closed, he backed out. I had just gotten all of my money back, and now I'm sitting here $30,000 in the hole. I had to reassess everything. I didn't know what to do. I called him the next day because we had a two-year lease that we needed to figure out. I was going to let him out of the lease completely. We filled out the paperwork on my dining room table and went our separate ways.

My wife asked me what I was going to do. I said, "I'm just going to have a dumpster come and load up all the equipment and throw it away." I was ok with it because we were going to recapture the money through another lease. I prayed again.

I came in here later that day, and I remember sitting down with my two-year old daughter. Something told me, "You've done this before, so... do it." I literally hired four people in about four hours. I designed the Front Street Sign Company logo, then went to Pinnacle Bank and deposited $1,000 in a business account. I still had not pulled my business license because, again, this was not my plan. I was like, "Ok, I just need to open. I'll get the business license tomorrow." We opened the doors, and it was like it never shut down. I made a post on Facebook and my wife said, "I thought you weren't gonna do it!"

I wanted to provide more than just a vinyl store. I want to be an asset to the community where we can do more and allow people to brand, recognize or promote their business at one place instead of having to go to a screen printer, a sign shop, a trophy shop, and an engraving shop. All that can be done right here. I know now as a business owner, if I can go to someone that's a one-stop shop, that's where I'm staying. I don't want to have to go chase down my shirts, my embroidery, my graphics, my graphic designer. We have a person on staff that does websites. We grew so fast and got busy very quickly

A month later, February 2017, I needed another full-time employee. The gentleman that backed out on me is the one I hired. He messaged me and said he'd love to come work for me. I had no hard feelings. I did question why- "why is this happening? Is this what I'm supposed to do?" I was the one throwing my hands up the whole time, but this is how it was supposed to be all along. He is the graphic designer that is still here today.

What is your favorite part about having a small business in Smyrna?

I love where I'm located. I enjoy the type of business we have. Also, it's business friendly. The mayor comes in. In Nashville, you are a business within a melting pot of thousands. I enjoy the smaller town feel. Yet, we feel so big in a town so small.

Front Street has curated some iconic projects, including the mounted Depot District display, as well as the 8' tall, six-hundred

pound Power 'S' at Smyrna High School. What was the process for making these structures?

The Depot District Projects came to us as ideas. They had an architect draw the sign up.

It is our job to make ideas reality. It's not even signage at the point, it's art. We had to decide on the materials, and the right way to do it. We educate customers on the best products. When you design for cities or towns, people may vandalize it. How can we provide a product that the only way it can be affected is if someone drives through it? Several people are involved in the process. It's our job to find high quality products that will last and be something that the city doesn't have to reinvest in because it wasn't done right the first time.

For the Power 'S', we drew that out on a computer and drew out what we thought would hold the weight. Smyrna Ready Mix donated and poured the footer. We did this during the pandemic when stainless steel was not readily available. We took the 'S' on a computer and spun it around. There are no exposed fasteners on the front of the 'S'. The finish on the front is all hand done.

That's an art installation. Smyrna High also asked us to light it. They wanted something in place of the fountain that would be maintenance-free. The 'S' is powder coated and stainless steel so if it does get spray painted, it will wipe off. The hardest part was choosing the right materials and constructing something we've never done before. It took about three months. It was a fun project. This was one of my favorite jobs.

We see these structures constantly. Customers ask if we did these structures, and we say yes. We love it. We also did the Depot stage sign. I enjoy the creative aspect and being able to take someone's idea and create something that's a reality and above their expectations.

What types of unique personalized gifts can customers find at Front Street Sign Company?

All of the catalogues are on our website. You can flip through each page of the sublimation tab. We can customize all sorts of unique gifts, such as tumbler decals, monograms, poster prints, window decals, canvas prints, corn hole board decals, cups, shirts, and hats. We can engrave barbecue sets, which would make a great gift for dad, with a turnaround time of two days, usually.

Another one-of-a-kind gift we offer is custom puzzles. If someone brings us a special family photo, we can turn that into a puzzle. An 8.5" x 11" custom puzzle costs around $15. We can do 16" x 20", which costs around $30. We can make as big of a puzzle as someone wants.

Also, we design a Town of Smyrna ornament every year. We are leaving a legacy in people's homes. It's going to go on a tree and will probably be handed down. It's about creating something that will stand  the test of time that can be passed down from generation to generation.

Your work is currently displayed at the Alaska Airlines and United Airlines terminals, and you have a mural at the Southwest Airlines gate at Nashville's BNA International Airport.

 **What is it like seeing your work displayed to a global audience at Nashville's BNA International Airport?**

Our work at Southwest is true art. That was a collaborative effort. Brian Tull was the artist. We do all of his stencils. He hand-painted the Rockabilly

Highway Mural in Selmer, Tennessee. He paints a lot of murals. He asked us to be a part of the Southwest project. The piece of art is seventy feet wide and fifty inches tall. It's in the whole new area of the Southwest terminal. It is so cool to be able to see that one of my clients and I came together to create something so massive on a wall that people from around the world see.

It's a humbling experience to walk through and see. We were at the Alaska terminal doing something to their gate and saw people stopping and staring at our work. It's amazing. It's actually a picture of a neon sign zoomed real close. It's simple, but you stare at it and get lost. I enjoy seeing it. Usually, my kids will say, "we did that." That's where it becomes more than a job.

Front Street Sign Company has been instrumental in paying tribute to Captain Jeff Kuss. In what ways were you involved with the memorial, and how big of an impact has this had on your business?

We did a lot of the signage. Mayor Reed called me at 9:00 p.m. one evening the weekend the Town had the memorial banquet and dedication ceremony. They didn't like the way the lights were reflecting from the plane on to the granite with LEDs. There were lots of dots. This is where we like to come in and problem-solve. I have never done anything like that before, but we figured it out. We did the photo display of Captain Kuss at the Smyrna Event Center. We also made the fans and programs for the dedication ceremony.

I was led to say we would maintain his name on the plane (at the memorial site) as long as we are open and the plane is in Smyrna. It was the very least I could do. Everything else on the plane is painted graphics. We

got to go to the hangar before they hoisted the plane up and put the name on it. The emotion behind that is hard to describe. I got to meet his parents. It's one of those projects that makes your heart happy that you were even asked to help. You are honored to help. It's not money at that point.

It's a connection with people and leadership in the community that your business has that exceeds any monetary value. This is how we can run our business differently. If we have room to give for something we  believe in, we will. Typically, those types of projects are the result of tragedy, but when you are involved in them it's a personal thing. It was a very touching project to be a part of.

What has been your biggest business milestone to date that you are most proud of?

Remodeling this building. The amount of growth last year during the pandemic. We didn't lay anyone off. There's no better compliment than asking one of my employees their future plans and them telling me they want to retire here. Providing a working environment where people want to be here and having a positive company culture. I see that being a big challenge in the future keeping that independent privately owned atmosphere and making sure the right people are plugged into key leadership roles.

I've pulled off impossible things before. The Town needed five-hundred Jeff Kuss shirts for the memorial in forty-eight hours. We made it happen.

What have been some of your biggest business challenges you have faced and how have you overcome them?

I'm a people pleaser, so I have a hard time saying no sometimes. I'll do whatever I can to make someone happy. There will be folks who aren't happy, and you just have to accept that. I've learned that it's ok to not do business with someone you aren't comfortable doing business with.

Being a leader of a business or nonprofit during a pandemic is probably the most challenging thing anyone could go through. Regardless of your opinion or where you stood, you were questioned. There wasn't a right or wrong answer. I stayed open. I outsourced some. I didn't have a CNC. We went during a pandemic because the people we were outsourcing CNC to closed. I decided to buy my own CNC. We can now do 3D signs, whereas we couldn't before. There's not that many people around that can do that. I cut the middle man out inadvertently because I needed to keep going. I chose to buy a $40,000 machine in April 2020 not knowing what was going to happen. Last year was the best year in twenty-six years a sign business running out of this building has done.

We've grown so much that we are 60% over last year. We were looking at purchasing some property in another city and opening another store, but that won't fix the problem we have in Smyrna. It's time for us to invest in Smyrna.

Do you ever stop to think that you are leaving a legacy since these structures and your creations will last for many years to come?

I think it hits me the most when my son or daughter brings it up. Front Street Sign Company is leaving a legacy. We are here to stay. I truly feel like whether I'm here or not, this business will keep going because of the community involvement. That's the one thing I will say to other business owners is the way you leave a legacy is to impact the community. You can't leave it only thinking about money. You have to make money, but that can't be your first priority.

I'm starting to see some of the fruits of the legacy that we're leaving, and being able to provide another legacy and that's building a new structure that hasn't been built on Front Street in decades. Part of Front Street Sign Company impacting this area is putting a building up that looks period and fits with the rest of the structures. It's not cheap to do that. I want people to question how long it's been here. I want it to last for years. I've always tried to be giving to where Carpe Artista has a place to use. I let the Arts Commission use the warehouse. I will let other organizations that may not have the funds to go rent something or private events that I want to host with friends or clients.

Since opening in 2017, Front Street Sign Company has won several prestigious awards voted on by the community, including a Firefly for Business of the Year and several Ruthie's Awards. Where do you see yourself and your small business 5-10 years from now?

I see the people that started for me being in leadership roles. In order for people to stay, they have to be able to grow. I plan on Shane, which is where part of the story started, being the director of creative operations. We will have a couple of stores and he will have a home base with graphic designers that will report to him. I want to keep the business and the product where it's made within my walls.

I see me employing and impacting more people. We do a program called Front Street Gives Back. One of my goals is to set up a scholarship fund for kids in Rutherford County in the graphic design field. I want to be more of a mentor in five years, not just a business owner.

I want to provide opportunities for this community that want to get things in a much faster way. Sure, you can sit at home and design your business cards online but it will still be two weeks before you receive them. I want it to be done here at our Smyrna shop, quicker. They may pay a few dollars more at our store than online, but they get it a week and a half quicker. We have people that come in on Fridays and they need something the next day. I love that people know they can call me and we will make things happen.

Who has been the most influential person or mentor to you during your entrepreneurial journey and why?

Jim Gammon totally fits that bill. He started pouring into me when I was twelve. I was always intrigued by Jim owning this business and his story. Jim was one of the top executives in the country for AT&T. He told me life is too short and the choices you make now decide where you are at when you are seventy.

What do you enjoy doing in your spare time?

Service to the community. Not only professionally, but personally. I serve on the Friends of Smyrna Public Library board and am also president of the local nonprofit, Antique Automobile Club of America, Stones River Region, as well. I love cars. We are trying to impact kids to appreciate the antique car hobby.

My love of cars started here at Signs Now when I was twelve. Jim had a 1970 Mercedes 280SL in the back. I enjoy customizing and preserving the history of an older car. That goes back to the buildings here. I enjoy the history that's here with the community. I remember when I bought the contents and I asked Jim if his Mercedes was for sale. I wanted that car since I was twelve. When I was thirty-two, I was able to purchase it. When he wasn't watching, I'd go back to the warehouse and sit in his cars and think about driving them with the top down. Now I own them.

How big of an impact has social media had on your small business?

When customers or fans share our posts, it has a huge impact on our business. It makes my heart so happy when you like something we've done, and you take the time to share. If we're involved in a community project that's dear to people's hearts, like the schools or parks, please share those posts. That way, not only are you impacting the business, you are impacting the community and sharing something positive. The Power 'S' was shared a lot. That's one of the best compliments a business owner can receive.

What does supporting local mean to you?

Supporting local to me means reinvesting in where you live. Without people supporting local, the face of this building, and the other building we are adding wouldn't have been possible. When you shop local, you are hiring someone to be the face of the community and change the landscape.

Local business owners change and directly affect what your community is. Can investors change it? Yes, but it's changed based on where they live and what they think the area should look like. They're investing money here, but they aren't invested professionally or personally. They don't live here. They're most likely just buying a building that's helping their portfolio. Whereas, for us, we want to be a light, we want to be more than just a sign company on the corner of Front Street. We want to be a place where people can have these interactive murals and take pictures. Investing in your community allows me to be able to do things like that.

We've loved being a part of your journey. What's coming next that we can be a part of to support you?

We are building a two-story period building with a rooftop deck. We look forward to growing and having expanded space. I'm excited to see what someone may do on the rooftop.

Is there anything else you would like people to know about you or your small business?

I spend no money advertising. We sponsor every school event we feel impacts people. Schools have been one of my favorite groups to work with. For me, it was money well spent because the amount of people we are impacting is what matters.

COURTNIE R. DUNN, AUTHOR
AS TOLD BY COURTNIE R. DUNN

Facebook: Courtnie R. Dunn
Instagram: @courtnie.r.dunn

Tell me about your (small) business.

At a very young age, I knew I wanted to be a writer. It's something inside of me that speaks to me that I am able to write down on paper. I kept it to myself mostly, but a year ago, I decided to just go for it. I broke out of my writing shell and wrote my first novel. I hope to provide a reading outlet for those who enjoy reading, but also inspire those who are on the fence and dream of writing, to actually do it. I published my first novel, *Squeeze the Lime* in 2020. I am currently working on a sequel that is completely unrelated.

What is your favorite part about having a small business in Smyrna?

Although, I do not have an establishment for people to walk in and relax, the beauty of a book is you can take it wherever you go. I also hope that the people of Smyrna are intrigued to support a local author.

How did your childhood in Smyrna shape you?

I have lived in Smyrna since I was four years old. I had amazing teachers all throughout my childhood who helped me become a better writer. Some of their methods I still use to this day, particularly my high school English teacher, Ms. Lori DiCiaula.

What inspired you to become an author?

I remember as early as nine years old just wanting to constantly write. My parents would buy me all types of diaries and journals to write my thoughts down in. I used to say I would move to New York City and become a writer. As I got older, I still felt that constant urge to write. I didn't graduate college with a journalism degree, so I did have my own insecurities about putting my work out there, but this has always been my dream. I want to put my stories out there for people to enjoy, but also represent the indie author life. I am a self-published author, so I not only write my own stories, but I also am responsible for putting "the word" out there about my novel. As well as seeking help for all that it takes to make a book come together.

Tell me about *Squeeze the Lime*.

Squeeze the Lime is a fiction novel based out of Nashville. It is about Heidi Mitchell, a twenty-seven-year-old waitress, looking to redefine her life purpose again. She had a plan, but plans changed when her mom fell ill. Now that her mom is better, Heidi is ready to rediscover and spice her life up.

But as the old saying goes, be careful what you wish for. Heidi's life may have gotten a little too spicy. A new man in town really brings the heat, but she is also faced with a stalker, the ultimate betrayal, and even murder.

Heidi will soon discover not everything is what it seems and the true power of love.

What are you most excited about for your small business?

I have the freedom to be able to write anywhere that I want. I could write about Panama City but from the comfort of my own home.

What's the first thing you do every morning to start your day on the right foot?

If there is any motto that I live by in this world, it would most definitely be, "...but first, coffee." I know that sounds so cliché, but it's my motivation in a cup. I am also a full time stay-at-home mom, so I need to be fueled by something to keep up with my two little ones.

What is the biggest lesson you've learned in owning and operating a small business?

My biggest lesson that I have learned is to be humble. What I mean by that is no, Reese Witherspoon will not be calling you the week after your book is released to include you in her monthly book club. Heck, not a year later, either. But that's okay, that is not how I measure my success. Although, I have been very fortunate to receive such a supportive response from a lot of different people, I am so happy that I actually did it. That I wrote my novel and put it out there for people to read. No one could give that to me, I had to do that for myself and it feels so good.

Are there any favorite mantras you live your life by?

Other than my coffee quotes, I have to admit that original Nike quote is my go to as well, "JUST DO IT." Again, it might sound cliché, but it's the truth, you have to, "Just do it". If you don't then only you will be holding yourself back from achieving what you truly desire.

What are your daily habits or systems that you live by that have set you and your small business up for success?

I always say what works for me, might not work for someone else. Trust me, I don't recommend anyone staying up until four AM. Speaking for myself, I had absolutely not a single clue where to start after I wrote my book. I didn't know how to put it out there or who I should give it to. So, I want to make myself available for anyone and everyone who has questions on the how factor of things.

What has been your biggest business milestone to date that you are most proud of?

My biggest milestone throughout this whole process is and will always be the first moment I held my book in my hand. It actually brought tears to my eyes. So cheesy I know, but it's true! It just felt so good to not just see it on a laptop or look at my notes I write down, but to actually hold the entire story in a printed book.

· · ·

What have been some of your biggest business challenges you have faced and how have you overcome them?

My biggest challenge now would be writing another story, which I am currently working on. Before no one knew what I was doing, so it was extremely easy to let it all come naturally to me, but now I feel pressure to write something to be as equally great as *Squeeze the Lime*. People that I don't know have reached out to me to let me know how much they loved the book, and although I am extremely grateful, I have a fear that I might let those readers down.

What advice would you give to someone wanting to pursue a career similar to yours?

I cannot say it enough, and I believe it with everything in me is to, "Just do it." There is no right or wrong way to write a book. If you want to write about a love story gone wrong with a twisted love triangle, aliens abducting cows for science experiments, or the next Stephen King scary plot twist; this is your world, and you can write whatever you want. It's extremely easy to doubt yourself and be in your own head with thoughts like, "People won't like this" type of stuff, and yes that is very true. Not every single person will like your type of writing, but that doesn't mean you shouldn't do it, either. You could be inspiring someone else!

What has been the best piece of business advice you have ever received?

I was venting to my dad about wanting to write a book, as I always have. Then he said to me, "Well if you're not going to do it, then maybe you're not a writer." When I asked him why would he say that he said to me, "If I really wanted to write, I would do it and figure it out as I go." Which is exactly what I did. I wrote my story and figured it all out as I went.

. . .

What 1-3 books have impacted your life the most and why?

I have all types of favorite books, but I would say I am more "impacted" by particular authors that I have read such as Lucy Foley, Jasmine Guillory Barbara O'Neal, Kristen Kemp, and more recently Jeneva Rose. All of these authors have a book that just really stayed with me and they have books that I can read again and again.

How has failure or apparent failure set you up for future success?

I wouldn't say I have a failure, because I have received an immeasurable amount of support. But the whole experience has taught me "what to do" versus just winging it as I was before.

Who has been the most influential person or mentor to you during your entrepreneurial journey and why?

My sister. She has such a confidence about her that it inspires me constantly. She doesn't care what anyone thinks, and she lives for herself and her family only, which I think all of us would like to do. But most of us, such as myself, tend to people please for the sake of others, whereas my sister doesn't let outside opinions influence what she wants. She has been one of the most supportive people throughout my entire life and I am so grateful to have her constantly reminding me to believe in myself.

Where do you see yourself and your small business 5-10 years from now?

In 5-10 years, I hope to have AT LEAST three novels out. I really want to push myself and keep writing for the rest of my life.

What does success mean to you?

My greatest success is that I did it. Even if it mounts to something small in the eyes of society, meaning I am not New York Times Bestseller, that's okay. I am very proud to see people reading my work, and even more proud that people are actually enjoying it. It would only be better knowing that I inspired someone else to go after their dreams, too.

What do you enjoy doing in your spare time?

My greatest role and title will always be being a mother. I quit my day job so that I would be able to be with my children more. They are only little once, and I want to soak up every second of it. I also really like baking, reading, and painting with a glass of white wine.

How big of an impact has social media had on your small business?

Honestly, social media plays a huge part in my role. If it wasn't for social media, I wouldn't have been able to announce it or reach potential readers. Because I am a self-published author, I don't have an agent helping promote me, I solely rely on friends and followers on social media to help "spread the word."

What does supporting local mean to you and why is supporting local businesses so important?

If 2020 taught us anything aside from being safe and respectful of others, it definitely taught us how much local business owners rely on the community to stay open. It's extremely sad but eye-opening to see businesses shut down. I think it is even more important now to show all of our support to local businesses. We are not only helping a business stay open, but also supporting someone's dream.

Where can people find your books?

People could purchase my book at local bookstores such as Parnassus Books and Duck River Books to not only support a local author but also a local business. Of course, it is convenient for Amazon to drop off at your front door step, but most local bookstores also have the delivery option available. The local book community has been amazing to work with. They have taken interest in my work as a local writer and put my book on their shelves. I could not be more grateful for all of the local support, not only friends and family, but those that have taken an interest in my work simply because I live here. It is truly amazing.

Also, it's available online at Amazon, Walmart, Barnes and Noble, and Books A Million. For E-Readers it is available on Apple devices and Kindle.

And check out the Smyrna Public Library!

We've loved being a part of your journey. What's coming next that we can be a part of to support you?

I am currently working on a project or two that I hope to have released by the end of this year!

Is there anything else you would like people to know about you or your small business?

I am truly so grateful for all that support that I have received whether it be purchasing the novel, help sharing my post on social media, or telling your friend about it. I honestly could not be more appreciative and I owe it to all of the readers that my book has sold as many copies as it has because of everyone that has taken an interest, so thank YOU!

DR. AUTOMOTIVE
AS TOLD BY DANNY BREWER

Website: www.autorepairsmyrna.com
Facebook: Dr. Automotive
Twitter: @sportzbrew

Tell me about your (small) business.

Dr. Automotive is an automotive repair business. Opening in August of 2004, my brother and I set forth on a mission. My son, Beauregard, is now also a vital cog in the business as we focus on repair and maintenance of cars and light trucks.

. . .

What inspired you to get into the auto repair space and open Dr. Automotive?

I had been managing the first Christian Brothers automotive repair shop opened outside the state of Texas. "Philosophical differences" led to my dismissal, and I needed a job. The space on Hazelwood was for lease, and with the financial backing from Butch Anderson, we took the plunge. We figured instead of working for someone else, why not just try and work for ourselves. Seventeen years later, here we are.

What is your favorite part about having a small business in Smyrna?

Being able to help people and trying to make a difference in my hometown is very rewarding. Focusing on the little things and the support of the community pays dividends in so many ways with the monetary aspect being one of the less important.

How did your childhood in Smyrna shape you?

Growing up, I remember playing in the local sports leagues and recognizing those who sponsored our teams. I looked up to guys like Gerald Lee (Lee Line), Bill Leckie (Tennessee Auto Supply), Doug Raborn (Raborn Insurance) and Frank Crosslin (Crosslin Supply). They were small business guys that always tried to make a difference. That is what I am striving to be… a guy who makes a difference.

. . .

What's the first thing you do every morning to start your day on the right foot?

I like to exercise and get the blood pumping and the gray matter working. Swimming in warmer weather and exercise bike or walking in colder weather.

What is the biggest lesson you've learned in owning and operating a small business?

Most worthwhile things do not come easily and if you sow the seeds the crops will grow. Faith is the most important part, faith in yourself, faith in your process, faith in God.

Are there any favorite mantras you live your life by?

Back a horse and get paid!

How have you grown your small business from an idea to where it is now?

Hard work, dedication, and faith. We have utilized our Smyrna roots and capitalized on word-of-mouth and a strong marketing program.

What has been your biggest business milestone to date that you are most proud of?

When we hit the fifteen-year mark and received a proclamation from Governor Bill Lee, it told me I was on the right path to becoming a pillar of the community.

. . .

What have been some of your biggest business challenges you have faced and how have you overcome them?

Focusing on the core principles of my life has helped keep the outside noise and shortsighted people from derailing our train.

What advice would you give to someone wanting to pursue a career similar to yours?

Be true to yourself and your customers. Honesty is always the best policy and if you take care of your customers, they will take care of you.

What has been the best piece of business advice you have ever received?

Don't be overly consumed with money. Just fix the cars and the money will be there.

What 1-3 books have impacted your life the most and why?

The Bible is a book that will never be outdated as these are lessons that can forever be learned.

How has failure or apparent failure set you up for future success?

When I was let go from my managerial spot at Christian Brothers the weight of my world was squarely on my shoulders. In their words, I just was not cut out to be in management. That doubt has driven me, and that fabulous failure was in fact one of the best things that ever happened to me.

Who has been the most influential person or mentor to you during your entrepreneurial journey and why?

My uncle, Butch Anderson, has been a guiding force for me. A fabulous success, he has never been afraid to take chances because he has the work ethic and determination to make things happen.

What does success mean to you?
Success is being able to truly look at yourself in the mirror and know you are living the right way.

What do you enjoy doing in your spare time?
Being community-driven, we sponsor different sports at many schools. I was a former booster club president for Smyrna High baseball, coached a summer team for Smyrna High baseball for six years, have been a volunteer assistant for Smyrna High swimming since 2001. I have been a sportswriter for a variety of publications since 1993 with a focus on high school and college athletics. I am a member of the US Basketball Writers Association and College Football Writers Association. I have acted as the chairperson of the Rutherford Reader's top ten high school football committee and am the founder of the Pigskin High School Football Award.

Since 2007, I have covered the sport of Thoroughbred Horse

racing in depth. Currently I have a website (horseracingscoop.com), am a member of the Turf Publicists of America, and a voter in the National Thoroughbred Racing Association's national poll. Covering the sport of kings has been a breath of fresh air, as it is the greatest sport in the world. I coached youth basketball at two different times for a total of about eight years and currently am the Vice-Chairman on the Smyrna High athletic hall of fame committee.

How big of an impact has social media had on your small business?

Through the hard work of Navigation Advertising (owned by Smyrna native Christian Hidalgo), we have established and maintained a web presence. This has been integral in the digital world we live in.

What does supporting local mean to you?

Local businesses are truly the backbone of America. It is important to support these people as they are the ones who support the community. Sponsoring local sports and schools normally falls on their shoulders as the corporate world seldom offers assistance in these areas.

AFFI PEST & WILDLIFE
AS TOLD BY JIM AFRICANO

Website: www.TheSkunkWhisperer.com | www.TennesseeBugs.com
Facebook: Jim The SkunkWhisperer and Affi Pest & Wildlife
Instagram: @JimTheSkunkWhisperer

Tell me about your (small) business.
We service mainly Rutherford County for pest control, moisture

control, and humane trap and removal of wildlife. I have serviced the community since 2003. Since that time, we have protected thousands of homes, and safely relocated about as many critters.

What inspired you to build a business around pest control and wildlife?

I've worked with animals most of my life. In the early 2000s there was room for a few more pest control companies, but a need for companies that dealt with wildlife getting into homes and businesses.

What is your favorite part about having a small business in Smyrna?

Smyrna is such a close-knit community, having a quality business in the area is strongly supported, welcomed, and shared.

What are you most excited about for your small business?

I have been able to build a business that is a value to the community, take care of my family, and focus on building my employees' dreams, while building my own.

How have you grown your small business from an idea to where it is now?

After having a couple of unprofitable restaurants, I built this business by bootstrapping. I followed a debt-free concept as much as possible that I learned the hard way from the other business. The lesson was that borrowing money can't save a failing business. That strategy forced me to mind every dollar coming in and out. It also taught me a great lesson on valuing and being considerate of our client's dollars as well. This idea put us in the black within two years, and only having a truck payment for the company's debt for a couple of years after that.

Smyrna Spotlights

- - -

You are known as the "Skunk Whisperer." Do you have any favorite skunk stories?

I have been called for things as small as bat mites, to a large buffalo, to rattle snakes in a sinkhole. Over the years, I have dealt with hundreds of skunks, and there are many stories. One of my favorite stories involves a maintenance man in Clarksville. It was a snowy winter morning, and I received a call about an injured skunk. I did not work that far out and tried to advise on how to get it to safely move on.

He was able to secure it. He asked again if I could help. He offered to bring the skunk to me. When a scared stranger is willing to risk so much on an injured animal, (time from work, driving in the snow, getting sprayed, getting bit, etc.), I freed up the rest of my day and met him.

We met in a parking lot. He pulled up in a pickup truck. I thought the worst. I thought the skunk was going to be in the back freezing. When I got up to the truck, I saw a box on the front seat next to him. As I looked closer, there was no top to the box, just a towel. No, the towel was not over the top, it was wrapped around the skunk to keep him warm. (Never attempt this).

I transferred the skunk to my front seat and left him in the open box. I thanked him for helping, and his willingness to drive the injured animal. This stranger's heart, and passion to help is exactly why I do what I do. I was able to get the skunk to a rehab facility. The skunk never sprayed.

What's the first thing you do every morning to start your day on the right foot?

My mornings usually start with a cup of espresso with just nature, and a short Tai Chi session. This sets my mind in balance. My job is different every day, and you must have a good mental balance.

- - -

What are some of the biggest lessons you've learned in owning a small business?

The biggest: be part of and active in the community. One is to understand your product, or service is to solve a problem, not make money. When you focus on solving the problem, your customers come to you. Another lesson, no matter how much you know there will always be more to learn. Last is to not take things personally. Your business is your life, but it's just a product or service to your customer.

Are there any favorite mantras you live your life by?

"What you are is what you have been. What you will be is what you do now."- Buddha

"In the midst of movement and chaos, keep stillness inside you." – Deepak Chopra

"When you properly educate you create acceptance, tolerance, and compassion." –Jim The SkunkWhisperer

"Success usually comes to those who are too busy to be looking for it." – Henry David Thoreau

What are your daily habits or systems that you live by that have set you and your small business up for success?

Since our business doesn't run on regular hours, we have a weekly dinner with the whole crew at my house. We do have a formal meeting at the beginning about the previous and upcoming week. Then I cook, and we share.

What has been your biggest business milestone to date that you are most proud of?

Working with our local State Representative and a rehabilitation facility to allow rehabilitation of skunks. Until that time, all skunks were to be euthanized.

Smyrna Spotlights 181

. . .

What have been some of your biggest business challenges you have faced and how have you overcome them?

COVID-19 was the biggest challenge. Though we came through it strong, there was the immediate regrouping, strategizing, and learning to stay above board in an ever-changing situation. The most valuable move we had made was having a business emergency fund. We were able to immediately tell the staff we were fine, and their jobs were safe.

What advice would you give to someone wanting to pursue a career similar to yours?

This industry can be lucrative, and fulfilling, but you must have a passion for it.

What has been the best piece of business advice you have ever received?

The old cliché, "love what you do, and you'll never work a day of your life."

What 1-3 books have impacted your life the most and why?

The Giving Tree by Shel Silverstein. It taught me at an early age the power of giving. *The Power of Habit* by Charles Duhigg. This book enlightened me on how to control my actions and reactions by looking for the root causes.

How has failure or apparent failure set you up for future success?

When I opened The Italian Market, I knew I was ahead of the time in Nashville. What my youth and lack of experience didn't show me was how important timing was. I could not sustain the curve to break even. It is now Coco's Italian Market and owned by my good friend, Chuck Cinelli. Chuck had the means and marketing knowledge to handle the rest of the curve and expedite getting over. To this day, he is doing everything I had started, but better and successfully. Chuck was a good friend before I opened the market. I had every opportunity to seek his counsel beforehand. I chose arrogance over accepting my ignorance and his mentorship. I didn't know my timing.

Who has been the most influential person or mentor to you during your entrepreneurial journey and why?

There have been some amazing people, and friends who have been influential. One person who stands above is my father. He taught me about hard work, integrity, and giving. He has not swayed from his beliefs in these. Though he was not the entrepreneurial type, he gave me the strength and encouragement to get out there and try.

Where do you see yourself and your small business 5-10 years from now?

I see myself doing a poor job of staying retired. Always keep moving.

What does success mean to you?

Success is about happiness. Family, friends, comfort, and few worries are my version. I am very successful in that realm.

What do you enjoy doing in your spare time?

I enjoy family, motorcycling, wine making, and volunteering. I serve on multiple boards, including the Better Business Bureau Advisory Board, Walden's Puddle Wildlife Rehabilitation, and Purple Paws Animal Rescue.

How big of an impact has social media had on your small business?

Social media has had a huge impact. People now use reviews to decide on who they use. It has changed the face of marketing to new customers. We love when you share stories of us serving you, and the experiences you've heard from others. Telling the wild stories our business takes us on sometimes.

What does supporting local mean to you?

The old adage of you do business with those you know, like, and trust comes to mind. Who can forget hearing "NORM" when he walked into Cheers. That's local. That's supporting your friends, and the community.

Nobody wants to just be a number. Online is what you want if you don't want the personal touch. Local business keeps you tied into the community. It treats you as an individual and a value to their business, not just a sale.

We've loved being a part of your journey. What's coming next that we can be a part of to support you?

Always exciting for us is our philanthropy. There are amazing rescues in the area. Being part of the charity events with us always inspires us to keep going and giving.

WILSON'S PHOTOGRAPHY | BRIDAL COUNTRY
AS TOLD BY GEORGE AND HELEN WILSON

Website: www.bridalcountry.net | www.wilsonsphotography.net
Facebook: Bridal Country

Tell me about your (small) business.

We opened Wilson's Photography out of our home in 1976. In those days, a lot of the photography studios were husband and wife and operated from their homes.

We have experience in many categories of studio and on-location photography including: children's portraits, wedding photography, school and graduation portraits, family portraits, prom portraits, and more. We have been capturing our clients' most special life moments and milestones for forty-five years.

One year later, in 1977, we opened Bridal Country, a formal wear store. We carry an assortment of formal dresses for prom, homecoming and special events, as well as bridal gowns and accessories. We also carry an extensive selection of men's tuxedos and formal wear for any special occasion.

Why photography? What inspired you to start a photography business?

George: I'd always wanted to do photography. We figured we were young enough to where I could try it out, and if it didn't work, I could go back to the computer world. It wasn't easy. I even loaded trucks in Nashville to supplement the photography business. This is our forty-fifth year in business.

What inspired you to start a bridal boutique business?

Helen: I was in the Jaycettes (women's networking group) at the time. We wanted to put on a bridal fair and fashion show. The Jaycees (men's networking group) helped, too. I went to a shop in Murfreesboro and asked the owner if she would provide the gowns. She said she'd actually like to sell her business and asked if I'd like to buy her store. All I wanted was to have a fashion show.

We went to the bank, but the bank wouldn't lend us the money to buy her dress business. So, we decided to buy a good amount of her stock. I was eight months pregnant.

At the time, we only had the photography side of the business. It was originally Dr. Frank's dentist office. We moved the studio around and built some walls and racks to hang wedding dresses throughout the photography studio. George had a small office. We ran both businesses out of the studio.

When Swagglers, the drapery business next door, left, I moved the bridal portion into its current location. We then had two buildings side by side, which gave us a lot more space.

We did end up having the fashion show at the country club on base. Marty Luffman was the father of the bride and a big help. All the local businesses set up booths. I couldn't afford to advertise at the time, so it was a great way to get the business out there.

What is your favorite part about having a small business in Smyrna?

Helen: The people. We were all friends. If I ran out of black dye, I'd call my friend, Judy. She'd tell me to come get it. Or, "I need a size eight shoe," or, "I ruined this dress," she'd tell me to come get it. We really helped each other out in the early days.

George: The people. You used to run into people you knew when you went to the store. There were five thousand people in Smyrna when we first started, and now it's close to fifty thousand.

What brought you to Smyrna?

George: We weren't originally from Smyrna. I am originally from the Mt. Eagle Mountain area. Once I was out of the Army, I got into computer work in Nashville. Helen had a job in Murfreesboro. We fell in love with Smyrna and knew this is where we wanted to start our business.

We've met so many people here, and a lot of people are still friends. That's the thing about a small town, our customers aren't just customers, they are friends.

How has the small business landscape changed since you first opened in 1976?

We used to park across the street from the railroad and walk across each day. That was before Nissan came to town. We had a gravel parking lot. Smyrna ended right about where Woodfin Funeral Chapel is. All the businesses on Hazelwood were built after we came in. You had the buildings on our side of the street and the businesses on Front Street. That was Smyrna at the time. Next door to us was a car dealership. On Front Street you had Sissies (now Breaking Bread), a popular restaurant, Joyce's Flowers, and Ben Franklin had the Five and Dime store. There was a dry cleaning business where Carpe Cafe currently is. There used to be a local hardware store where Joe B's is. We have seen Smyrna change a lot over the years.

We started having a Smyrna Open House on Sundays. We had food, and the local businesses could show their goods. We did that for several years and it was great for the town. All the merchants knew each other and participated. A lot of citizens partici-pated as well. It benefited everyone and helped raise a lot of awareness for our local businesses.

Then we took the bridal shows to the Murphy Center. It got really big. It all started with the Jaycees and Jaycettes. We had a few shows at The Town Centre for several years in the eighties.

In what ways have you seen bridal trends change over the years?

Times have changed. It's not as formal as it used to be. In the beginning, we saw a lot of wedding dresses with high necks and long sleeves. Weddings were always in the church. Years ago at the Atlanta Market, I told the vendors that Smyrna would never buy strapless wedding dresses since we were in the Bible Belt. Eventually, however, they did. That was a huge change in the bridal industry.

Now, it's all about venues. There are fewer church weddings. When we did weddings and photography, we would have the wedding at the church, go to the Fellowship Hall, have some cake and punch, then we were out of there. Now, you are going to stay for a while because they are having a big party. We used to be able to do two weddings in a day, on some occasions even three. People had no desire to stay around for long periods of time.

A lot of our brides were straight out of high school. Mom would come and help pick out the gown. In many instances, we helped the bride's mother pick out her wedding gown.

On the photography side, we used to have a lot of repeat photography customers. We would take the senior photos, then prom, then wedding. We would sometimes photograph fifty weddings in one year.

We have seen photography change a lot over the years. We used to shoot children's photos on the floor. We also photographed The Dance Academy for years. We had a background and lighting. Most photography is all about location now.

What has been your biggest business milestone to date that you are most proud of?

We've been in business for over forty-five years. People ask us all the time, "how long are you going to go at it?"

. . .

What are some of the biggest lessons you've learned in owning a small business?

Time management. Sometimes, we look back and don't know how we did all of this when we had two kids. We were always on different ball fields. Some years we had over one-hundred games.

What have been some of your biggest business challenges you have faced and how have you overcome them?

George: In 1988, we had a fire that wiped out both businesses. We had the old ceilings with the chords running across the top and lightning struck.

We were at the ball field taking pictures for various teams, then we came to the studio. We had a class reunion at the Town Centre that night. The neighbors called to inform us that our buildings were on fire. We came across Front Street and saw the smoke. Once we got to the railroad tracks, someone tried to stop us from crossing. We told him those were our buildings, and we were going across. However, we couldn't get in. I snuck in the front and got our money bag and book. You could see the fire underneath the floors. I got back out. People were lined up outside on the hoods of their cars watching.

Helen and Mayor Sam Ridley lighting the Town Christmas tree, early 1980s

We went to the Town Centre and got the microphone from the band and announced that we had an emergency and needed everyone up front immediately. I took the class reunion picture in five minutes, gave the woman the receipt, and we were back at the studio. We didn't know what to do. There was no back-up plan. The Fire Department was at the studio, and there was nothing we could do, so we went ahead and took the photo. We also figured we would really need the money since both of our businesses had just burned down. We had several people with trucks that helped us load up as much of our burned businesses as possible. We laid stuff out to dry, and went through all the photography negatives.

One thing that really helped was that we placed the negatives in a plastic container after learning that at a photography seminar. The containers melted, of course, but sealed the negatives, which really helped to salvage some of the photos. We lost an entire wedding. The bride came that day and her wedding album had been on the coffee table. The fire destroyed it. However, the negatives were still good.

We lost a lot of dresses but ended up replacing almost all of the bridal gowns. Some of the other bridal shops helped. One customer became upset because she ordered a hat. We told her, "Honey, we have just burned down. You are lucky your hat is not here."

We had a lot of photos all over the floor that we were getting ready to deliver the following week. We lost a lot of those. However, we were able to retake some. Sometime later, Steve at Bella Vita Tattoo next door let us use part of his attic for storage, and it caught on fire. We had smoke damage and had to go through this process again.

What makes the experience of shopping for formal wear at Bridal Country so unique and special?

Personal service. If you want something special and unique, shop local. There may be some big chain shops, and they have a lot of dresses in all the sizes and colors. I have one dress for each style. We can always order additional sizes and we price match.

Also, I track all the local high schools for prom so that no two girls will show up in the same dress. I tell her the girl from Smyrna High has already purchased that dress, and you don't want to show up with the same dress. The first thing I ask the girls is where they go to school. The chain stores won't do that. Different schools like different styles. I keep a master spreadsheet each year and have done so for many years. Up until about five or six years ago, on the first day after New Year's, the girls would line up to start coming in here to hurry and pick out a dress so another girl wouldn't buy it first, but that has since gone away.

COVID-19 hit us hard. There were no proms. We were doing great in February 2020. We were dead March 1. The girls and their moms came in on Friday to buy a dress, then the school cancelled prom on Monday. Also, 2021 was bad because the schools couldn't decide whether to have prom or homecoming.

How big of an impact has social media had on your small business?

When customers share our posts or leave reviews, it helps others discover us. Most of our business has been word-of-mouth, for which we are grateful. We have mothers and grandmothers that will come in and say, "I bought my wedding dress here!" Or, "They took our ball photos when we were little."

What does supporting local mean to you?

Helen: It means that our people are shopping with us. We really like helping people. You know what she likes, and you do a good job for her. Small business owners put a great deal into their businesses. They need support.

Unfortunately, a lot don't succeed. If we don't support them, then we're not going to have anything left but big box stores. If we don't quit ordering everything online, we won't have any small businesses. Now, online retailers are designing and selling bridesmaid's dresses. I altered one dress from a major online retailer but won't do that again. It's often cheaper material, and so hard to work with. You may pay $40 for the dress, but I'm probably going to charge at least $45 to alter it. We saw Walmart come to Smyrna, and we like Walmart. We used to have a little shop nearby called The Sewing Basket. They could not compete and went out of business. The Five and Dimes are all gone.

LEGACY WINE & SPIRITS
AS TOLD BY GARY PATEL AND KETAN PATEL

Facebook: Legacy Wine & Spirits
Instagram: @legacy_wine

Tell me about your (small) business.
Legacy is the largest liquor store in the Smyrna area. We have a massive inventory spanning 8,000 square feet, including a premium selection of fine wines, spirits, and a large selection of craft beer. In addition to top brands, we carry local favorites. We have a cigar room with a walk-in humidor containing the area's largest selection of cigars. We also own Shell Legacy Station. Legacy is a one-stop shop

for you to buy your gas, food, liquor, cigars, breakfast, and coffee. We are family owned and operated since 2016.

What inspired you to open a both a liquor store and later a gas station?

Gary: When I came to America in 1999, I was working at a family gas station. I then started in the liquor business with my brother-in-law, Charlie, in his Murfreesboro store, Stones River Total Beverage. Then, we decided to build a bigger store. We didn't have much money and didn't know if we would survive or not. We started with 7,500 square feet. We built a small beer store next to our liquor store. In Tennessee, you couldn't sell beer and liquor together in those days. We started growing and kept growing. I was going back and forth to India at the time because my family was still there. I finally gained my legal status and I decided to bring my family to Tennessee.

In 2004, I decided to go out on my own. Charlie and I bought our first liquor store in La Vergne. It was the only liquor store in La Vergne. I bought the land two years later. That store was only 2,000 square feet. Finally, we opened La Vergne Beverage Depot in 2007.

Smyrna was dry at the time. We started thinking about opening a store in Smyrna because we had regular customers from Smyrna coming to our La Vergne store. We bought land in Smyrna in 2008 when the market was going down. In 2009, Ketan came to La Vergne and worked with me. Then, we decided to go to Smyrna and build a liquor store on the land we previously purchased. We made Ketan a partner and started envisioning the future and Legacy together, Ketan, Charlie and I.

Ketan worked very hard from day one. In March 2016, we had our grand opening for Legacy Wine & Spirits. In April 2016, we opened the Shell Legacy Station located on the same property. From there we kept growing and haven't stopped.

. . .

What brought you to Smyrna?

Ketan: My sister lived in Rutherford County, and I really liked it. I didn't want to live up North any longer. I needed a break from the fast life and wanted to start something new. I came here and joined Gary and learned so much. I knew I wanted to work for myself eventually

What has been the best piece of business advice you have ever received?

Ketan: My uncle told me there are two ways you make it in America. You can work eighty hours until you are forty, or forty hours until you are eighty. Those are your options. I knew I wanted the second option. This October, I turn forty. I'm where I want to be. All I know is one way. I was very motivated and still am.

Gary: My dad was in the construction and financial industries in India. I'd go to work with him in the morning building houses, then class at night. He always told me that if you do good, I'm still going to find a mistake. That's the only way you are going to learn to be better. My dad also always told me to help people  when I could, which is why giving back is so important to us.

I never had to work this hard in India. In America, you have to work very hard if you want to be successful. I started with a small store. Now we have seven businesses. I used to sleep three hours a night. I worked the night desk at a hotel and at the liquor store seven days.

What makes the experience of shopping for wine and spirits at Legacy so unique and special?

Gary: We provide excellent customer service and vast knowledge to customers they won't find at a box store. Ketan knows all about wine. We offer one of the biggest craft beer selections and have a major cigar inventory. We also take customer requests and fill special orders.

We believe in offering the right price and having the right attitude. You have to treat customers well.

When I was in a small store, we learned something new every day. The ladies like a clean store that is bright, open, and safe. They want to spend their time and money in a good environment. Our gas station is very safe, clean, and lit up bright at night. We care very deeply about customers' safety and shopping experience. We like customers to be able to move about freely throughout the aisles and see other customer's faces while they shop.

What do you enjoy doing in your spare time?

We enjoy going to hockey, soccer, and football games. We also enjoy giving back to the community. We provide wine and beverages, and sponsor events such as the Rotary Fish Fry and Senior Activity Center spaghetti supper. We have supported the Law Offices at the Victory House's Court Appointed Special Advocates ("CASA") Christmas benefit for ten years.

What does supporting local mean to you?

We have to support local. In Tennessee, all the big chains came into the wine and beer market. Now wine is in grocery stores. One day liquor will be too. They will eat the small stores and local liquor stores will likely be forced to shut down. We don't know what the future holds. You don't see any local grocery stores owned by 'mom and pop' like you did fifty years ago.

When you spend money at local businesses, the money stays here. We have worked hard to get here. Big chains come with a lot of money. If a chain isn't doing well in a certain state, they can often shift resources around or file for Chapter 11. Local businesses don't have those options, so it's much harder.

Convenience causes local businesses to shut down. For example, drive-thrus. "I want to pay for the food through my app and not go inside." This hurts small businesses. A small restaurant may not be able to have its own app or drive-thru. You can have something shipped to your house overnight, so you don't even have to go to any businesses.

Oftentimes, CEOs from out of state make the business and financial decisions when it comes to revenue generated from sales, whereas local business owners make these decisions locally. That has a much bigger impact on the local economy and community.

Whenever you spend money in our store, it stays in Smyrna. That money is reinvested back to the community. When you buy wine from a big box, it goes to a corporate chain. People have to support local businesses if they want them to stay.

What has been your biggest business milestone to date that you are most proud of?

Ketan: We love sharing our knowledge of wine and spirits and helping people pick out something to enjoy or the perfect wine for special occasions. I want you to know what you're buying. I'm proud of the level of customer service we provide. We have a lot of repeat customers.

. . .

What have been some of your biggest business challenges you have faced and how have you overcome them?

When a customer comes in for the first time, we have to figure out what we can do to bring them back. Building a clientele is the hardest part.

How big of an impact has social media had on your small business?

When you go to a new restaurant or liquor store, the first thing customers do is read reviews and look at photos. One bad review can turn people away. We are judging businesses by someone else's reviews. Positive reviews are huge and really help.

Where do you see yourself and your small business 5-10 years from now?

We want to expand.

Is there anything else you would like people to know about you or your small business?

Our gas station is not a franchise, so many gas stations are. We buy gas from Shell but we are locally owned.

CLOUD 9 MOBILE GROOMING
AS TOLD BY SUSAN GATES

Website: www.Cloud9MobileGrooming.com
Facebook: Cloud 9 Mobile Grooming

Tell me about your (small) business.

Cloud 9 Mobile Grooming is a mobile pet grooming business that covers parts of four counties. We have six mobile grooming rigs at this time and want to expand as we can hire or train groomers. We offer full-service grooming for dogs and (well-behaved) cats.

I have been mobile grooming since 2008. Cloud 9 Mobile Grooming came into being in January 2011. I have been the sole proprietor from the beginning, and I like it that way, even when things get hard. Starting a business in the Great Recession was maybe not the best move, but I stuck with it and made it to where I am now with hard work, a great team built over time, a LOT of mistakes, and some luck.

What inspired you to open a mobile grooming service?

I spent twenty-eight years in corporate information technology. My job description changed many times over those years but suffice to say, if it involves computers, I pretty much have done it. I had no plans to find a new career. I thought I would retire still a nerd when the time was right.

Life decided differently, though. I was laid off twice in the space of six years. That second time, I decided that was not going to happen again. I was going to find some way to work for myself. A friend was doing mobile grooming and I said to myself, "Hey, why not? I like dogs…"

I had no idea if I was going to be good at it. No idea if I was even going to like it. Turns out, I'm pretty good at pet grooming. And I love it! Now that most of my time is spent on management of the business, I really do miss the hands-on grooming.

One of my most memorable grooming experiences was when a client with an ancient springer spaniel called and wanted his dog made comfortable in his old age. He hadn't been groomed in a while and was pretty matted. The client carried him into my mobile grooming rig because he couldn't walk. I shaved and bathed him, mostly while he was laying down. Anything else would have been cruel. When I finished, I picked him up and put him down on the grass outside, figuring he couldn't go anywhere so it was safe. Well, he got up and took off running, he felt so good! That one made me proud of what I do.

What brought you to Smyrna?

I grew up in Connecticut and moved to Tennessee in 1990 to take a job in Hermitage. I've been in Smyrna since 2002. I love this town, and the fact that I can work here, too, is the best!

How does the grooming process work? What can clients expect?

We bring the grooming salon to client's homes or workplaces. All the messy stuff happens in our mobile grooming rigs and Rover or Fluffy is back on their couch in the space of an hour, maybe a little longer depending on size and coat type. Clients love that there's no mess, the convenience, and the much lower stress on their pets because they don't have to leave familiar surroundings.

What are you most excited about for your small business?

The possibilities for expansion of mobile grooming in general and my business specifically. Mobile grooming is exploding. There aren't enough mobile groomers to serve everyone interested in the service.

What does a typical day look like for you?

There are no typical days for me, which I like. There is maintenance to address, employees to manage, bills to pay, the future to plan, etc. I may start one day and work right through my To Do List. Other days, I may have to throw that list away and handle emergencies all day.

· · ·

What is the biggest lesson you've learned in owning and operating a small business?

How all-consuming it is. Business ownership is 24/7/365. There is always something that has to be done, someone who has to be talked to, some issue that has to be addressed. I'm not a sit around the house type anyway, so I thrive on the pace.

Are there any favorite mantras you live your life by?

Work smart, and hard. I think things through before starting on any task and it helps those tasks go easier.

How have you grown your small business from an idea to where it is now?

I really just bought a rig and away I went. I made a name for myself by being able to handle pets that had been deemed "difficult" by other groomers. I groomed all by myself for many years until the demand got to be more than I could handle. I built my second rig and hired my first groomer in 2014. That was a big step!

The next rig came in 2015, then 2018, then pretty much every year since we have put another rig on the road. I transitioned a groomer to Operations Manager in 2019 and added a full-time scheduler just last year. Two more big steps!

What are your daily habits or systems that you live by that have set you and your small business up for success?

Work, work, work... I am transitioning responsibilities to others as I am able, but there is still plenty that I have to take care of myself.

My ultimate goal is to make myself 100% dispensable, so the business will be more valuable when it comes time to let someone else take the reins.

What has been your biggest business milestone to date that you are most proud of?

Adding the second rig and my first employee. Also, starting in the Great Recession and not only making it through, but building a thriving business that will hopefully be viable well after I retire.

What have been some of your biggest business challenges you have faced and how have you overcome them?

My biggest challenges have been people-related. I am not naturally social; I work better with dogs and cats. Some employees have left because I'm not what they wanted me to be. I have let some clients go because they wanted to dictate how I do things. It is only in the last few years that I have become comfortable with who I am, and who I am not. I no longer try to please everyone.

What advice would you give to someone wanting to pursue a career similar to yours?

Be the manager *you* would want. I learned how *not* to treat people in my twenty-eight years in corporate America.

What has been the best piece of business advice you have ever received?

Employees come first. Nothing works without them, and a manager needs to understand that. Support them, mentor them, address mistakes and shortcomings in a professional and productive manner, show them you value their input and contributions.

. . .

What are some of the biggest lessons you've learned in owning a small business?

Oh, there are so many mistakes I've made. The biggest were all employee-related. Like hiring someone I knew wasn't a good fit simply because I needed a groomer desperately at the time. Or delaying firing a groomer when they really needed to be let go. I have learned from every single mistake and the experiences have made me a better business owner and manager.

How has failure or apparent failure set you up for future success?

The treachery of one employee in particular set me up for future success with all of my employees. It was a very hard lesson to learn. That is, that when an employee needs to be let go, just do it. There may be chaos for a time as you handle the fallout of losing that employee, but it is far better to rip off the bandage than to suffer the damage to the team by keeping them around.

Who has been the most influential person or mentor to you during your entrepreneurial journey and why?

We are surrounded by influences, those that help us and those that don't. Nobody gets to where they are without other people helping or hindering. We learn a lot of lessons from both types, and arguably the hinderers are more valuable to our development than anyone else.

Where do you see yourself and your small business 5-10 years from now?

When I started this business, it was with the intention to expand to such a level that I could sell it as a turn-key business and make enough to retire on. Cloud 9 Mobile Grooming is a large part of my retirement planning.

. . .

What do you enjoy doing in your spare time?

I enjoy fly fishing and watching my Red Sox play baseball. I read voraciously and my library card is my most valuable possession.

When I first started this business, it took a long time to develop a clientele. The best advertisement was, and still is, the mobile grooming rig. So, I would park in a neighborhood I wanted to cultivate. One day, Laurie Green stopped by and asked if I would groom a dog that belonged to one of her clients. (Laurie is the founder of SAFPAW, which helps homeless and low-income people take care of their pets.) I said sure, but I would not accept payment, it would be donated grooming. Since then, we have continued donating grooming for SAFPAW clients as we have time in our schedules. It makes me feel good to help these people who are struggling. But it has also been great for the business.

How big of an impact has social media had on your small business?

The biggest impact social media has on my business is making my employees feel appreciated. Clients post comments and reviews that validate their experience and expertise. Everyone likes a pat on the back at times.

What does supporting local mean to you?

Supporting local means my neighbors have the opportunity to live the same life I want for myself.

Small, local businesses employ the majority of people in this country. And most do it the right way, viewing employees as people, not line items on a financial statement. Large corporations have their place, but I would much rather do business with a small local company.

. . .

We've loved being a part of your journey. What's coming next that we can be a part of to support you?

We are starting a bath-centric route so we can hire pet bathers and train them to be full-fledged groomers. Training people who want to learn and become part of our great team will help us continue to expand.

We are also working towards putting a cat-mobile (mobile grooming for just cats) on the road. This will help us serve the very under-served mobile cat grooming market in the area.

Is there anything else you would like people to know about you or your small business?

Starting with nothing really can turn into something if you work hard, accept that there will be setbacks, and pay attention to the details. I am humbled by all the clients we have had over the years, their loyalty, and their patience as we have experienced bumps in the road. I am grateful for the employees I have had over the years, even the ones I had to let go or those who left on their own. I learned something about myself from every single experience building this business. It is very important to know yourself first, I think.

JANARTY'S HOMEMADE ICE CREAM
AS TOLD BY JANELLE AND MARTY SCHIFF

Facebook: Janarty's Homemade Ice Cream
Instagram: @Janartys
Phone (text or call): 615-918-0085

Tell me about your (small) business.

We named our shop Janarty's for "Janelle and Marty." We are family owned and operated since 9/8/2018.

Marty and I met over ten years

ago when he was a musician. We started dating in 2015. That story in and of itself is a good one. Things happen in life for a reason!

Marty was a musician for over twenty years, then worked at a grocery store (aspiring for management). I (Janelle) was going to nursing school. We had our first daughter together, Audrey, in 2017, and knew we wanted to spend more time together and build something we could be proud of, and our children could be proud of. His twenty-one-year-old daughter, KJ, works in our shop as our manager.

Part of our inspiration was watching the shows Chopped and Shark Tank. We would sit up after work and school watching them and dreaming of owning our own business, something food related. We didn't want to do a restaurant because there's a lot of overhead and moving parts. We decided instead to focus on something more specific- to do one thing and do it really well.

We then began researching what our area didn't have, (little did we know very few places do what we do, exactly) and we found that our area did not have a homemade ice cream shop!

Then, fate took hold! A friend of ours owns the building we are in now and was renovating it to try and find someone to lease to. He knew Marty always wanted to open a food establishment, so he invited us to come and take a look at it. It was perfect! This was in May 2018. We went home that night and got to work and haven't stopped since!

We did a lot more research on how to make the best possible ice cream we can. We visited a lot of other shops, ate a lot of ice cream (difficult research for sure) taking notes on what we liked and what we didn't. What we found is very few, if any, make their product on site, and even fewer make the base from scratch! We decided then that we would do just that! We knew we had to make a profit and that profit margins are important, but more importantly to us, we promised ourselves we would make the highest quality, from scratch ice cream and baked goods that we could.

Marty makes *all* of the ice cream and I make all the baked treats and chocolate dipped goodies. We use a high-quality Belgian chocolate for our dipping. We make all treats in-house (all gluten-free) including homemade fudge, Rice Krispy Treats, lemon bars, brownies, chocolate covered Oreos, chocolate dipped strawberries, cookies, and we are constantly thinking of new dessert ideas to add!

We make over fifty ice cream flavors and put out eight at a time. They are so small batch that the ice cream pans change out several times a day! *That* is fresh!

We have an amazing, kind, caring team we could not do this without. They are trained to make the waffle cones, our homemade whipped cream, take great care of customers, do lots and lots of dishes, and *lots* of cleaning!

When we first opened, we had two outside bakers. We can say proudly now that we make everything in-house! Marty has had celiac disease since he was very young, so he knows how nice it is for those who have to or choose to eat that way to find a place that has those options.

One of the most special things about our shop has been the relationships we've made. So many of our customers have become friends, and some like family. The support and love from this community has been incredible!

. . .

What inspired you to open an ice cream and sweets shop in the heart of Smyrna's Historic Train Depot District on the Front Street roundabout?

We looked into having our business in other places, Sam Ridley being one of them, but it just doesn't have the same appeal- the same feel. We absolutely love the part of Smyrna we are in. Front Street and the historic district we are in has such a special feel you just don't get in busier areas. We wanted to be in the downtown, old Smyrna, where the charm can't be beat! We believe every downtown needs an ice cream shop and we are so happy and proud to be the one in downtown Smyrna!

What is your favorite part about having a small business in Smyrna?

We love this town! People are kind and so happy to have us here. It is a large enough town without being too overwhelming. We are close to Nashville, but not too close.

What is so special and unique about your formula?

Quality and incredible customer service are two of our top priorities. A lot of ice cream shops either order their ice cream in pre-made or they order the base in. We make our ice cream on-site, extremely small batch from scratch (half gallon at a time, which is unheard of). Small batch ice cream is often referred to as five or ten gallons at a time, we make it a half gallon at a time!

Also, we don't add any additional preservatives and no additives. We slow-churn our ice cream to minimize overrun (the air whipped in -believe it or not, most ice cream you eat is 40-60% air!! Ours is less than 10%). We end up with less product but a higher quality one, which matters SO much more to us!!

What are some of your favorite flavor combinations?

Salted caramel and coffee; Chocolate and cinnamon brown sugar; Sweet lemon and vanilla; Blueberry Lavender and sweet lemon; Campfire and chocolate.

Our flavors change out several times a day- they all sell so great! Chocolate, sweet lemon, butter pecan, cookies and cream, and cinnamon brown sugar are some of the most popular!

What is your favorite part about working together? What's the most challenging?

We love to collaborate and come up with new ideas together. We love the pride we have in our shop and that we created it together. I love to clean so Marty has to remind me to get back to the product!

What have been the critical key ingredients to Janarty's success?

Quality, customer service, not cutting corners, and caring. We truly care about customers having the best possible experience they can while enjoying the best product we can make.

A trip to Janarty's is more than just a sugar rush, it's a magical experience and a sweet break from life's stresses. How does it make you feel when loyal customers come in for a tasty treat, whether it be to celebrate happy occasions, reward themselves for making it through another week, or, just for some 'scoops'?

It means so much to us to know it's more than a sweet treat, it's memories! We have a mother and daughter (Carrie and Colleen) who have been coming every Friday for several years. We've come to know and love them! The Mom has said she loves the idea that our shop will be a place where her daughter will have childhood memories and someday possibly bring her own daughter!

There's a couple who started as regulars in our shop, Don and Sandra, and are now like family. They were high school sweethearts and never able to have children, so they treat our girls like their own grandchildren.

Being a part of people's memories and sweet moments is priceless for us! We love that!

What's the first thing you do every morning to start your day on the right foot?

Coffee (at least once a week from Carpe Cafe next door!) and spending time with our two young daughters before bringing them to daycare. Those moments are the best.

What are you most excited about for your small business?

To see continued growth and success and continue to meet new people!

What does a typical day look like for you?

Marty works seven days a week (until we close Mondays and Tuesdays again in our off season). He is able to come home early some nights when his daughter KJ manages.

I (Janelle) am only able to work when our girls are in daycare, but I put in as many hours those days as I can (6:00 a.m. to 5:30 p.m.). We make baked treats and ice cream every moment we are there.

. . .

Are there any favorite mantras you live your life by?

"Comparison is the thief of Joy" - FDR. "Commit to the Lord whatever you do and He will establish your plans." Proverbs 16:3

Janarty's has won several prestigious awards voted on by the community, including a Firefly for Best New Business, and several Ruthie's Awards for Best Ice Cream, Best Milkshake and Best Dessert. Where do you see yourself and your small business 5-10 years from now?

Those awards mean so much to us and are so humbling, especially the local Firefly awards! Our hope and vision for the future is to continue to keep up with our growth (God willing it continues at this pace. We are up 78% this year so far), and are able to produce a lot more ice cream without changing our small batch, from scratch process. The first step will hopefully be to get another location, not for retail, but for production space. We would still oversee every part of it, and Marty and I would still make the treats and ice cream at our main location, we would just have a few other people making it with us.

Our other goal/vision in the near future is to get a food truck so we can be mobile and attend events, do parties, catering, etc. We have been asked to cater events in the past and we haven't been able to.

What does success mean to you?

Happy customers, happy employees, memories made at our shop, and people associating our business with quality, friendliness, cleanliness, and care.

. . .

How big of an impact has social media had on your small business?

Online reviews and posting and sharing on social media outlets has been invaluable to our success! We don't/can't afford to advertise very much being a small business, and we would rather save that marketing money to donate to schools, and local nonprofits such as Carpe Artista. We rely heavily on word-of-mouth. We read every review and they all mean so much to us. We want feedback, good or bad, and if ever bad, we want to know how we can be better. Thank you to anyone who has helped spread the word about us!

Janarty's does a great job supporting and promoting locally owned businesses. In what other ways does Janarty's partner with locally owned small businesses? Why is this so important to you?

We love partnering and working with other small businesses. We are a team and it's important to stick together and do what we can to support one another.

We use Carpe Cafe beans in our coffee ice cream, and we note that on the ice cream sign as well as mentioning it to as many customers as we can. Front Street Sign Company is our go-to for any signage. We order lunch religiously from Front Street Pub, and we frequent Breaking Bread and Carpe Cafe for the best greens and coffee in town.

What does supporting local mean to you?

Supporting local means so much to us. We try as often as possible when we travel and especially in our town to support local. You typically will get a better product, made with care, and better customer service. You can generally feel the love and dedication when you're in a small business.

Also, you are supporting someone's hopes and dreams, their family, and the money is going back into your community. Gift cards are such a wonderful way to support us and any small business, especially to someone who hasn't been to our shop before.

Is there anything else you would like people to know about you or your small business?
We love what we do and feel so blessed and grateful we get to do it every day. We will never take for granted or lose sight of the fact that our customers and incredible staff are the reason we get to!

STEVENS LAW, PLLC
AS TOLD BY ROBERT S. STEVENS

Website: www.stevenslawtn.com
Facebook: Stevens Law, PLLC
Instagram: @stevenslawpllc

Tell me about your (small) business.

I started my business in 2009 after I passed the bar exam and became a licensed attorney in Tennessee. Prior to this, I worked for another local lawyer for several years. My primary areas of practice include estate planning, probate, divorce and child custody, litigation, and consumer bankruptcy.

What inspired you to go into law and become an attorney?

I have always enjoyed research and writing. Law is a perfect fit for these. A career path test in high school also indicated that law would be a good profession to pursue based on my interests and talents.

What is your favorite part about having a small business in Smyrna?

The best part of my business is interacting with clients. People in our community are very friendly and have been great to work with over the years. Many clients have become like family.

What are you most excited about for your small business?

We're able to assist so many people through various phases of life. When their cases conclude, it is rewarding to see the relief they experience. Experiencing the finality clients face and being there to support them from a legal perspective through it all is what keeps the office going.

How have you grown your small business from an idea to where it is now?

Providing high quality service and good networking have helped to grow the business. Recently, the office has enhanced our web and social media presence.

. . .

What's the first thing you do every morning to start your day on the right foot?

I always look at my calendar first and try to plan a schedule that allows me to get everything done that I need to do. Lawyers work best with deadlines, so if I have set expectations for things to finish, they are more likely to get done as planned.

What does a typical day look like for you?

I am normally at my office by 7:00 a.m. to plan the day and catch up on correspondence. Depending on the day, I either have client meetings or court in the mornings. Afternoons and evenings are either client meetings or time to research and draft documents. I try to return phone calls at the end of the day and if needed, I stay at my office to finish matters that need to be done before I leave.

What is the biggest lesson you've learned in owning and operating a small business?

Good planning is critical. Planning includes time management at the office, making and following a sound budget, and also managing client intake to not overload the office with more than we can handle.

Are there any favorite mantras you live your life by?

"So in everything, do unto others as you would have them do unto you." Matthew 7:12 (NIV)

Stevens Law has won several prestigious awards voted on by the community, including several Best of Main Street Awards and

several Ruthie's Awards for Favorite Attorney. What has been your biggest business milestone to date that you are most proud of?

My office has consulted with over two thousand clients since 2009.

What advice would you give to someone wanting to pursue a career similar to yours?

Be willing to work hard and put in long hours. Also, if someone is interested in law, it is good to start planning early on to learn good time management, analytical skills, and how to wisely control money.

What are some of the biggest lessons you've learned in owning a small business?

Managing time and money are critical.

Things don't always go as planned, so it is important to be flexible and have a "Plan B" ready.

Giving back to the community is more important than people realize.

Who has been the most influential person or mentor to you during your entrepreneurial journey and why?

Imogene Bolin hired me to work for her after my first year of law school, and I worked several years out of her office. I learned how a law office actually operates from the inside and how to manage clients, expectations, time and money. She was very good to me and to her clients, and this impacted how I run my office.

One of the highlights each year

while working with the attorneys at the Victory House from 2009 - 2019 was the annual Christmas party. This annual event served two purposes: an open house to fellowship with friends and clients, and also as a fundraiser for a great non-profit called CASA (Court Appointed Special Advocates). Through the generosity of event attendees, we were able to raise tens of thousands of dollars and carloads of toys for CASA of Rutherford County, an organization that does so much unrecognized work for abused, neglected or dependent children in the juvenile court system. Meaningful experiences like this make working in this community so worthwhile.

What do you enjoy doing in your spare time?

I have been a proud member of Smyrna Rotary since 2010, and am currently serving as president this year (2021-2022). I have been a sponsor of its annual Wings of Freedom Fish Fry for many years.

In 2018, one of our members named Bill Hays brought forward the idea of Rotary leading the effort to construct an all-inclusive playground in Smyrna that allows everyone to participate regardless of ability. The board accepted the proposal and began due diligence on how to best approach this large task. When Bill Hays had to step away from Rotary, the board asked me to chair the playground committee. After narrowing down designs, our club began fundraising for this much-needed playground to expand recreational opportunity for people and families with disabilities. Freedom Playground was completed in mid-2021. Between Rotary's fundraising from individuals, businesses and foundations, plus the Town of Smyrna's significant contribution and partnership, well over $800,000 of value was gathered for the project. Phase Two of Freedom Playground is an ADA compliant restroom facility that will be constructed nearby, and Rotary will be making a substantial contribution toward this component, as well.

Working on this project has been a major highlight in my career, and I look forward to Smyrna Rotary's endeavors in the future.

The business has also sponsored numerous other causes and events over the years. Being involved and giving back are very important for the success of any local business.

I currently serve on the Rutherford County Commission and previously served on the Motlow College Foundation board of trustees for eight years. My favorite hobby is traveling and visiting new places, from local to international.

How big of an impact has social media had on your small business?

Online reviews and engagement on social media are very important for the business. Clients often note the positive things they have seen online about Stevens Law when they come in for initial consultations. We make an effort to stay connected online and do ask clients to leave reviews so others can better understand the level of service we provide.

Why is supporting local businesses so important?

Local businesses give back to the community and also support each other. It is important for local businesses to be successful to keep people here employed.

SMYRNA READY MIX
AS TOLD BY JEFF HOLLINGSHEAD

Photo courtesy of Eric Adkins Photography

Website: www.smyrnareadymix.com
Facebook: SRM Concrete

How did Smyrna Ready Mix get its start?

SRM Concrete is a family owned and operated ready-mix company founded by Melissa and Mike Hollingshead in 1999. Our first plant was built in the backyard of our first home. We had no experience in the business, nor did we know anything about concrete plants. It was a struggle buying our first plant, but by hard work and the grace of God, we made it. The plant has been up and running for two decades. So much of our history is right here in Smyrna.

We started Smyrna Ready Mix to service our own concrete needs for our business, Hollingshead Concrete. Hollingshead Concrete is a concrete finishing company mainly doing residential work such as house slabs, driveways, sidewalks, etc. At that time, local ready-mix companies weren't able to provide reliable service, so we formed Smyrna Ready Mix to not only provide ourselves with exceptional service, but to other local finishers and contractors as well.

As our company continues to expand, our mission remains the same which is to provide every customer with quality concrete and unmatched service.

The dedication and determination from an outstanding group of mixer operators drives the business growth and has allowed SRM Concrete to add more than four thousand employees with over three hundred locations that span across thirteen states.

What is your favorite part about having a business in Smyrna?

It's home to us, and we love Smyrna. We all grew up here and went to school here. This is a special town made up of special people. We are just glad to be a part of it.

How did your childhood in Smyrna shape you?

Smyrna has shaped our entire family's childhood. My parents, my brother, and I went to Smyrna schools and were born and raised here. There have been so many teachers and people that have touched not only my life, but my parents as well. People like Mr. Raikes and Coach Trumpour.

.   .   .

Did you ever dream your family's 'backyard' business would experience such exponential growth? Why do you think SRM has been so successful throughout the years?

First and foremost, we have been incredibly blessed. We had a vision to become the largest ready-mix producer in the country and surrounded ourselves with great team members. In business, it's not one decision that makes you or breaks you. It's making good decisions every day and fixing the bad ones. SRM has been successful due to our dedication and work ethic. Our goal is to get up every day and out work our competition.

In addition, you also founded Hollingshead Cement, Hollingshead Harbor, and Hollingshead Aviation. What was the inspiration behind these ventures and what purposes do they serve?

Hollingshead Cement buys and sells bulk cement. We import cement from Europe into the east coast and from there, rail the product across different parts of the country for resale. It was primarily formed to service SRM Concrete's cement needs, but we do sell to other third parties as well. We have a cement terminal in Savannah that services the coastal areas of the Carolinas, Georgia, and northern Florida. We currently have plans to build other cement terminals in other areas of the country in which SRM Concrete operates.

Hollingshead Harbor is a raw material handling and transport business. We have multiple river ports and terminals spanning the country in which we transport and unload raw materials such as rock and sand with the use of our own boats and barges. We currently have locations in Nashville, TN, Houston, TX, Detroit, MI, Panama City, FL, and Jackson, AL. Hollingshead Harbor operations directly integrate into the supply chain of how SRM Concrete receives its raw materials at many of its locations.

Hollingshead Aviation is a fixed-base operator (FBO) providing a variety of different aviation services and amenities. Due to the growing footprint of SRM Concrete, our need to travel grew as well.

We saw the aviation business not just as an opportunity to provide the services we need to travel, but a separate business opportunity in a niche industry.

In 2019, Smyrna Ready Mix unveiled plans for a new headquarters in Smyrna. Why did you decide to move your headquarters from Nashville to Smyrna? What is the significance behind the name "Cornerstone"?

We named it Cornerstone because Smyrna has been a cornerstone for us. We could not have done as well as we have without being a part of this town. For the last five years, our corporate office has been in downtown Nashville, but eighty percent of our workforce lives in Rutherford County, with many of them living in Smyrna. Everybody in the company is elated to not have to fight the Nashville traffic and be back home. The building will house a corporate staff of two-hundred to three-hundred people. It will have a fitness center and a daycare center for employees to use. The company will occupy the entire building.

What all types of ready-mix concrete services does SRM provide?

We design and supply many types of concrete mixes for an array of different jobs. For example, we do many high-rises, warehouses, schools, but also patios, driveways and sidewalks. Whatever the job, we can fulfill it.

We sell to do-it-yourself homeowners who can use our SRM Concrete app to help them through the process of planning a new driveway, patio, sidewalk or any other concrete related project. Also, finishers and other contractors can use the app to track their truck, view their order and tickets, pay invoices, and anything else they may need as it relates to the details of any job.

· · ·

What has been your biggest business milestone to date that you are most proud of?

We have made over seventy successful acquisitions, but I am most proud to be able to run a successful family-owned business. My dad, brother, and I get to work together every day and are best friends. That is basically unheard of.

What have been some of your biggest business challenges you have faced and how have you overcome them?

Our business has grown significantly over the last ten years. So that in and of itself is challenging, but we have overcome the challenges by just getting up and going to work every day. I am a big believer that if you work hard then things will work out. They always have for us.

What is the biggest lesson you've learned in owning and operating a business?

I became the CEO of SRM seven years ago. For me, the most important aspect of a business is culture. Our business wouldn't be successful without a team of people that are proud of the company that they helped to build. We have a story, and I think that in itself is powerful. My parents founded this business in our backyard with nothing, and now we have grown to be a good-sized company. Businesses need a soul. Without it, they just aren't as successful in my opinion.

SRM has partnered with many charitable and civic organizations throughout the thirteen states it services, especially here in (Smyrna) Tennessee. SRM regularly sponsors Little League teams, donates an immense amount of concrete, monetary support and other in-kind contributions to various projects. Smyrna has been significantly impacted by SRM's generosity over the years. Why is

giving back to the community and your employees so important to SRM?

We think it's important to give back to the community that has given us so much opportunity. Especially giving back to kids in the community. That is where our heart is. My dad grew up in Smyrna in the trailer park next to Gil's Market. He had a tough upbringing, but was able to live the American Dream. We want other kids to know they can do the same.

SRM has won several prestigious awards voted on by the community, including winning the Local Legacy Award in the Light Up Local Firefly Awards, founder Mike Hollingshead was presented with the A.F. Bridges award as Contributor of Year, and was inducted into the Smyrna High School Hall of Fame as a contributor to the school. Where do you see yourself and SRM 5-10 years from now?

I was very proud of Dad for getting inducted in the Smyrna High School Hall of Fame. Over the next ten years, we want to keep growing. We want to be the largest construction materials company in the country. This would entail us growing about four to five times bigger than we are today.

What do you enjoy doing in your spare time?

I am the pastor of Calvary Apostolic Church. This is where all my free time goes. We have a large family. I have three kids and my brother has four, so we constantly have a lot going on!

How big of an impact has social media had on your business?

It's very important to us for people to be engaged with our business online. We are constantly looking for ways to engage with our customers online and for them to see what we are up to.

· · ·

What does supporting local mean to you?

It's helping where needed, whether it be local schools, churches, or the town itself. It's about making ourselves available.

Business is hard. Every business owner knows that each customer matters and we wouldn't have business without them.

THE SOCIAL NUTRITION
AS TOLD BY JULIA HAMILTON & HARLEY STEWART

Facebook: The Social Nutrition
Instagram: @thesocialnutritiontn
Tik Tok: @thesocialnutritiontn

Tell me about your (small) business.
　The Social Nutrition has been in business for almost one year. We offer healthy protein smoothies packed with vitamins and nutrients, and clean energy teas that boost your metabolism and burn calories!

We also offer one on one coaching to anyone who wants to lose weight, gain muscle, or learn more about nutrition.

What is your favorite part about having a small business in Smyrna?

Being able to bring a healthy option to Smyrna and getting to know the community! Smyrna is growing, and we are here to grow with it.

What brought you to Smyrna?

We did not grow up in Smyrna, but we love the hometown feel. Harley moved here in 2014 and does not plan on leaving!

What inspired you to start a healthy lifestyle business?

Harley: I really decided to start a healthier lifestyle in 2020. I have always been active, but I lacked on nutrition. I was spending hours in the kitchen on Sundays trying to prepare for the week and every diet I tried, I could never stick with. I met Julia through social media and The Social Nutrition was created shortly after! We teach people how to make this a lifestyle change, this way you don't have to worry about a "diet." We want to create a healthy, non-restrictive lifestyle for people.

Julia: We wanted to create a healthy fast-food option for people and simplify basic nutrition.

What are you most excited about for your small business?
To grow, both as a business and as individuals, and to really get to know and make a difference in the community! We love the Smyrna community, and we are all about supporting other small and local businesses here.

What's the first thing you do every morning to start your day on the right foot?
We each say three things we are grateful for.

What does a typical day look like for you?

Our lives are pretty busy. We are both full-time college students pursuing bachelor's degrees. Depending on the day, we may work at The Social in the morning and have classes in the afternoon, or vice-versa. Our days do not end there. We have clients that we have to follow-up with to make sure they are staying on track and have everything they need. We are also always working on our business.

We want to create an environment at our shop that anyone can come and enjoy! We also like to go around to other businesses to get to know them and figure out ways that we can partner to help each other! We like to stay active, so we try to set some time aside to workout or get some movement in.

What is your go-to favorite menu item that you offer?
    Favorite Blended Coffee: Caramel Macchiato
    Favorite Iced Coffee: House blend with our fat burner creamer
    Favorite Shake: Banana Nut Bread or Fruity Pebbles
    Favorite Tea: Strawberry Peach Ring or Hydra-Bomb

What is the biggest lesson you've learned in owning and operating a small business?

There is a *lot* of work that goes into any kind of business, but with that comes so much reward. Having a business partner is like having another relationship as well. It is something you must work at consistently. We have also learned how important it is to show up your best self because we are not only showing up for ourselves, but also our customers and our community. We come into our shop every day with a smile on our faces, ready to shine light on anyone who comes into our path.

Are there any favorite mantras you live your life by?
    "Develop success from failures. Discouragement and failure are two of the surest stepping stones to success." "If you want to keep happiness, you have to share it." -Dale Carnegie
    "Let others lead small lives, but not you. Let others argue over small things, but not you. Let others cry over small hurts, but not you.

Let others leave their future in someone else's hands, but not you."
-Jim Rohn

How have you grown your small business from an idea to where it is now?

We both worked at a smoothie and energy bar similar to ours in Murfreesboro. We knew very quickly that creating and owning one of our own was definitely in our future.

What are your daily habits or systems that you live by that have set you and your small business up for success?

If someone comes into our shop not having the best day, we want to turn that around for them. We also know how important it is to work on ourselves to be the best version we can be. Reading and doing things to work on our personal development is something we really focus on.

What has been your biggest business milestone to date that you are most proud of?

Opening a brick and mortar location! We are both full-time students, but we took a leap of faith and pursued something that we set our minds to!

We also had our grand opening celebration about a month after opening and had such huge success!

. . .

What have been some of your biggest business challenges you have faced and how have you overcome them?

Learning how to run a business and balance our personal and school lives has definitely been a challenge. I (Harley) am a perfectionist. This can be a blessing and a curse. Learning how to start up a business was also challenging. There was no one that could walk us through the entire process and if you try to call the State, they will send you in so many different directions. A lot of it is learning as you go.

I remember shortly after we signed our lease, Julia was out of town, but I was eager to get the build-out process going, so I went ahead and got our electric and water turned on so we could start cleaning the building. Of course, the companies can never tell you a time of when they will be there to turn things on, they just tell you to make sure everything is off. So, as I am still working my full-time job in Murfreesboro, I stop by on my lunch hour to make sure things had been turned on and I walk into a pipe that is blasting water into the air. There was a huge puddle and no way to turn the valve off except at the pump. I had to call the water company and wait almost ten minutes before they sent out a maintenance man to turn off our pump.

These are things no one will be able to prepare you for. This was just a couple days into the process. It wasn't easy, but it has been so worth it. We have learned so much in such a short amount of time.

What advice would you give to someone wanting to pursue a career similar to yours?

No matter what you want to pursue or how old you are, go for it! We are both in our twenties making our dreams come true! If you want something, set your mind to it, and go all in. Make your dream your reality!

Quitting my full-time job was the scariest thing I have ever done. So many things went through my head such as, "Is this going to work?" and, "Are we going to make money?" or, "Will I be able to pay my bills?" I knew that I would make it work and opening this business has been such a blessing. The reward you receive is something no one can prepare you for. It is truly a blessing every day that I get to go to work to a place that I love! I can't wait to see how we grow as individuals and how our business grows along with Smyrna.

What are some of the biggest lessons you've learned in owning a small business?

How much work they are! Thankfully, we have a partnership so we have been able to lean on each other.

No one can prepare you for the amount of effort and time you will have to dedicate to your business, but no one will be able to prepare you for the reward you will receive in the end, either. The hard work and tears will be so worth it in the end.

What 1-3 books have impacted your life the most and why?

How to Win Friends and Influence People by Dale Carnegie. It is one they recommend you read a couple times a year because you will be able to learn something new every time. It has helped us grow into better friends, better business owners, and overall better people.

How has failure or apparent failure set you up for future success?

As Dale Carnegie says, *"Develop success from failures. Discouragement and failure are two of the surest stepping stones to success."* Every failure is a lesson learned.

. . .

Where do you see yourself and your small business 5-10 years from now?

We see our business having multiple locations! We want to bring healthy options to multiple locations in Smyrna and surrounding cities! We love what we do, and we love being able to teach others!

What does success mean to you?

Success is freedom and happiness. Success is being able to wake up every day and absolutely enjoy what you get to do. It is us making a positive impact on the lives and community.

What do you enjoy doing in your spare time?

We both like to stay active and love being outdoors! So, lots of hiking, kayaking, fishing, swimming.

I (Harley) also love to travel. I love learning the culture behind each state. I used to work in the dental field, so my goal is to participate in a dental mission trip somewhere in another country.

How big of an impact has social media had on your small business?

Social media has the potential to reach thousands of people in a matter of seconds. Instagram has probably been the most helpful as far as reaching people and letting people see what we are all about. Reviews, reposts, shares, and tags mean so much to us! We appreciate everyone that takes time out of their day to interact with us on social media.

Someone once told us that if someone has a bad experience at a franchise, they will forgive and continue to go. However, if someone has a bad experience at a small business, they hardly ever go back.

What does supporting local mean to you?

Supporting local is everything to us! Whether that be supporting a business that is similar to ours or completely different. There is room for everyone to succeed. So, stop by your favorite local businesses and show them how much they mean to you!

Local businesses pour their heart into their business. They are able to express their passion through their business, and even the smallest purchase or repost on social media mean the world!

We've loved being a part of your journey. What's coming next that we can be a part of to support you?

Expansion! We want to expand our team, hours, and locations.

We also want to become more involved in the community.

We will also be hosting pop-up shops and participating in community events.

Is there anything else you would like people to know about you or your small business?

You can become a VIP member and purchase our items to make at home at a discount.

Our smoothies can effectively replace a snack or meal providing twenty-one vitamins and minerals. Our teas are loaded with vitamins, will boost your metabolism, burn calories, and give you some good, clean energy.

We have options for everyone! Gluten-free, caffeine-free, low calorie, low carb, kid-friendly and pup-friendly. We have it all!

Having a bad day? Need a little more energy? Need a friend to talk to? Need some advice on nutrition? Stop by The Social Nutrition! We can't wait to meet you!

FADED UNIVERSITY
AS TOLD BY MARQUISE MARTIN

Website: www.fadeduniversity.com
Facebook: Faded University Barber College
Instagram: @FadedUniversity

Tell me about your (small) business.
　　Faded University Barber College is a barber training program that opened in October 2017. The training courses include Master Barber, Barber Technician, Barber Instructor, and Cosmetologist wanting to obtain a dual license as a Master Barber.

In addition to barber training, Faded University offers a variety of low-cost grooming services to the public, including haircuts for adults and kids, skincare, hot towel shaves, hair color, and chemical texture services.

Why barbering? What inspired you to open a barber shop and college?

After serving in the military, I returned home and worked a few years in a job that I did not particularly enjoy. I had a friend who enrolled at a barber college in Murfreesboro, and he suggested I visit to see if I would be interested.

During my visit, I was instantly intrigued with the idea of becoming a barber and enrolled in the program. People skills and attention to detail came relatively easy to me. Barbering allowed me to become an entrepreneur. Faded University Barber College has allowed me to become an educator and mentor others who wish to become professionals.

What is your favorite part about having a small business in Smyrna?

Being able to give back to the community that I love.

How long does it take for someone to become a licensed barber?

The Master Barber course requires fifteen-hundred hours of training and ranges from twelve to eighteen months.

The Barber Technician course requires three-hundred and forty hours of training and ranges from three to six months.

The Barber Instructor course requires three-hundred hours of training and ranges from three to five months.

The Cosmetologist dual license course requires three hundred hours of training and ranges from three to five months. This course is for licensed cosmetologists that are also wanting to obtain a master barber license. Faded University does not offer a cosmetologist training course.

What are you most excited about for your small business?
The ability to mentor and help young people.

What does a typical day look like for you?
A typical day starts with 9:00 a.m. theory class. We offer guest services from 11:00 a.m.- 5:00 p.m. The afternoon theory class is from 5:00 p.m.- 7:00 p.m.

What is the biggest lesson you've learned in owning and operating a small business?
You are never too old to learn a new skill.

Are there any favorite mantras you live your life by?
Trust the process.

How have you grown your small business from an idea to where it is now?
Community outreach. Being able to visit high schools, attending community events, partnership with the Boys and Girls Club, and sponsoring an annual back to school haircut event has helped the business grow.

· · ·

What has been your biggest business milestone to date that you are most proud of?

Opening the first barber college in Smyrna.

What have been some of your biggest business challenges you have faced and how have you overcome them?

COVID-19. Being able to adapt and create some normalcy for the students so that they could continue their education via virtual theory classes.

What advice would you give to someone wanting to pursue a career similar to yours?

In addition to trusting the process, I would tell them to put God first.

What has been the best piece of business advice you have ever received?

Always have a business plan.

What are some of the biggest lessons you've learned in owning a small business?

I've learned that owning a business is not as easy as it may seem.

. . .

What 1-3 books have impacted your life the most and why?

I consider the Bible to be the instruction manual on how to live life. *The Milady Standard Barbering* textbook because I feel this book has made me a true master barber.

How has failure or apparent failure set you up for future success?

I feel that if you have not experienced failure, you may not have taken chances that are necessary for growth. "Growth doesn't come from comfort zones." - Roy T. Bennett.

Who has been the most influential person or mentor to you during your entrepreneurial journey and why?

Gary Gratton, because he pushed me to do what I thought I could not do.

Where do you see yourself and your small business 5-10 years from now?

Faded University would like to have a bigger presence in the community by opening a larger facility. This will allow us to offer more opportunities for future students and placement programs for new barbers.

What does success mean to you?

The ability to be able to provide for my family and being happy.

What do you enjoy doing in your spare time?

My most enjoyable hobby is golf. Faded University also takes part in some of the following community events:

- Faded University Father's Day Golf Tournament

- Free Back to School Haircuts
- Depot Day Celebration
- Thanksgiving Nourish Food Bank Can Food Drive
- Smyrna Christmas Parade
- Front Street Christmas- with Front Street Sign Company
- Home Street Home – haircuts for the homeless

How big of an impact has social media had on your small business?

Social media is huge. It allows us to reach a broader audience and stay in tune with industry trends.

What does supporting local mean to you?

It means investing into the community and giving local small business owners an opportunity. Supporting local businesses is important because local businesses support the community.

MARTY LUFFMAN, STATE FARM INSURANCE

AS TOLD BY MARTY LUFFMAN

Website: www.martyluffman.com
Facebook: Marty Luffman

Tell me about your (small) business.

We celebrated forty-five years in 2020. We offer home, auto and life insurance.

. . .

What inspired you to become an insurance agent?

After graduating from David Lipscomb University, I was offered a position with the State of Tennessee. I went to work for the Department of Public Health as an analyst. My first job was to audit one of the hospitals in Davidson County. Apparently, I did pretty well. They sent me out on another audit, then a third, then a fourth. The following year, a position became available with the Department of Agriculture. They had never had a personnel director. Surprisingly, out of fifty candidates I was selected for the first Director of Personnel for the State. I was twenty-three and worked this position for two years. It was very stressful. In 1974, the governor called and wanted me to apply to be the Chief of Personnel. A few months later, I was selected.

Well, come election time, and a new governor is voted in. One day my Commissioner calls me in his office. Guess who's sitting on the sofa smoking a cigarette and he's got a drink in his hand? I'm certain I smelled scotch. The Commissioner said, "we are having trouble justifying you in our administration." I snapped back, "I'm having trouble justifying working for this administration." Very quickly, Governor Ray Blanton snapped back and said, "Why don't you just get yourself out since we agree?" I was officially terminated that day.

I spent the next year playing, traveling, and horseback racing and even made a horse race track in Smyrna. I sent my resumé out. No one offered me a job by this point. Then, State Farm called me in for an interview a year later and offered me a position. I took it and loved it. I worked in management for the next five years and applied for an agency. I got my agency, and forty-five years later I'm still with State

Farm and have no intentions of ever retiring. Being an insurance agent has supported my many opportunities to serve the community.

What is your favorite part about having a small business in Smyrna?

The small-town attitude, where everyone is friendly and courteous. Children and teenagers are respectful.

How has Smyrna and the small business landscape changed since you first started in 1975?

My very first State Farm office was just down the sidewalk from Smyrna Printing & Design, Wilson's Photography and Bridal Country. I shared office space with two attorneys.

As I think back over the years watching Smyrna grow prior to Nissan moving in, it's absolutely amazing. On Front Street, there was a women's clothing store, a dry cleaner, Sissies, the Post Office, a store for ladies' linens and sewing classes, and a general merchandise store. The Smyrna newspaper was next door to the Snake Pit, which was next door to the Rescue Squad. We also had a movie theatre, a library, and Smyrna Birite.

We had one streetlight. The businesses on Lowry were very casual. Over the railroad tracks in one square block was Smyrna Printing & Design, Wilson's Photography and Bridal Country, businesses that still stand to this day. A shoe cobbler, Mr Peebles, Regal Furniture, and Smyrna Hardware in the old livery barn. There was a car service center (currently Donut Palace) Oxbow Restaurant, and Sushi House. Down the street was Crosslin Supply. Sam Ridley Parkway was a gravel and dirt road. Bill's Bar was on Sewart Air Force Base. The Smyrna Country Club sat near where Whitt's Barbecue is currently. Around the corner was Gilsville.

I opened a Western store in Smyrna called Bridle and Saddle Co. in 1989. It did so well that I opened a second one in Nolensville in 1992. This location did not perform as well, so I decided to donate what was left to the Tennessee Children's Home since they had an equestrian program. A spot became available in Opry Mills in 2009. I opened a store there, but then the flood came one year later and took almost all of my inventory. I auctioned off the remnants and gave the money to St. Jude Hospital.

In the late 1970s, Charlie Daniels had a barn in Smyrna on Jefferson Pike across from Gilsville. My barn was on the other side of Smyrna. Charlie had Arabians. I had gaited horses, nothing expensive like his. We rode together on occasion. He would ride one of mine. He favored a big black walking horse, good disposition, and easy ride. There was a bait shop in the middle of Smyrna, Ed's Bait Shop, with picnic tables out back. We would meet there occasionally, have a sandwich and a beer and chat. He had been invited to be the Grand Marshall in the Nashville Christmas Parade. He asked to ride the big black walker, and of course I was good with it.

A few days later, Charlie called wanting a gaited horse for Hazel, his wife. She was not a rider, so I was extra careful selecting one. I delivered it on Christmas morning. We sat in his barn telling stories. We lost touch with each other. Occasionally, I would hear from him, but he was just checking in and saying hi. I never went to his ranch again, or ever saw him again.

History & Horses

I have always loved and appreciated local history and historical storytelling. I have seen Smyrna change so much over the years.

One project I took on was helping to create the Smyrna Christmas Parade in 1974. I helped organize the parade for ten years. I'm truly proud of that. It's still going strong today, but much larger. I was the Grand Marshall in the Smyrna Christmas parade for years.

I have many wonderful memories as far as local history is

concerned. I gave historical tours of the Grand Ole Opry from 1966-1968. Another proud memory I have is producing the very first Smyrna Heart Ball in 1978 at the former country club at the Base. Also, when President-Elect Reagan came to Nashville in 1980 and landed at the Smyrna Airport, I had the honor of being one of his drivers and got to shake his hand.

I ran for Police Commissioner against Paul Johns in the eighties. Paul beat me by one hundred and thirty-three votes. That was an interesting time. Paul and I enjoy telling stories and laughing about it to this day.

Then, in 1989, the Department of Interior contacted me about building a horse and hiking trail on the original Natchez Trace. So, being a historian, I was really excited about this. For three years, I organized and recruited volunteers. Today, we have the Natchez Trace horse and hiking trail. I did several years of interpretative trail rides. This led to giving historical talks to various organizations and three different magazines asking me to furnish stories.

What are you most excited about for your small business?

The pleasure I receive when folks come by the office to chat. Chatting about anything- the weather, cars, horses, John Wayne, guns, history, politics, or, the growth of the town and how it used to be.

What is the biggest lesson you've learned in owning and operating a small business?

Well, there is no denying I was an academically pathetic student. I couldn't make being happy and having fun work with having to study. Opening my business was a slap in the face of reality. I had to learn all about government regulations, bookkeeping, taxes, underwriting claims, and a lot of discipline. Also, budgeting my money, this was something I had never done.

What has been your biggest business milestone to date that you are most proud of?

There have been so many. I look back and there is no way can I pick just one. I was asked to co-chair the Smyrna Bicentennial with one of the greatest icons I have ever met, Walter King Hoover. After the event, we met for our last meeting, and he stood with the others, giving me a standing ovation. My love of history has created many opportunities as a speaker and a writer. Being the Town of Smyrna Historian, following in the footsteps of Hoover and Ernie Johns is humbling. Receiving a plaque and being recognized for my historical stories by the Rutherford County Historical Association was overwhelming. But without question, being recognized by Rutherford County as their Favorite Insurance Agent in 2020 was probably the pinnacle. It rewarded and reinforced my efforts of community service and integrity.

What are some of the biggest lessons you've learned in owning a small business?

Taking a leap of faith that all will end well, and picking yourself up if it doesn't. When I built my office, the area was isolated. Nothing but farms and a couple of businesses within a few miles. It was a risk, but thankfully it turned out well.

What 1-3 books have impacted your life the most and why?
The Bible, *The Celestine Prophecy*, and *Why Did I Survive*

What does supporting local mean to you?
Smyrna is a town, but more of a community. I could ride my horse up Enon Springs to Lowry Street. There was a Dairy Dip where the Trading Post car lot is now. I would ride over there, eat an ice cream and get back on my horse and ride down Lowry Street to Washington, across to Front Street. There were always folks sitting outside to chat with and small business owners that came outside just to say hi. I would continue my ride to Hazelwood and get back on Enon Springs to make the trek home. Very little traffic in those days.

Supporting local means going to local restaurants like the Omni Hut, Sissies, and The Castle, some of Smyrna's most iconic locally owned restaurants. Sadly, these restaurants have closed over the years. I have so many fond memories in each of those places. It means going to Gil's Ace Hardware for tools and supplies, and not ordering online.

It was small business that built Smyrna, and it was the residents that built the small businesses. It's very important to support the local business owners. They have employees that live and shop in Smyrna. They pay taxes that support our schools, and make numerous donations to schools.

What do you enjoy doing in your spare time?
Some years ago, a magazine that catered to horse folks called *The Trail Rider* invited me to start writing for them. I saw a story about John Wayne's movie studio in Texas. This was his original Alamo

movie lot. I called and talked to one of the owners and made plans to fly down. The family and I became very good friends and I visited quite often and would take a horse with me. It was about this time that I was getting involved in horse competition mounted shooting. I asked permission to host a shoot in the movie studio. We had three or four of the best adventures I can remember. I traveled across America with my horse, Doc Holliday. We competed in forty-seven states. Doc and I went three years as national champions, and were also invited to Canada, Sweden, Germany and France.

I enjoy speaking to school children about local Smyrna history. I've been a regular as a living history tour guide and have done a lot of re-enactments.

I also enjoy being active in the community. I am in the Smyrna Rotary Club and Lions Club. I have partnered with the Smyrna Court Clerk's Office 'Clerks for Coats' Coat Drive since 2017. I have also sponsored a lot of Little League teams for close to twenty years.

Photo courtesy of Dan Epright

How big of an impact has social media had on your small business?

Most of our business is word-of-mouth, but we love positive reviews.

BARBARA POTTER PHOTOGRAPHY
AS TOLD BY BARBARA POTTER

Website: www.barbarapotterphotography.com
Facebook: Barbara Potter Photography
Instagram: @barbarapotterphotography

Tell me about your (small) business.

Creative, Fun, and Professional! Barbara Potter Photography is a full-service photography studio located in the Historic Depot District.

My early beginning in concert photography naturally led to creating creative images for artist albums, websites, and marketing. This has evolved into providing a complete line of portrait photography services such as corporate and creative headshots, branding, family, maternity, newborn, children, high school seniors, glamour, engagements, couples, and boudoir.

Our studio can create beautiful products from your images such as prints, canvas, metal prints, wall collections, and image boxes. All our sessions include a consultation to plan your session in detail. A professional photographer has the experience and knows the technique to consistently capture high quality images. We will also provide the artistry and vision for your session.

The renovated 1,700 square foot space has multiple shooting bays, props, hair and makeup, wardrobe change room, and a lounge area. There is also a covered outdoor area that is available for sessions. On location and travel destinations can be arranged as well.

Barbara Potter Photography is a two-time Photographer of the Year (2020 and 2018) with NIMA (Nashville Industry Music Awards). We were also awarded the Top 10 Photographers Award in 2020 with the Tennessee Professional Photographers Association. I am a very active member of the Professional Photographers of America and currently serve on the Tennessee Professional Photographers Association executive board as Vice President. Barbara Potter Photography has also received many awards at the state and international print competitions.

. . .

Why photography? What inspired you to start a photography business?

I spent over thirty years in the warehousing, transportation, and distribution business. It was a great career, but I was experiencing burnout. Deep down, I always felt something was missing. Then, in 2008, I met my husband Ben, a singer/songwriter/musician. Everything changed when he took me on my first trip to Nashville. I was in love! Not only with him, but also with the music scene. We made many trips after that one. Of course, I took a lot of photos and started building relationships with various artists. Finally, in 2013, Ben convinced me to leave my career and pursue photography as a business. So, I did just that and never looked back. We lived in both Nashville and in the Seattle area for five years, then finally in 2018 we decided to live in Tennessee full-time and made Smyrna our home!

When I look back, I realize that I have always been inspired by the beautiful imagery in magazines and movies. But I have also always been a shutterbug. My first camera was one of those mail order min-spy film cameras. I believe that is where my love of taking candid photographs came from. The joy of capturing the essence of someone in their totally natural state when they don't know the image is being taken of them. Now, I love creating images, because of the connection made with my clients and having it come through in the images captured.

. . .

What is your favorite part about having a small business in Smyrna?

I love living here and having my business here. It is super convenient and most of all, I love the support of the community.

What brought you to Smyrna?

My husband and I had friends that lived here, and they always liked the vibe of it.

When I settled down in Smyrna, it was very important to establish myself and set up shop in my community. I wanted to be active and serve my community. In all my years of traveling and moving around, I really wanted to be rooted in Smyrna. As far as the artists go, having my studio in Smyrna has its benefits.

It is a large and spacious studio that is easy to get to with free parking! Plus, my clients can enjoy Zama Park across the street, the Train Depot, and other local businesses before or after our session!

It seemed to have all the conveniences nearby, but it wasn't like living in a big city. Everything is nearby, the lake, walking trails, parks, restaurants, shopping, Farmers Market, the arts. There is not a lot of reason to have to ever leave!

What have been some of your most memorable artist album photos?

Each one is memorable since it is usually such a large and milestone project for each artist. There is a lot of planning and work that goes into it. But my most memorable one was Lillie Mae Rische's "Forever and Then Some" produced by Jack White. Ten of my images were used for the insert for the vinyl and CD. The cover had already been shot by another photographer, but I was honored to have this opportunity and will forever be grateful.

You offer a wide array of photography services. Do you have a favorite that you like to shoot?

I really love them all! It's all about connecting with the clients and making them feel comfortable but most of all to have fun and have a truly memorable experience.

What does a typical day look like for you?

I wear many hats- all of them! But depending on the day of the week, I spend time with client consultations, booking sessions, planning photoshoots, shooting, ordering prints and products, networking meetings, and volunteer work.

What is the biggest lesson you've learned in owning and operating a small business?

What you put in is what you get out. However, you need to set boundaries, otherwise you will be working 24/7. It is important to keep and make time for family, friends, personal time, and God. I am constantly working on this one. When you are passionate about your business, it can be very difficult to separate it from personal time! Many times, I will purposely leave my camera at home, otherwise I find myself not being present in the moment with those I am spending time with. When I was on my ten-year wedding anniversary trip to Hawaii several years ago, I only brought one camera and two lenses and locked them in the hotel safe. They only came out three short times!

Are there any favorite mantras you live your life by?

Vision without action is just a dream.

. . .

How have you grown your small business from an idea to where it is now?

Dedication, hard work, perseverance, overcoming adversity, and a positive attitude.

What has been your biggest business milestone to date that you are most proud of?

Opening the studio in Smyrna.

What have been some of your biggest business challenges you have faced and how have you overcome them?

Signing a lease for a new studio one month before the pandemic hit and having zero business for months was very challenging, but so far so good!

What advice would you give to someone wanting to pursue a career similar to yours?

Start slow and build up your technical skills and your portfolio. Make sure you are sustainable with your business flow.

What has been the best piece of business advice you have ever received?

Treat others as you would want to be treated.

What are some of the biggest lessons you've learned in owning a small business?

Not everyone is your client, and that is ok!

What 1-3 books have impacted your life the most and why?

The Power: Secret by Rhonda Byrne. This book shows the power of the law of attraction. Positivity breeds positivity!

Hero by Rhonda Byrne. This book will tune you into what your true calling is and why you should start living it. I never imagined I would be a photographer but looking back there were so many things that were guiding me and pointing me to it.

How has failure or apparent failure set you up for future success?

Every failure is truly an opportunity to learn and grow. There are too many to count. Losing everything in a previous marriage and having to start all over from scratch.

Who has been the most influential person or mentor to you during your entrepreneurial journey and why?

My husband, Ben. He is also a small business owner and an entrepreneur and understands the crazy schedules and demands. But he works hard and does an amazing job of balancing personal and work life.

Where do you see yourself and your small business 5-10 years from now?

Hopefully as a very well-established business in Smyrna that everyone will know of. Possibly with multiple locations.

What does success mean to you?

When a client refers someone to Barbara Potter Photography, that is the biggest compliment. My business has primarily been built on word-of-mouth.

What do you enjoy doing in your spare time?

Spending time with Ben and our two pomskie dogs, Rosie and Lillie, working on home projects and working in the garden. I am a member of SiMA, the Smyrna Rotary Club, and am a sponsor of the

Rotary Fish Fry, and a volunteer for Meals on Wheels. I also contribute my services to various organizations such as the Boy Scouts of America.

How big of an impact has social media had on your small business?

Social media has had the biggest impact for growth of my business as new business, which has primarily been built on word-of-mouth and social media posts.

What does supporting local mean to you?

Purchasing products and services from locally owned business owners as much as possible. Also, promoting them as much as possible to friends and family, even if they do not live here! It is important to support local business for small businesses to survive and to boost Smyrna's local economy.

We've loved being a part of your journey. What's coming next that we can be a part of to support you?

Stay tuned for the grand opening date!

Author's note: Barbara Potter is an absolutely amazing photographer and person. I cannot recommend her enough! I am incredibly honored that Barbara photographed my author images for this book, including my author headshot (p. 345) and my photograph on the back cover. She is a joy to work with!- BSS

DESIGNS BY SYLVANYE
AS TOLD BY SYLVANYE "SAM" ROH

Website: www.designsbysylvanye.com
Facebook: Designs By Sylvanye
Instagram: @designsbysylvanye

Tell me about your (small) business.

I am a kiln-formed glass, silversmith and metal clay artist, and instructor. I have been creating for about twenty years. I create wearable art jewelry, wall art, glass tiles, desktop accessories, dishware and more with fused glass. I also teach a wide range of workshops from beginning level classes to master's level in kiln-formed glass and more. I teach from four years old and up! I have taught classes on paint pouring and jewelry making, and classes on how to use microwave kilns. I teach on location in my studio and also can travel to do workshops and classes for larger groups, for corporations or businesses looking for creative team-building classes. I love sharing the creation process with others and seeing something new through the students' eyes in a design I may have done many times before.

I am the number one distributor in the U.S. for selling both the MicroKiln and the Grande Microwave Kiln. I am also a certified Precious Metal Clay artist. I have been somewhat of a pioneer in the testing and teaching of how to fire-to-sinter with almost all brands of silver metal clay as well as Art Clay Copper using the MicroKiln (microwave kiln). I developed a blog dedicated to the use of microwave kilns, called "Microwave Kiln Help Desk". Last year, I started working with 3D laser engraving and cutting. In case you are wondering, the MicroKiln is a kiln that can be used in a conventional microwave oven at nine hundred watts preferable to create glass and pure silver metal clay jewelry designs.

Why art? What inspired you to open a design studio?

Art came to me later in life. I retired from a position as a corporate executive with a top Fortune 500 company where I had started and ran a department for five years. It was during my last four months of employment that I discovered a passion for glass while attending a glass conference in Nashville. There were glass artists, vendors and instructors from all over the US selling their equipment and teaching how to design with glass. Of the four main disciplines: glass blowing, stained glass, lampwork glass and kiln-formed glass it was the kiln-formed glass that inspired me the most. It's funny- glass is all around us, but most people don't think about it very often- how it's created now, or the history of it. I never did.

When I learned about how over thirty-five hundred years ago, ancient Egyptians were creating molten glass in many colors in furnaces more than twenty-five hundred degrees and I could do something similar in a more updated way, I was fascinated. It was old and new at the same time. I didn't have any formal training, but I immersed myself in learning with books and videos and within three months, I opened my Smyrna studio. I started making whatever I could- from clocks to dish ware, and I started selling at artisan craft shows. It wasn't until then that I found out I had a knack for teaching. People would ask me about my designs, and I found myself offering to show them how to make them. So, a studio was a natural next step.

You make beautiful handmade lattice glass dish designs, which would make a lovely gift for the hostess, new homeowner, or 'just because'. What is the process for making these dish designs?

They really do make great gifts. You can use them to hold fresh fruit, or as a piece of art, or you could put your mail in them, if you want. They are both pretty and useful! The lattice designs are made with fused glass. Fused glass is made with pieces of already formed colored glass that are re-melted and fused together. I cut individual strips of glass out of large sheets and glue them together. The color choices of cut glass are endless, and that becomes even more true with fusing. When fusing, you can place different colored pieces of glass on top of each other and they melt and fuse together without the colors blending. Students can make the lattice glass designs in class. The class takes just a couple of hours, and then after that kiln time is eighteen hours.

. . .

What is your favorite part about having a small business in Smyrna?

There is a vibrant and supportive arts scene in Smyrna. We aren't Nashville, and we may not offer the breadth of arts and cultural activities that bigger cities offer, but there are lots of creators here, and many of us are working together and supporting each other in our creative journeys.

What brought you to Smyrna?

I was born in Nashville but grew up in the D.C. area. I moved back to Nashville as an adult and then my husband, Doug, and I moved to Smyrna. We were looking for a house and Doug found the perfect place for us here. There was enough room for my studio to be on the same property as our house, and that was important. I love being able to spend time with my husband and then take just a few steps away from the house and be in my studio.

What's the first thing you do every morning to start your day on the right foot?

I wish I could say I sit on the back porch and spend twenty minutes with a cup of hot tea or some fresh squeezed juice and contemplate art and my life, but the truth is that it depends on the day. I have two dogs, a Bichon Frise named Khloe and a German Shepherd named Miss Daisy, so my mornings always involve them. Having my own business allows me to structure my mornings. Of course, when I am teaching, I like to get the studio set and ready for classes. When I am not teaching, I might spend some time chatting with artist friends who inspire me, or going over my calendar for the week. It really just depends. It's fluid and I love that. Probably one constant in my days is that I am always learning.

. . .

What are you most excited about for your small business?

I am just excited to still be creating, and to still be able to get excited about new things. I am so excited about the new direction I am taking with 3D laser cutting and engraving. I can now create with so many more materials than just glass. I can now create with wood, leather, and acrylic, with paper and rubber and coated metal, and even marble. The possibilities are endless and it's very exciting. I'm never bored, and I'm so thankful that God gave me endless curiosity. It has served me well.

Where are your designs displayed, and where can people purchase your designs?

I have had work displayed in Zama, Japan, in the Renwick Gallery of the Smithsonian Gift Shop in Washington, DC, and in the gift shop at The Frist Museum in Nashville. I have a small gallery space at my studio as well, and you can purchase from my website.

What creation that you have designed to this point are you the most proud of?

One of my favorite pieces was a custom glass bowl that was a gift to the city of Zama, Japan, Smyrna's sister city. I love that our Town has a sister city and that they include sharing local art with each other as part of their relationship. I was honored to be asked to contribute, and it's hard to believe that my work is displayed in a city hall in Japan.

What is the biggest lesson you've learned in owning and operating a small business?

What I have learned is that most people are creative in some way. Everyone is not an artist and not everyone wants or needs to have a job in the creative industries, but most everyone has a little creativity inside. Most people enjoy the creative process so much more than they think they will. We all loved to create as children. Lots of people just forget how. I love helping people reconnect with that lost part of their lives.

Are there any favorite mantras you live your life by?

"I love what I do, and I do what I love."

How have you grown your small business from an idea to where it is now?

It's really just about continuing to learn and try new things and continuing to evolve as an artist or a business owner. If you have ever spent much time with me or dropped by my studio you have surely found me watching a YouTube video on a new process, or taking an online class, or even learning from a tutor. I really do love to learn and I think that love of learning, a drive to work and a good work ethic have carried my idea from just an idea to an actual business.

I collaborate with other artists and join groups on social media, read blogs and sign up for email lists. Education is key, and it doesn't have to be formal in-classroom learning. There is so much to learn just from others around us.

What has been your biggest business milestone to date that you are most proud of?

Being able to retire from the corporate world and open my design studio. It happened so fast that I don't think I appreciated it as much in the beginning as I would come to later. It may not have always been my dream, but it's definitely a dream come true.

. . .

What advice would you give to someone wanting to pursue a career similar to yours?

Just do it. If the passion is there and the drive and determination is there, why not? Of course, the hard work must be there. And surround yourselves with creative people. That is important.

What has been the best piece of business advice you have ever received?

Listen to people, and be genuine when communicating. It sounds too simple, but it's true. I never would have started teaching without listening to people tell me that I was good at explaining my designs. I listened to the ideas of friends and associates about artists I should teach and later those artists ended up recommending me to teach at some of the top Southern arts and crafts schools like the Arrowmont School of Arts & Craft in Gatlinburg, TN, the John C. Campbell Folk School in Brasstown, NC, and the Appalachian Center for Crafts in Smithville, TN. I think that's what makes me a good teacher. It's not just about what I have to say to you, I have to be able to listen to my students, to listen to their feedback and questions and what they need. It has to be *real* listening- not just polite conversation. I have to be invested in what other people are saying. How can I expect people to listen to me if I'm not willing to listen to them?

What are some of the biggest lessons you've learned in owning a small business?

There is no coasting. There is always something new to learn. It's important to keep trying to improve yourself and your business, to stay inspired and not get into a rut with either business practices or the way you create, or even the things you create.

What have been some of your biggest business challenges you have faced and how have you overcome them?

Marketing is challenging. I have several different things to market including my kilns, glass designs, workshops, jewelry, teaching, and consulting, and now also the engraving and cutting. It's all different markets and different target audiences.

What 1-3 books have impacted your life the most and why?

The Power by Rhonda Byrne and *The Artist's Way* by Julia Cameron. I don't necessarily buy into every aspect of what Byrne is saying in *The Power*, but my takeaway from that is I do have to really look into myself to find what I need to reach my goals and realize my dreams. No one is going to tell you the answers. I read *The Artist's Way* with a group class. The insights that came from hearing other artists talk about their struggles, and the way we opened up to each other and worked through that book was very inspiring.

Where do you see yourself and your small business 5-10 years from now?

I hope I am still here in Smyrna, still loving what I do and doing what I love!

What does success mean to you?

Doing what I love and loving what I do! It doesn't get better than that. Also, being able to have a real quality of life is important. I had success in the corporate world, but that doesn't come without a price. Being able to set your own hours, to work when you are inspired, to make your own way and own your journey. That feels like success.

What do you enjoy doing in your spare time?

I like spending time with my husband, friends, and family. I love to support other artists and creators and attend artist shows and fundraisers. I am involved in the community with several arts organizations including the Rutherford Arts Alliance, of course, and I am an appointed board member of the Smyrna Arts & Culture Advisory Committee. This year will be my second year helping organize the Depot District Art Crawl that is held every June. I also serve on the Friends of the Smyrna Public Library board and am in charge of curating displays at the Smyrna Public Library from local artists. I have met so many artists through that work and I love being able to help them share their art. I am also working with Rutherford Arts Alliance and the Art Department at MTSU right now regarding a 3D laser workshop to create wooden "living hinge" clutch purse.

How big of an impact has social media had on your small business?

It makes a huge difference! Recommendations and positive reviews are so important to small businesses.

What does supporting local mean to you?

Get out and see who is in your city or town. Who is creating? There are so many wonderful undiscovered artists right in your town. It's easy to go online and buy gifts, but plan to take a little extra time to see what's around you that you can purchase at the holidays, or for special occasions. It literally means everything to local businesses and local artists.

I can tell you from experience that it's terrifying to take the jump into owning a small business. Being supported by your community makes it a little less terrifying, and it makes you feel like you made a good decision, not only about your business, but about the city you chose for it.

. . .

We've loved being a part of your journey. What's coming next that we can be a part of to support you?

I will have lots of new offerings with the 3D laser, engraving and cutting. Stay tuned for more workshops and think of me for gifts and special occasions. When I was teaching classes, gift certificates for art classes were perfect for date nights, kids' birthday parties, or girls' nights out or church group activities. There is something special that comes from creating with friends. Your hands are busy and your mind kind of relaxes. You remember what it's like to create for the sheer joy of creating. There have been lots of laughs and warm memories made in my studio. Thinking about that makes me happy!

Of course, I sell all kinds of glass gifts- bowls, sculptures, business card holders, clocks, vases, and paper weights! I sell microwave kilns so you can create silver or copper or clay jewelry in your own home. I sell jewelry. Of course, there are many glass creations such as rings, pendants, bracelets, and earrings. I also sell stamped brass and copper jewelry. With my new line of 3D laser engraving and cutting I can make so many things! Front door signs, holiday signs, wooden handbags, Christmas ornaments, keychains, and plaques. If you imagine it, I can probably make it!

CARPE CAFE & CARPE ARTISTA
AS TOLD BY RON ALLEY

Photography courtesy of Karen Smith

Website: www.carpe-cafe.com | www.carpeartista.com
Facebook: Carpe Cafe | Carpe Artista
Instagram: Carpe Cafe | Carpe Artista

Tell me about your (small) business.

The most visible part of our business is Carpe Cafe. Our artist cafe was the first part of our nonprofit that opened in February 2012. We took up residence here because we had a bigger vision for the Depot District. It expanded from there. Carpe Cafe is our front porch to the community to bring people in to build relationships, especially with creatives, to talk about our vision for the town, and now the county. We really want to see the arts influence our quality of life and affect the economics because the arts have a huge economic impact on the community as a whole.

As far as our menu is concerned, we have soups, salads, sandwiches, and local roasted coffee. Our roaster, Raphael's Roasters, is in Tullahoma. They offer small batch roasting. We have worked together to create a custom roast, particularly our Carpe Grog, which is a favorite. He was able to help create that to our specifications.

We started off with a bakery type feel and have gone through some changes over the years. Our cinnamon roll is a signature staple. We are in the process of ramping our bakery back up. We just purchased a new refrigerated display and came to a baking arrangement with the Smyrna High culinary arts instructors to offer some of the baked goods along with some grab-and-go items to help facilitate people coming in during their lunch break so they can grab our salads or wraps, or pre-prepped cold sandwiches like our spicy pimento cheese, if they are in a hurry. We are also increasing our drink offering.

Carpe Cafe celebrated our eighth anniversary in 2021.

What inspired you to open a cafe in the heart of Smyrna's Historic Train Depot District on the Front Street roundabout?

When we started in 2011, there really wasn't much going on in the Train Depot. I came down and took pictures one day and several of the buildings weren't active or maybe they were open one day a week, the sidewalks and parking area next to the Depot may have had one or two cars. As I walked around and took pictures, there was a lot of passenger traffic with the roundabout, but nothing to cause people to want to come to the Depot District, or to live in this historic area, or even just hang out. There wasn't any space because the Depot hadn't been developed as a place to hangout- no sidewalks, tables, benches, or anything.

We did a presentation for the Town administration that had photos of the buildings and the area, and it was a, 'let's dream', 'what if' presentation. What if this building was used for this, and what if this building was used for this, what if the area was used for this? Literally that presentation was what if this building we are currently in, what if this building were used for a restaurant, what if the Assembly Hall were used as a venue, what if the Train Depot (which was closed at the time, and had been closed to the public for thirty years), what if it were used as an art gallery and for events? What if the Carpe Artista building we now have was used as an art center? A place for artistic activity. What if the streets and parking lots were used for festivals and cultural activity, what if there was public art in the area?

I looked at that presentation at our fifth anniversary and was like, "Wow, it's already happening." It had already been renovated. The Assembly Hall had already been renovated and open to the public for activity. We started festivals and had seen them grow. We had taken up  residence at the Cafe and we had acquired the Carpe Artista building. It was amazing to see how things had transformed in a five-year period and continue to do so.

Carpe Cafe is where we started. We started meeting with people asking, 'What if?' and sharing our vision for this area, and how it would be a great place for community and creatives, for Smyrna and its residents, and for things culturally that we didn't have at the time. We are still working on that, and envisioning things even grander than what it is now, but we are starting to see some of those things happen. There is still a ton of potential.

We are so grateful to the leadership of the Town. The Town Council has been very great to work with. At the time, we didn't have a track record, but they gave us a chance to create and have been supportive.

History, culture, and the arts go together. Our ultimate goal is to train young artists at a high level and instill mission-driven passion for doing something that's bigger than them and giving back to culture and impacting it positively. Ultimately, what we hope to do through our training programs is help aspiring artists develop their skill levels in different art genres so they can go into those industries and be successful at a local or national level. Also, we strive to instill leadership development, so they are learning character development, entrepreneurship, marketing, management, event planning, civic engagement, all those things they don't usually get in a traditional program, so that they can go directly into the industry so that one day they may lead and influence the culture in a positive way.

With that in mind, you have to create an environment locally that gives them the opportunity to lead and be engaged, creating that environment here that helps them in that growth is key. If we infuse it with education and cultural events it does two things: it helps our community and helps our students get that experience they need. It's a great pair. Every time you spend a dime at Carpe Cafe, you are directly supporting the arts in Smyrna and beyond. When you enjoy a meal at Carpe Cafe, you are helping to fund Carpe Artista's programs and tuition assistance for deserving students. We hope someday the Cafe will fund scholarships.

. . .

What is your favorite part about having a small business in Smyrna?

Smyrna is such a great community. I like that there has been a decision early to remain constituted as a town, as opposed to a city, even though we are very much the size of a city as we continue to grow. It's the people and being able to work with locals who care about where they live and continue to have vision to make it a great place to live and raise kids. We have something to offer.

What brought you to Smyrna?

I was an independent Christian artist. I knew the former pastor at First Baptist. He reached out to me, so I helped lead choir and worship. That snowballed and I moved into that position. The church exploded and grew from five hundred to about thirty-five hundred at the time (2011). I was focused on building the arts there, and knew it was time to move to a new segment.

God led me to start a new organization moving outside the church walls to try to raise up new artists that have values and want to make an impact on the culture. We started making those connections and my family fell in love with it, that was in 1995. We have no plans of ever leaving.

What does Carpe Artista do? What types of lessons do you provide?

There are three main divisions of Carpe Artista. The first is Carpe Academy, which is all our education. The second is Carpe Artista Events, and the third is Carpe Cafe. Carpe Academy provides training, classes, and private instruction in just about every instrument you can think of. Piano, voice, violin, viola, acoustic and electric guitar, bass, drums, banjo, accordion, mandolin, ukulele, as well as songwriting. We were actually going to take our theater group to England during the pandemic. Our theater group will be traveling to Houston to perform *The Little Mermaid* in their live festival. We want these groups to grow so that we can represent the arts in other places and say, "We are from Smyrna, we are proud of the arts, and we want to show you what's going on in Smyrna."

We have theater, visual art, painting, sculpting, mixed media photography, we hope to have a pottery training center in the near future.

We also have Rock Band Camps which is a full set of camps during the summer with musical theater and visual art camps, for all ages. With the Academy, we start at age five and go to one hundred. Most of our camps focus on school age, but we do offer Rock Band Camp for adults who once enjoyed playing an instrument and had dreams of being a rockstar and performing under the lights, but then the reality of having a family and other obligations forced them have to put those instruments down. This gives them the opportunity to check something off their bucket list. We pull them together one night a week for six weeks and pair them with band managers who have played on the biggest stages of the world. Leanne Womack's bass player, drummers for Trick Pony and Blake Shelton, Kenny Chesney's bass player. These are some of our instructors and band managers. They are instructors in Rock Band Camp and Juke Box Hero for kids and adults. Our students get great instruction and connection with people who work professionally in the music industry. It's an amazing opportunity that we have to offer.

Carpe is one of Smyrna's favorite destinations for live entertainment due to a full schedule of local musicians, performers, authors, artists, and other creatives, as recognized by numerous community awards and accolades. Do you have any memorable

performers or events that really stand out over the last eight years?

We are very grateful to be here and plan to stay. There are several things that stand out. The Battle of the Bands that we've had with Juke Box Hero for adults is one. It's just amazing what the students can pull together in such a short time. It's a lot of fun.

We've watched some of our students over time as they've grown and started their own festivals. Our cafe manager, Ernie Fabian, has a band called Idle Threat that just signed with Tooth and Nail Records. Four years ago, Ernie started a rock alternative festival called Threat Fest that was based in the Depot District, and it has grown in attendance each year. Now it is a two-day event with ten bands and two hundred and fifty fans in attendance from all over the country. It's very niche, but very significant. It started at the Depot and migrated to the Carpe Artista parking lot. We hope to expand and have a venue for festivals in the back. These events are very niche but bring tourism and create notoriety for Smyrna.

What are you most excited about for your small business?

I'm a visionary. We are still excited about the possibilities for our Carpe Artista building and having an arts center. Also, I am excited about the residential development that will create the population density to drive more traffic to the local businesses in the Depot. We still have so much potential for further development.

What does a typical day look like for you?

It changes depending on what's going on. Certain days are filled with meetings and connecting with people and asking- how do we move things forward, how do we get people engaged, how do we connect with businesses to do arts advocacy, why do the arts matter, how do they affect our quality of life, how can they bring economic growth? I start at 8:00 a.m. and sometimes don't finish until 9:00 p.m. Weekends in the summer months are just as busy- the Farmers Market, recitals, tech meetings for upcoming productions. Thankfully, our team is growing and I can release some things to some key people which I am grateful for.

During the pandemic, my wife and I started a new entrepreneurial endeavor with real estate development. This will be a key component of a for-profit piece coming alongside the nonprofit piece for future developments in other communities. We need to be able to bring that actual real estate development to communities that have realized that in their overlooked historic areas. We believe we can support the nonprofit with the for-profit and support the for-profit with the programming that a nonprofit brings as far as the event and cultural sides to those developing businesses. As if I don't have enough to do! One of our goals is to create affordable housing, cooperatives, and co-working spaces for artists not just in Smyrna, but other communities.

How does Carpe partner with other locally owned small businesses? Why is this so important to you?

We sell artwork from local artists at the Cafe. We sponsor events in our Carpe Artista building. For example, we host Business Before Hours and partner with other small businesses to help get them involved in those events in order to make connections throughout the county.

Also, we created the Farmers Market, which creates opportunities for local farmers by giving them the opportunity to bring their wares and produce to sell to the community. We provide opportunities for local food vendors, entrepreneurs, and arts and craft vendors partnering with SiMA and supporting each other to bring attention to our community.

Our cup sleeves come from Custom Cup Sleeves. We serve coffee from Raphael's Roastery. We partner with Front Street Signs for special event banners and Janarty's uses our coffee beans for their ice cream. We have to support other local businesses.

What makes the dining experience at Carpe Cafe so unique and special?

It's a historic building. When you walk in you can smell the coffees. We try our best to instill in our staff that they aren't responsible for customer service, they are responsible for hospitality. So, they are inviting customers into our dining room and treating them as their guests, not patrons. There is a big difference. We let people know what our bigger purpose for being here is. Of course, the artwork we sell, knowing it's local and supporting local artists.

What is the biggest lesson you've learned in owning and operating a small business?

I can't do it all. I've coined a new phrase, "If I'm overwhelmed, I've under delegated." I'm trying to learn to release and be a better manager and delegate to strong leaders.

Also, do not be afraid to ask. I've always been timid to ask, but people are willing to give and participate when they feel valued. It's all about people and relationships. That's what matters.

. . .

What has been your biggest business milestone to date that you are most proud of?

I'm most proud of when I see those kids confidently smiling at the end of a recital. To see them find identity in themselves and in their art. One of our high school seniors managed the entire Farmers Market during the pandemic and made it grow. She started our programs in middle school and went through our pilot program at Carpe Studio. We won the Tennessee Department of Agriculture award as well as a Firefly for the Farmers Market for Smyrna's Favorite Event. It is awesome to watch students grow.

What have been some of your biggest business challenges you have faced and how have you overcome them?

The biggest challenge is financial. The arts are not a heavy heart-string for people to donate to. I spent most of the first year doing volunteer work primarily myself. But we are starting to see some things turn around. I've had to navigate never running a nonprofit before. I'm a slow study, but we are still here. We've been blessed.

GLAM HOUSE | GLAM HOUSE SKIN
AS TOLD BY TIFFANY GRANSTAFF

Website: www.glamhousesmyrna.com | www.glamhouseskin.com
Facebook: Glam House | Glam House Skin
Instagram: @glamhouse513 | @glam_house_skin

Tell me about your (small) businesses.

Glam House is a full-service salon that specializes in balayage and custom hand-tied extensions. The atmosphere is rustic and glam. You feel like you are at home or hanging with your best friends when you come in. We are staffed with the most amazing stylists in the industry that continue their education yearly.

Glam Skin & Extension Bar is a quaint 1920's historic house turned Medi Spa located right in the heart of downtown Smyrna. We offer botox, filler, microblading, microneedling, HydraFacials, microdermabrasion, lash lift and tints, facials, PRP treatments, lip injections, chemical peels and more. We have a nurse injector, a nurse practitioner, medical estheticians, lash artist and more. The moment you walk through our pink doors, you are our number one priority. We will talk you through any procedure you are getting and make your time spent here an escape.

What is PRP, aka, a Vampire Facial?

This procedure involves extracting blood from the patient's arm and using a centrifuge to separate the platelets and plasma from the red blood cells. From there, microneedling infuses skin with platelet-rich plasma (PRP) that stimulates collagen and elastin fibers to promote cell turnover for your most brilliant complexion. This 'tricks' the cells into 'thinking' the skin surface is injured and generates new tissue. The skin responds to this action by plumping up and thickening, getting to work on those wrinkles, lines or scars, large pores, stretch marks, and loose skin.

This treatment is a little fountain of youth miracle. Collagen starts to decline at the age of twenty-five. This is what keeps the skin looking youthful. You're one quick blood draw away from turning back the age clock a few years.

. . .

What is derma planning and what are the benefits?

It is a physical exfoliation method that requires the use of a sterile surgical scalpel to gently remove the top layer of the skin. This treatment results in ultra-smooth, fresh, and brighter skin. By removing that dead layer and peach fuzz from the face, the skin is evened out, and it helps with cell metabolism, which helps new skin come to the surface.

What have been some of your biggest business challenges you have faced and how have you overcome them?

Most definitely COVID-19. It was such a scary time for all small businesses. We got past it by selling products and getting creative with online sales. Our clients were amazing! Many sent money just to help keep the doors open.

What is the biggest lesson you've learned in owning and operating a small business?

I figured out that I couldn't do it all by myself after about five years. My husband has taken over the business side and I have hired a wonderful person to help with booking.

What has been your biggest business milestone to date that you are most proud of?

Taking the leap and opening. It was so scary at first. When we opened Glam House, I was eight months pregnant with my third baby. There was no time to waste and there was no time to not succeed.

Where do you see yourself and your small business 5-10 years from now?

I see us opening up more locations in surrounding areas.

What does supporting local mean to you?

Everything! This is how we feed our babies. We small businesses have our heart and souls in this town.

How big of an impact has social media had on your small business?

For both Glam House and Glam Skin, social media is everything! Our clients live to see those before and afters. Today's world is so visual, so we try to show real-life content. We now have a website where clients can purchase products. I tell them to shop local, not at major online retailers.

We've loved being a part of your journey. What's coming next that we can be a part of to support you?

We will be hosting a Christmas sip and save this year. We would love for you to attend.

GIL'S ACE HARDWARE
AS TOLD BY GINNY OLERUD WILLIAMS

Website: www.acehardware.com
Facebook: Gil's Ace Hardware

Tell me about your business.
We carry everything from tools to lawn and gardening supplies,

cleaning supplies, home repair and cooking, paint, everything you need for your DIY projects, and pool and spa supplies.

We carry a huge selection of nuts and bolts. We have power tools and hand tools in electrical and plumbing. We also carry seasonal items such as Halloween and Christmas lights and decor. In the cooler months, we have a great selection of what you will need for snowy weather such as faucet covers, ice melt, heaters, sleds, and shovels. We also sell grills (and deliver and install). We sell a lot of bird seed and carry local honey from Lynchburg. In the summer, The Peach Truck sells peaches out of our parking lot. We've got top-quality products for all your needs to take care of business.

We also have a section featuring local authors. For example, *Smyrna, The Church, The Town,* by Walter King Hoover. All proceeds benefit Friends of the Smyrna Public Library. We sell books written by Michael Hendrickson, Darren Long's *Omni Hut: Celebrating Tennessee's Tiki Treasure*. We also sell some of Greg Tucker's books.

We have ten employees. Everybody has their area of expertise and is very helpful. We all take our life experiences, and it works out well. I'm blessed with good people.

The right tools make all the difference. We are 'Ace the helpful place,' nationally known and *locally* owned. We offer a big box store selection with small-town service from our helpful and knowledgeable team.

We celebrated our forty-fifth anniversary last year.

. . .

History of Gilsville

We started out in 1953 as a grocery store. My parents were from Fargo, North Dakota. My grandfather always had a little corner market. I'm a third-generation retailer, you could say.

My dad was stationed here at the Stewart Air Force Base. Rather than re-up, my dad decided to go into business. We started out on the other corner, which at the time was Gambill's Market. As the story goes, Mr. Gambill won it in a poker game. The week I was born, my dad bought that little country grocery store, tore it down, and eventually built Gilsville.

My parents were pretty conservative. They built their dream house, and when Daddy went to borrow money to build Gilsville, the bank told him they wanted our house as collateral. He said no, he couldn't do that. Mr. Chaney of First Tennessee Bank took a chance on my dad.

In our first store, we had a non-food section where we cut keys and sold all kinds of things, including hardware items, that most grocery stores didn't have. We were sort of like a general store. I may have been the one that planted the seed. I said to my dad, "Daddy, this aisle is a mess. By the time I find what customers want, they have already left." I told him we just needed a whole separate store. Next thing you know, we have a store on the other corner on Jefferson Pike.

My dad always wanted to meet a need when something was needed in the community. He felt like the grocery store had everything in it, but then realized that the hardware store needed to be separate in order to have more space and merchandise.

In 1972, my dad started thinking about how crowded it was in the grocery store, so he built the Gilsville shopping center. That's when we bought the Radio Shack and decided to have a hardware store. We had all these empty spaces on the other side. It's always been different things. There's always been a barber shop.

My husband and I met in college at MTSU, where we both graduated. I was supposed to be a teacher but decided I really didn't want to teach kids. I minored in business administration thinking I probably would go back into the family business. My first husband, Bob Lee, who is now deceased, and my dad started the hardware store in 1975.

I was in charge of training in the grocery store, so, in a way I was student teaching. I feel like as manager of Gil's Ace Hardware, I'm teaching, too. People are smart with YouTube, or they bring in a picture of what they need. Some people even create things that don't exist. I jokingly tell customers they will have to manufacture and patent their idea and make a million.

My dad was the promoter and always wanted to build things to make them bigger. Mom was the bookkeeper, "wait- we can't do that, we can't afford that." They were the perfect team. He promoted and she kept the books.

At one time, we had a second grocery store, which is now Smyrna Printing & Design. Of course, they didn't have enough parking, it still doesn't. Richard and Mike are customers here, too. We enjoy talking about the old days.

In the time that they've been in business they have been in the restaurant business, the appliance business, we used to own the Radio Shack, and the service station turned convenience market. Service stations weren't as popular, but convenience markets were up-and-coming. So, in 1976, he converted the service station into a convenience market. We sold that in June 2020.

We opened Gil's Ace Hardware in 1975. We got out of the grocery business in 1984. I've been here ever since.

What inspired you to stay in the hardware business?

Everyone that walks through that door has a problem. I love solving problems and helping people. When I was in the grocery business, we carried your groceries out to your car. Sometimes, people come in grouchy because something's not working right, you hope they leave with a smile. We hear people tell us they were at a box store and weren't able to find a product we carry. I make a mental note not to ever run out of that product.

How has Smyrna and the small business landscape changed since you first started in 1975?

I remember seeing my mom washing dishes at the restaurant, which was behind the convenience market. It started out as Skyway Restaurant, home of the big 'Ole Hamburger,' we called my grandpa 'Ole.' Then it became a meat and three called the Oxbow, then a barbecue place, then Yates, and now it's Chappy's.

What is the story behind the iconic Gilsville sign?

That was a refurbished sign that was originally a Minnie Pearl's chicken sign. It's been there since 1973. It definitely has the seventies motif. We've thought about redoing it, but our customers love it because it's so unique and retro. We've even had people offer to buy it. The lights used to race, but that's against the sign ordinances. It was very bright and flashy and looked like an emergency vehicle.

What is your favorite part about having a small business in Smyrna?

I have a lot of friends that shop with me and I am always making new friends. I love helping people. I love supporting the community, especially ball teams and my alma mater, Smyrna High.

How did your childhood in Smyrna shape you?

I grew up in Smyrna. I went to a little country school called Jefferson School. It was like its own little community. We had two grades in every room. I loved all of my teachers, recess and playing outside.

I got a good education here. I was in the first class at Thurman Francis. That's when it was seventh through ninth grade. Then, we went to Smyrna High where I was a cheerleader. I've lived here my whole life except for one year in Murfreesboro. Growing up with the air base, I had a lot of friends come and go. I enjoyed the swimming pool, tennis court, bowling, and the movie theater when we had the air base. A lot of people from my graduating class have remained in Smyrna.

What are some of the biggest lessons you've learned in owning and operating a small business?

One of my favorite childhood photos is my sister and I in a shopping cart. Mom was probably working the register. We grew up in the business. I remember chopping chickens when I was twelve. Luckily, I still have all my fingers. When I was sixteen, there weren't that many jobs. People used to say, "I worked for Mr. Gil." When I was younger, I used to say, "Oh, I have to work." People would tell me how lucky I was to have a job. It really made me rethink how lucky I was.

In 1980, my dad died at fifty-seven. I was twenty-six and a new mom. I admired the hard work my parents did. My dad only had a fifth grade education but was brilliant. I think he thought he had something to prove. My mom had two years of business college.

We have had businesses that failed. The appliance store didn't work out. I talked my mom into selling Radio Shack. We sold it and it moved behind Gold's Gym. It's still there to this day.

Are there any favorite mantras you live your life by?

"When life gives you lemons, make lemonade."

. . .

Gil's Ace has won several prestigious awards voted on by the community, including Fireflies for Business of the Year and Local Legacy, and several Best of Main Street Awards. What has been your biggest business milestone to date that you are most proud of?

Being in business for forty-six years. At our fortieth we had barbecue, birthday cake and door prizes. Each year we try to get bigger.

Another milestone was surviving COVID-19. That was one of our most successful years.

What have been some of your biggest business challenges you have faced and how have you overcome them?

I have always told people you have to ride the waves. You would love for your business to increase every year. 2020 was insane. I got stressed out and ended up going to the doctor. Our business accelerated so much, which was a challenge to keep up. Our orders doubled, then we had to figure out how to get the product in. Then, getting the product on the shelves stocked. We were blessed. My prayer was to thank God for blessing us with good business but help us to keep up. I felt like the duck that sits on the water gracefully but is frantically paddling underneath. People were furloughed or working from home. A lot of people wanted to convert that third bedroom into an office. Some bought grills from us, and a lot of customers did landscaping.

Also, in 2020, we had an ice catastrophe on the front of our building that caused our awnings and bricks to collapse. It caused a lot of damage. When the second sign went down, there were bricks in front of the front door. That's where I would have been standing to lock the door. We  thanked God that no one got hurt. We had to put a new roof on. Not only are we in the hardware business, but we are commercial property owners trying to keep these spaces filled. So when the HVAC goes out, we have to come up with the $25,000 to replace it. It's all about adapting and flowing.

Community Service Throughout the Years

I was the first woman elected to the Smyrna Town Council in 1989 and served until 1993. I really enjoyed doing that and having input regarding the community. I was a commissioner of Parks and Recreation. But, at the time I was getting married, and my daughter was going to high school. I had to get back in the hardware business. I got that political bug and wanted to do it.

I used to be involved with the Smyrna Street Festival in the eighties, now it's called Depot Days.

One of the things I'm most proud of that had the biggest impact for the community was that I was the first chairperson of the Smyrna & La Vergne Food Bank. Nissan was being built and hundreds of people were moving to Smyrna not knowing whether they would have a job, not having any friends or family here. They would come into the grocery store needing food. I directed them to Rutherford County Food Bank.

Patsy and Hiram Wright were connected to the air base. They were customers of the grocery and hardware stores. They said we need a food bank here, and wanted me to be the chairperson. I agreed because I saw a major need. I would go pick up the food with Carolyn Peebles. It got to the point where we had to fundraise, get the food, get volunteers, and process and vet people coming in.

It was so hard doing all of this. I convinced them we need to become a United Way agency. All I knew was that they funded nonprofits. They were resistant at first, saying it was too much paperwork. The first time I went to a Rotary meeting was to ask for money for the food bank. The server and I were the only women. I thought,

"We are going to get some money because these are the movers and shakers in Smyrna." I was so excited to talk to Rotary. It was very satisfying because you saw how many people got food. Now look at the food bank.

Also, I love supporting Eagle Scouts. Last year, the first female Eagle Scout came by for help. She built a moveable obstacle course for the K-9 dogs at the Rutherford County Sheriff's Office.

Anybody that goes for their Eagle Scout is working really hard. I'll sit down with the Eagle Scout and ask what they are doing. They have drawings, plans and a supply list.

I'll ask questions like, "Are you sure that's a long enough bolt?" One Scout I'm helping now is building a moveable plexiglass partition at Stones River Manor so families can visit each other. We have helped over twenty Eagle Scouts. We try to help several each year.

What do you enjoy doing in your spare time?

I have been in Rotary since 1987. We have been a proud Fish Fry sponsor for nineteen years.

I enjoy my church, St. Luke Catholic Church. A lot of church members shop here. I enjoy volunteering. I've done stream cleanup, Boat Day, Meals on Wheels, Habitat for Humanity, blood drives through the American Red Cross, as well as the 'Clerks for Coats' Coat Drive. I also love supporting Carpe Artista and all they do for the community.

. . .

How big of an impact has social media had on your small business?

Facebook is really effective. When our building collapsed, we had so many people ask if they could help clean up and ask if we were okay. It's so heartwarming that people cared and were offering help.

What makes the experience of shopping for appliances at Gil's Ace Hardware so unique and special?

A lot of customers tell me they like that our employees ask if they can help. You won't hear our team members say, "That's not my department, I can't help," or point to products across the store. We will personally escort and help you find what you need. We talk to each other on the radio all the time to make sure we find what our customers need. We have amazing customer service.

I think a lot of people discovered us in 2020 because they wanted to support their locally owned businesses. We had our best year last year.

We actually may have more plumbing repair parts than some of the big box stores. Sometimes, they want to sell new fixtures because it's more money. We may spend thirty minutes with a customer and only sell a ten-cent part. If we don't have it, we try to tell people where to go, or we can order it for them.

We're focused on convenience and savings with perks like our in-store pickup option when you order online, plus our Ace Rewards program, which rewards customers for shopping with us. You get a $5 gift card on your birthday and coupons throughout the year. It is local perk and customers love it.

A lot of people think we are a part of a chain or franchise. We are actually a cooperative. This is an Ace store, but Ace gives us enough freedom to do what we want. There are five thousand Ace stores.

. . .

What does supporting local mean to you?

Doing business with local people. Supporting local nonprofits like the Senior Activity Center, Carpe Artista, the Smyrna High School Bulldogs football, Springhouse Theater, and Rotary.

A lot of my customers are small business owners around town. We support each other. People will call us for referrals. I have a business card section. I'll ask, "Have you checked with Steve Johns?" Or, if we can't cut a key, we'll send them to A Lock and Key Center. They have to do good work for me before I refer them. Allen's Air Care does our air conditioning. Sometimes, the front window is like a big community bulletin board. If somebody sends me a flyer to help promote a community event, we usually will. I've seen people come up and take a picture of all the signs on the window.

It was really sad when we had to sell the grocery business in 1984. It was sort of like the end of an era. We had that store from 1953-1984. The big box stores started moving in and we couldn't keep up. In 1989, Food Lion came in and our former family grocery store officially went out of business.

Is there anything else you would like people to know about you or your small business?

Thank you for the support. We wouldn't be what we are today without you. We've been a part of Smyrna since 1953. We love living and working here. I can't imagine living anywhere else.

AZTECA BAKERY AND EATERY
AS TOLD BY FIDEL BELLO

Facebook: Azteca Bakery
Instagram: @azteca_bakery_

Tell me about your (small) business.
　　Azteca Bakery is a small bakery that has been open since 2018. We

combine rice and beans with almost everything: carnitas, chicken, tamales, chiles rellenos, and barbecue ribs.

In addition to serving authentic Mexican food and delicious treats, we also cater large parties.

What is your favorite part about having a small business in Smyrna?
Smyrna has a small home-town feel. Everyone knows each other.

What inspired you to open a bakery?
I have a degree in business and have always dreamed of being a business owner.

What menu item(s) would you recommend to someone new to Azteca?
Tamales, without a doubt. We have the best tamales in town. There are many treats but my three top are tres leches cake, flan, and chocoflan. My favorite go-to lunch is the rotisserie chicken.

What are you most excited about for your small business?
When customers return and give thanks.

What's the first thing you do every morning to start your day on the right foot?
Prayer and positive thinking are essential parts of my day.

. . .

What does a typical day look like for you?

I have three jobs now. I teach Spanish at a high school located approximately ninety minutes from Smyrna. I help coach soccer, so practices and games take up a great deal of my time, I keep odd hours at the bakery. My third job has no salary, as I am working on my PhD.

What is the biggest lesson you've learned in owning and operating a small business?

The biggest lesson I have learned is to treat customers with respect and appreciation because they have options of where to take their business. Customers are the life of any business. If they bring their business to my bakery, I want them to know that I appreciate them.

You learn how to be a strong person. Problems are part of life. I am learning the importance of faith.

Are there any favorite mantras you live your life by?

"Do not be anxious about anything, but in every situation, by prayer and petition, with thanksgiving, present your requests to God." Philippians 4:6

What has been your biggest business milestone to date that you are most proud of?

We are the first Hispanic business to participate in the Town Christmas parade. In fact, we won. In 2020, we received the Main Street Award for the best Mexican Flavor.

What have been some of your biggest business challenges you have faced and how have you overcome them?

COVID-19 has tremendously impacted my life and Azteca

Bakery. Also, in 2020, we had an ice catastrophe on the front of our building that caused a lot of damage, but thankfully, no one was hurt.

What advice would you give to someone wanting to pursue a career similar to yours?

To have perseverance, determination and to trust God's plan for your life.

What has been the best piece of business advice you have ever received?

Keep going, God has this. Believe in yourself.

What 1-3 books have impacted your life the most and why?

The Bible is a roadmap of how to live.

The Miracle Book by Morris Cerullo made me recognize that every day is full of miracles.

A Course of Miracles (Un curso de Milagros) by Kenneth Wapnick. There are three hundred sixty-five exercises. Everything is about the law of love.

How has failure or apparent failure set you up for future success?

Failure is simply a part of life. "Success is counted sweetest by those who never succeed," is a quote by Emily Dickinson, meaning without the struggle, success would not mean as much.

Where do you see yourself and your small business 5-10 years from now?

I hope to open additional businesses.

. . .

What does success mean to you?

Success is not necessarily the amount of money you make. People can be wealthy monetarily, but unhappy. Striving to be more Christ-like every day, showing kindness to others, and knowing I have done my very best is success to me.

What do you enjoy doing in your spare time?

I worked hard to become bilingual, so I could communicate with diverse customers. Since I am a teacher, I take a special interest in young people and their future. Food was sometimes given to families who were experiencing hardships, or, when a family member was diagnosed with COVID-19.

How big of an impact has social media had on your small business?

Reviews and food photos help us tremendously! Many new customers have come to the bakery because of social media.

What does supporting local mean to you?

A community in which people are there for one another by supporting locally owned businesses. Supporting local businesses keeps the local economy strong.

GINGER FARMS
AS TOLD BY AMBER JOHNSON MORTON

Website: www.thegingerfarms.com
Facebook: Ginger Farms
Instagram: @ginger_farms

Tell me about your (small) business.

Ginger Farms is a family owned and operated farm aiming to provide the highest quality produce and meats for our local communities. Our vision is to be a learning farm, where folks of all ages can come and learn, play and grow. We own about nineteen acres, and since we've been so fortunate and blessed with this land, we want to give back. We do that through a couple of different avenues. We grow about an acre's worth of garden, which changes every year. We always do wildflowers to promote pollination with all the other plants, including sweet potatoes and okra for this year. We grow that and we usually just give it away or barter with people. We have the garden, and we also have chickens that lay eggs. My family consumes so many eggs that we don't even sell those because we don't have enough left over.

What inspired you to start a learning farm?

Our land has been in our family for over one hundred years. It belonged to my grandparents. They actually used to be pig farmers. Our grandparents built a house on the land when I was in middle school. My mom was given five acres of the land next to it. I grew up on five acres next to the current property that we owned. When they passed about five years ago, the opportunity came for any of their sons or daughters to buy the land. They were all well-established but not interested. My mom didn't want to buy it, either. Then, it opened up to the grandkids.

Being one of the older grandkids, I really wanted this land to stay in the family. It's right next to my mom, and I thought it would be perfect to raise my three kids, but my husband wasn't interested. Lord willing, I remember praying, "God, please let my husband change his mind, I know he's never been a farmer, and this is way out of his wheelhouse, but please change his mind or release me from desire." I felt released from wanting the property. I told the family, "You can put it on the market, or do whatever you want with it." Then, one month later, my husband changed his mind. We sold our house and moved into this house.

It's a great home. My grandparents built it with plans to give back to their kids and grandkids. They were members of the Stones River Baptist Church. They would host their church often, and they would host neighbors on the street often just to say, "We love our community, so come dine with us!" Their table seated twenty people. My husband and I had the same desire to build community. We love to open our home and host people.

What is your favorite part about having a small business in Smyrna?

Ginger Farms really is a small community building place because we love to get to use our farm to bless and host others. We love to use our land to have other kids experience things that they probably might not experience. Our Airbnb tent is for others to experience camping. It's so much a part of what we did growing up that I love for others to have the opportunity to share the experience.

What types of produce and cuts of meat do you offer?

Our money maker on the farm front is our pigs. We raise pigs, so that we can get them processed for meat that we consume and sell to friends and family. We are USDA approved. It's a small number of pigs, the most we've had is five. We usually never get to sell them to the public that often because we run out.

Ginger Farms is known for its wildly popular farm camp that offers hands-on experiences and has become so loved that it was nominated for a Firefly for the Best Event in Smyrna in 2021. What types of activities do kids get to partake in at farm camp?

We host farm camps, which are camps for ages entering Kindergarten to exiting fifth grade. It's a three-and-a-half-day camp, just to get kids outside and enjoying nature. We do one day of plant activities, one day of nature appreciation activities, and one day of understanding animals. This is my fourth year doing farm camps. We've got farming, homesteading and we just added our first Airbnb tent. We have one bell tent that we host campers through Airbnb to have a glamping experience. It's a tent but it has a mattress and a stove for heating that you can use in the winter. We have a hot water heater, so you can have hot showers, and it has a sink. There's no plumbing because our nineteen acres is all limestone runoffs. We make sure that everything's eco-friendly because we are next to the lake.

Where do you see yourself and your small business 5-10 years from now?

I would love to see more Airbnb sites on the property. We

currently have the tents. I'd love to have a treehouse and an air stream trailer. I'd also love a common campfire area so that multiple families or friends could have their own individual experience and have a place to come together. I would love to see Farm Camp grow. For now, keeping it small is really fun. I'd love to be able to grow the farming with the animals and host more animals. We're building more fencing to bring in goats to clear that land and eventually cows, too. I'd love to be able to rescue other animals.

We both have full-time jobs and hobbies that we love that give back to the community. It's just praying through the balance. It's kind of unknown what could happen in the next five to ten years. I hear from so many adults that say they'd love to attend a day at Ginger Farms.

What do you enjoy doing in your spare time?

We love pouring into our community. My husband coached at Smyrna High over the past twelve years. He really felt led to look at those kids' foundations. He moved to Smyrna Middle in 2020 to coach. I worked as a Preschool Director at LifePoint Church for many years and was very involved. I was also a teacher for six years in the Rutherford County School system. I work for a Smyrna company called Syndicate that designs construction, because I love my hometown.

Not only do we love sharing what we've been blessed with others, but we love being outside and getting kids to work outside with us. This is how I was raised. My education was in science education. We were always outside, exploring, appreciating, and learning about nature. I naturally gravitate to doing things outside, so gardening was kind of our first dig into our hobby homestead. We were partnering with a ministry in Brazil through LifePoint, and had just started gardening. My husband latched onto this. Even in our old house, we had a small garden box. Once we moved, it just grew. As my kids get older, I want them be a part of it.

. . .

What is the biggest lesson you've learned in owning and operating a small business?

I never garden the same way twice. I always love trying new systems and seeing what works and what doesn't. People ask me all the time, "What should I do?" I'm constantly trying new things. We're moving our garden around a lot, trying different fertilizers, different methods of composting and landscaping tarp and cardboard. There are so many parallels to daily life. You go outside and you're just drawing those metaphors, like weeding out the garden and weeding out those things unnecessary in life so that the true plant can grow. There are so many things that I love about gardening. Tending to your flocks and keeping relationships with your animals so that they know, trust, and love you. I love reading books about gardening, farming, and talking to other farmers and gardeners in the area because there's such a deep connection with the land, plants and animals and getting outside and enjoying it.

TONY'S SHOE REPAIR
AS TOLD BY TONY REINA

Business Address: 304 S Lowry St #A3
Phone: 615-587-9101

Tell me about your (small) business.
I've been in business for nearly sixty years in New York and downtown Nashville in the Arcade. After five years of retirement, I decided to reopen a business closer to home in Smyrna. I do shoe repair for all types of men's shoes and boots, and women's soles and heels. I fix

luggage and repair handbags, leather goods, and replace zippers. I can also dye shoes and fix some rips.

What is your favorite part about having a small business in Smyrna?

I chose Smyrna because it is closer to my house and realizing that there is not this kind of service in this town.

What brought you to Smyrna?

I was a school kid about nine or ten in my hometown. When vacation came, many kids used to go have a good time. Boating, swimming at sea, fishing, and many other things. In my case, my father obligated me to go to a cobbler's shop to learn how to make shoes. It was not my desire to become a cobbler, but in my time, you had to do whatever your parents told you to do. Sometimes, that was where I would spend my vacation. When I was growing up, my father tried to suggest to me that he would like me to be a doctor. Another thing that never crossed my mind.

When I was learning to be a cobbler, my father kept telling me, "Learn something like this because you never know, one day you might need it." Well, that was reality. While I was growing up, my dream was always to go to the city and see the world. That dream came true when I was fifteen or sixteen. I joined the Columbian Navy. I went to Navy school in Barranquilla for six months. Then, shipped to the Navy base in Cartagena where I stayed for several years. After that, I sailed in the Columbian Merchant Marine for several more years, until one day I flipped a nickel to decide to come to the U.S. and become a U.S. citizen. And here I am.

. . .

What's the first thing you do every morning to start your day on the right foot?

Eat a good breakfast. Say my prayers and head to work.

What are you most excited about for your small business?

Entertainment and fun. Meeting new people, especially getting in contact with my church members.

What does a typical day look like for you?

Take in work to do. Ordering supplies and seeing new faces. After I leave at 4:00 p.m. or 5:00 p.m., I start doing the heavy work at home in my garage.

What is the biggest lesson you've learned in owning and operating a small business?

The satisfaction of being your own boss.

How have you grown your small business from an idea to where it is now?

I started making shoes when I came to the U.S. We made them by hand in the 1940s. When I started in Long Island, New York, it was after two months practicing shoe repair machinery. After two months in New York City at an Italian Company, LaSpada sent me to Nashville. That is when I started in the Nashville Arcade for Walsh Shoe Repair Company from New York in 1970. After that, I had the idea to open my own business. I borrowed some money from the bank, and started one by one purchasing my own machinery. And to make the story short, this is where I am now.

What has been your biggest business milestone to date that you are most proud of?

The opportunity to cruise almost every year in the company of my wife.

What have been some of your biggest business challenges you have faced and how have you overcome them?

Finding affordable supplies.

What has been the best piece of business advice you have ever received?

Attending school at Ball State University in Indiana. I earned my orthopedic certification to improve my ability to help customers with severe podiatry issues.

What are some of the biggest lessons you've learned in owning a small business?

Always pay your bills on time. Keep up with your taxes. Also, it's good to know a specialty skill that others cannot perform.

What 1-3 books have impacted your life the most and why?

The Bible!

Where do you see yourself and your small business 5-10 years from now?

Selling is my best option because there are not too many people interested in this trade.

. . .

What do you enjoy doing in your spare time?

Sleep. I used to go to Honduras for years to build houses, hand out food and visit hospitals and prisons. Also, attending the men's Bible class and prayer groups at church.

How big of an impact has social media had on your small business?

That impact has been really impressive for lots of new neighbors and all around. I made the front page of the newspaper earlier this year after you (Brittany) posted about my business on Facebook. It was liked and shared many times. This brought in many new customers, and I fixed a lot of shoes.

What does supporting local mean to you?

Frequent local businesses like restaurants. They help grow the economy and it is an opportunity for them to grow.

I guarantee my work. I am an artist, and my canvas is your shoes. Just bring in those shoes!

STEVE JOHN'S APPLIANCE & PARTS
AS TOLD BY STEVE JOHNS

Website: www.stevejohnsappliance.com
Facebook: Steve Johns Appliance

Tell me about your (small) business.

We've been in business since 1971. My brother, Paul Johns, former Smyrna Mayor and Alderman, and I first started off as an auction company called Colonial Discount and Auction. I was fifteen-years old when we first started, and Paul was thirty-three. Two years later, we turned it into an appliance and TV store. We started next door to Omni Hut. In June 1978, we moved into the location we are in now. In 1991, I bought Paul out. I've had the business myself for thirty years.

We are a platinum dealer, and the largest displaying dealer of Speed Queen in the United States. We keep around one hundred and twenty on display at all times. I won't sell any other brand of washers and dryers.

We offer a wide selection of appliances to fit your lifestyle, from washers, dryers, stoves, refrigerators, freezers, dishwashers, microwaves, ovens and more. We carry the top-name brands and offer Smyrna's best selection of brands like: Whirlpool, Speed Queen, Maytag, Amana, and Frigidaire. We also have do-it-yourself appliance parts. Our store is filled with new, used, and some scratch and dent appliances that we mark down. I would say 99% of what we sell is brand new.

We do home delivery and installation. The people that do our service are local qualified electricians and plumbers that have been doing it for thirty years. We are one stop, one shop and one hop.

What inspired you to open an appliance store?

The business evolved over fifty years. We are one of the oldest businesses left on on Lowry Street. It's a great feeling.

Purchasing major appliances such as a washer and dryer for one's home or business is a large investment. What advice would you offer someone when shopping for appliances?

The only washer and dryer I'll sell today is Speed Queen, which has been made in America since 1908. Speed Queens are old school washers and dryers like your Granny had in 1920. They are built to last for twenty-five years. Your big-name washers and dryers typically last two to five years.

A lot of people don't realize that there is not a major price difference between Speed Queen and major washer and dryer brands, even though Speed Queen lasts much longer and has a three to seven-year warranty, whereas big name brands generally have a one-year warranty. The Speed Queen cycle time for both washing and drying clothing is around twenty-seven minutes. Most other brands' cycle time is one hour or more.

You will save a lot of time, as well as money on both your water and electric bills by purchasing Speed Queen. Not to mention, your washer and dryer will last a lot longer. I recommend Speed Queen to all my customers. It's sort of like buying a 1957 Chevrolet. We have people coming in to buy them from all over the region.

Smyrna Spotlights 311

. . .

What is your favorite part about having a small business in Smyrna?

The local community. I'm proud to be a part of the Smyrna community. I've been here sixty-six years and have no plans of slowing down.

How did your childhood in Smyrna shape you?

I was born and raised in Old Jefferson Community. I was the first class to go through Thurman Francis in 1967. We are old school Smyrna.

What makes the experience of shopping for appliances at Steve Johns Appliance so unique and special?

When you come to my store you will get top-notch customer service. As soon as you walk in the door, we will ask- how can we help you, what do you need, why are you here, when can we get it to you? Your local people are smart. They generally can tell you more about the product than anyone else, especially us.

What have been some of your biggest business challenges you have faced and how have you overcome them?

Help. I work 'eight days' a week and I'm only open six.

What has been your biggest business milestone to date that you are most proud of?

Being in business for fifty years.

. . .

What is the biggest lesson you've learned in owning and operating a small business?

The importance of customer service.

Where do you see yourself and your small business 5-10 years from now?

I hope I'm still in business. I've worked all my life. I love working.

In what ways have you seen Smyrna change over the years since your first started your business?

Time changes everything. In the 1950s and 1960s, you went to stores, often via word-of-mouth. You got to know the store owner. Today, people want to order everything online. Online isn't always the best option.

In 1991, I was elected to the Rutherford County Commission when the County only had eighty-eight thousand people. We've come a long way and have grown a lot. I was chairman of Public Safety for eight years. We were responsible for setting up the first SRO Program in the state, which I'm proud of. We built the new jail. We had the take-home car program for the Sheriff's Office. Those were some of my most enjoyable years, listening to the more seasoned politicians after I was newly elected.

How big of an impact has social media had on your small business?

We get good reviews. If they come see me they will have a positive experience. We love when people share our content and leave positive reviews so that others can discover us. We had one bad online review. We have a cat I rescued named Boo Boo. Boo Boo came to me when she was three weeks old. Someone kicked her out. She stays in the store. Now, she's six. Someone said we don't need to have a cat in the store. Boo Boo is very popular among many customers. She's brought us about $50,000.00 additional revenue. She gets anything she wants. Come see us, we'll take care of you.

What does supporting local mean to you?

Supporting other local businesses. Eating at local restaurants and choosing local businesses for services. We are the only local appliance store left in Smyrna.

People look at price, not always service. I may not always give you the lowest price, but I will give you the best service.

Is there anything else you would like people to know about you or your small business?

I appreciate the people that have traded with me over the years. I've had a good life.

CRIMSON SECURITY SERVICE
AS TOLD BY NICK JOHNS AND BRANDON & NIKKI SASSER

Photo courtesy of Angel Pardue Photography

Website: www.crimsonss.com
Facebook: Crimson Security Service, Inc.

Tell me about your (small) business.

Crimson Security Service is a contract security officer firm. Our services include protection for residential and industrial property, corporate security, and more. We are first responder owned and operated and committed to maintaining the highest integrity and offering a superior customer experience.

Crimson Security Service provides customized security guard

services for a wide variety of clients. Some of our security services include HOA and apartment community patrols, industrial and warehouse security, hotels, hospitals, retail complex (mall) security, event venues, corporate office, or any other dedicated security job.

Each of our patrol vehicles is fully lit, lettered and stocked with a first aid kit, traffic vest, rain gear, and dedicated phone for the client.

Our owners have a combined twenty plus years in the security industry, and thirty years in the emergency services field as professional firefighters.

What inspired you to open a private security company?

Working in the security field, we recognized the gap in customer service and employee satisfaction that many other service providers ignore. With a heart for service and genuine initiative to leave things better than we found it, we knew we could close that gap between great customer service and positive employee satisfaction.

What impact, if any, has serving as professional firefighters had on your security business?

It has prepared us both for leadership within the company as well as working in stressful situations. This knowledge is shared in training with our officers to lead to a well-rounded officer for each client.

What is your favorite part about having a small business in Smyrna?

The connections you make turn into an extended family. You always see a familiar face, have someone to bounce your ideas off of and most importantly, you have a network who genuinely wants to see the community as a whole succeed.

. . .

What brought you to Smyrna?

Brandon: I grew up in a small farming community in North Florida. I moved to Tennessee in 1999 to begin my career as a firefighter with the Town of Smyrna. I learned that honesty, dedication, and initiative are the building blocks of any success story.

Nick: I moved to Smyrna when I was five. I grew up in a neighborhood with a ton of friends that played sports sunup to sundown. This is how my love of sports was created. My father was a firefighter in Smyrna. I was always proud to say he was a firefighter. This is what led me to my career as a firefighter in Smyrna as well.

Together we have brought all our lessons learned to build a company that truly seeks to serve our clients and employees with the utmost integrity and dedication.

What are some of your top security tips the everyday citizen can adopt when it comes to home security?

Communication with fellow neighbors is one of the best deterrents. When the neighborhood knows what is and isn't supposed to happen, criminal activity will be deterred.

What about when performing mundane tasks such as safe shopping or going to the ATM?

Take ten seconds to look around and gather your surroundings and details of the situation. Make mental notes of individuals and vehicles as well as any dangerous obstacles. Always make eye contact with someone walking towards you. This little act will let them know you are not distracted and will not be an easy target. If you hear someone or something behind you, turn around and look at them. Again, simply recognizing your surroundings is the best way to stay safe. If you are uncomfortable, find help.

·   ·   ·

In 2019, Crimson Security Service provided security for the Blue Angels and The Great Tennessee Airshow, and again in 2021 for the Airshow and the U.S. Air Force Thunderbirds. What were these experiences like?

Successfully serving the Airshow network and the Smyrna/Rutherford County Airport Authority was a rewarding experience. Both in the business sense by leading to new clients due to the visibility of our officers at the event, but also in serving our local community.

Crimson Security Service was presented the Employer Support of the Guard and Reserve Award from the US Secretary of Defense as a Patriotic Employer, which is the highest recognition given by the Department of Defense to employers for their outstanding support of National Guard and Reserve employees. How significant was receiving this award?

We are honored to employ members of our armed services as well as first responders. Thirty to forty percent of our employees are military or first responders (firefighters, police and EMTs). Our employees' dedication in service to both their country and our company is priceless.

How have you grown your small business from an idea to where it is now?

Nick: I started working security as a part-time job secondary to my career as a firefighter. The structure and attention to detail the fire service provided me led us to believe we could start our own successful security company. We have always taken pride in doing things the right way and not cutting any corners. I feel our level of professionalism and attention to detail has driven our success higher than we ever imagined.

What is the biggest lesson you've learned in owning and operating a small business?

Brandon: Not everyone is out to see you succeed. But only you can walk the path to success.

Are there any favorite mantras you live your life by?

"Wrinkles are engraved smiles from all the happy times to see you through the tough times." "He who waters shall be watered."

What are your daily habits or systems that you live by that have set you and your small business up for success?

Nick: I am a firm believer in prayer and starting and ending my day with this. We believe in a structured system and holding people accountable.

What advice would you give to someone wanting to pursue a career similar to yours?

Nick: The fire service and security industry are very similar in regards to chain of command and structure. Training and education are vital and are an ongoing thing throughout your career.

What has been the best piece of business advice you have ever received?

Nick: My dad told me when I was a young guy just getting started to never turn down an opportunity when it's in front of me. There have been many times that I have accepted an opportunity when others passed them up. I believe continued education is vital to growing your success.

What 1-3 books have impacted your life the most and why?

Nick: *Quiet Strength* by Tony Dungy and *Pride and Ownership* by Rick Lasky

Who has been the most influential person or mentor to you during your entrepreneurial journey and why?

Nick: I don't believe I have one single person that has influenced me throughout my journey. I have been blessed to be around several great leaders that I have aspired to mirror in my own life. I would say that I try to live my life and make my decisions on what God has set forth for me to follow.

What has been your biggest business milestone to date that you are most proud of?

Brandon: Signing our first government contract in 2019. Followed by surviving and actually growing during the pandemic.

What have been some of your biggest business challenges you have faced and how have you overcome them?

Competing with stereotypes of security officers has been a struggle. Most think of the old man in the bank sleeping or Paul Blart-Mall Cop. Crimson focuses on training to ensure our officers are vigilant, effective, and still approachable.

What do you enjoy doing in your spare time?

Crimson enjoys working in the community. Whether it is food drives for Nourish Food Bank, helping with the Smyrna Court Clerk's

Office 'Clerks for Coats' Coat Drive, Rotary Fish Fry, Depot Days or Simply Smyrna. This is our hometown, and we know that you have to be involved in order to make a difference.

Brandon: I also enjoy time hiking, camping and traveling with my family.

Nick: Golf, camping, and watching my children play sports.

Crimson Security Service has won several prestigious awards voted on by the community, including a Firefly for WGNS Good Neighbor of the Year. Where do you see yourself and your small business 5-10 years from now?

Crimson has a five-year goal of serving clients in at least two different states and a ten-year goal of five or more states.

What does supporting local mean to you?

Live where you sleep. Shopping and eating at the locally owned businesses where you woke up that day. Even if you are out of town, look up that town's local businesses and support them. Local business owners have a vested interest in their community surviving. If they see a need and they have support, they will fill that need. Those are the businesses that will be there in the hard times to support their neighbors and fellow business professionals.

We've loved being a part of your journey. What's coming next that we can be a part of to support you?

We have partnered with IdentoGO to facilitate background and fingerprinting for TBI and FBI.

FAMILY AND COSMETIC DENTISTRY OF SMYRNA
AS TOLD BY DR. STAN RICHARDSON

Website: www.smyrnasmiles.com
Facebook: Smyrna Smiles

Tell me about your (small) business.

Our practice is family dentistry. For over thirty years, we have seen patients from four to ninety-nine years old and have been privileged to have served several generations. Most of the staff have been here around twenty years. We offer everything from esthetic restorations, fillings, teeth whitening, porcelain crowns, dentures, bridges, veneers, oral surgery, dental implants, and gum treatment. We enjoy improving smiles and we have dental services to meet just about everyone's needs.

. . .

What is your favorite part about having a small business in Smyrna?

It has been a blessing to have been able to serve and be trusted by so many people in this area for their dental needs. My staff and I feel like many of our patients have become like family. We have been invited to family events, and unfortunately, attended many funerals as well over the years.

What inspired you to become a dentist?

My interest has always been in medicine and serving others. When I was in my last year of college, I met my father's dentist and was impressed with the modern practice he operated versus the old traditional dental practices I was familiar with. I was hooked.

What brought you to Smyrna?

I grew up mostly in Hickman County. When I first arrived in 1989, the people were so friendly, and it immediately felt like home.

What's the first thing you do every morning to start your day on the right foot?

I try to kiss my wife and tell her I love her and have a great day! Then, when I arrive in the parking lot, I pray for all who will enter the building that day. God has been good!

What are you most excited about for your small business?

We continue to grow and expand our services as well as continue to gain great staff.

Smyrna Spotlights

. . .

What is the biggest lesson you've learned in owning and operating a small business?

Treat people well and fairly, and not only will you grow, but you will sleep well at night. Also, you can't be successful by yourself. It takes a team.

Are there any favorite mantras you live your life by?

Every day you are given is a blessing!

What has been your biggest business milestone to date that you are most proud of?

We have taken on another new dentist, Dr. Taylor Reeves, who is local to this area.

What advice would you give to someone wanting to pursue a career similar to yours?

Follow your passion and don't let others steer from it!

What 1-3 books have impacted your life the most and why?

The Bible and *How to Win Friends and Influence People* by Dale Carnegie

How has failure or apparent failure set you up for future success?

They say you learn the most from your failures. My best learning situation was not heeding the wise words of Ronald Reagan who said, "Trust, but verify."

. . .

What do you enjoy doing in your spare time?

I enjoy hunting and some farming. We have supported the Smyrna Rotary Club Fish Fry for nineteen years and feel it does so many amazing things. We enjoy getting to meet new people at Depot Days.

What have been some of your biggest business challenges you have faced and how have you overcome them?

The biggest challenge has been making sure we got the best and brightest as staff. We have been blessed to get a super staff which took a disciplined hiring system approach that involved the whole office.

Where do you see yourself and your small business 5-10 years from now?

We continue to grow exponentially while increasing our range of modern dental services.

How big of an impact has fans/followers posting about your small business on social media had on your small business?

We always appreciate positive reviews so potential patients can find us!!

What does supporting local mean to you?

We enjoy the benefits of being a small community. It's great to be able to serve friends and business family.

SMYRNA PRINTING & DESIGN
AS TOLD BY RICHARD MINOR AND MIKE MITCHELL

Website: www.smyrnaprinting.com

Tell me about your (small) business.

We started in 1981. We do commercial offset printing. Our primary focus is basic items such as letterhead, envelopes, business cards, postcards, and business forms. We incorporate some digital new printing, but most of our work is basic offset typography, like what we call old school type printing. We accommodate some of the newer digital formats. This is a newer modernized full color process.

We are actually still capable of printing the way it was done fifty years ago. We have equipment that old. Everything is done by hand and wrapped with butcher paper. It's old school and classic. Nothing like modern printing. We have binder tables, and one of our presses is a twenty-two-inch Harris Press, which is a big offset press that prints 17 x 22 inch paper.

We can still shoot film. We also do typesetting layout artwork, which is essentially the composition of text by means of arranging physical or digital type used to create a drawing or paste up of a whole page.

We liken ourselves to the offset version of Hatch Show Print. They print old style letter press and woodblock letterpress. The more modern full color process used to be super expensive to have full color process negatives made, now it is digitized and it has become very affordable. Richard does the design and layout, then outsources it. We can produce the full color process with the modern look.

As far as off-set negatives, it's a different kind of photography. Someone could bring a picture in, and we could screen that and edit a piece of printing. It's not an exact reproduction. It's a reproduction using printing techniques. A primary example of this is photographs in the newspaper. It's not the kind of photograph you would frame and put on your wall to use as artwork, but it can be reproduced in volume that way. People can bring in old newspaper articles and we can repurpose them for them to frame and hang on the wall.

We have industrial accounts that are manufacturers all the way down to the guy that says, "I want to go into business for myself." He may bring his idea in on a napkin.

We found a niche working with small businesses, the Town of

Smyrna and the City of La Vergne. They have been very supportive over the years.

What inspired you to start a printing and design business?

Richard: When I first opened, I had another partner. Mike came in after three years and bought the other partner out. We've been partners ever since.

Mike: Richard and Tom Hutton were the original partners. Those guys took the leap of faith to start a printing business, but neither one of them were printers. I came down here and looked around. I realized right away when I met Richard that he had great artistic talent. He is a fine artist, a commercial artist, and a great layout person. He's done plenty of design work for local businesses. I knew the business was a gold mine. I tend to be the technical person leaning towards the manufacturing side and keeping the presses running. Richard does the typesetting and layout and builds a great rapport with customers. I count him as my best friend. It's hard to be in a partnership sometimes. We've had great luck with it, and I think very highly of his artistic abilities. We've made it work all these years.

I'm an old musician. It was either feast or famine for me. My father was a commercial artist at Triangle Printing Company in Nashville for years. I worked at Triangle for about ten years. My dad taught me a lot about printing. I had a great friend  who was an equipment dealer that knew Tom and Richard. He told me to go to Smyrna to meet those guys. I had a dream to get back to my hometown of Smyrna. I came out and met them and liked both immediately.

. . .

Richard: I was at the Department of Education for six years at a media center. They prepped information for printing, dissemination through media like slide presentations for state specialists and the Department of Education to take to various schools.

A new administration came in and they were looking for ways to legally 'unload' people. Our situation was decided for us. I was at the point and age to either go back to doing what I was doing and work for someone else, or, take a leap and start something for myself. I figured I was young enough to try. If I failed, I could always go back to doing something else. I took the leap and it worked out. I had to build this business over time.

How did your childhood in Smyrna shape you?

Mike: My family has been in Smyrna for six generations. I loved growing up here. I graduated from Smyrna High in 1968. I love Smyrna, and didn't want to leave.

What is your favorite part about having a small business in Smyrna?

We love the small-town atmosphere. We are our own bosses. We live here, we are in a small town, we don't have a long commute, and it's laid back. We'll see customers and classmates around town, which is always fun. Sometimes we don't always recognize a customer around town, but the moment they walk in our shop, we know their name immediately.

We love that Rotary tells the membership to support the local businesses. Rotary is very loyal and sends their people to us. They do a great job carrying the torch for a lot of these community causes. We like pitching in, but Rotary does all the heavy lifting.

How has Smyrna and the small business landscape changed since you first started in 1981?

Mike: Richard and Tom bought the building from former Smyrna Mayor Sam Ridley. We have watched the Train Depot develop, and we've seen businesses move in over the years.

We had a great relationship with Sam Coleman and Rusty Griffin at Regal Furniture next door when they were our neighbors years ago. We carried on, we were just a bunch of young guys. We had Halloween parties and had a lot of fun. We even had get-togethers to watch the Smyrna Christmas parade from our front lobby.

As far as history of the building, Ginny Olerud William's (Gil's Ace Hardware) dad put in this storefront back in the 1950s. At the time it was very modern. He put his grocery store in here. The old school Smyrna people are getting few and far between.

What have been some of your biggest business challenges you have faced and how have you overcome them?

These online services where people can order business cards has really put a lick on us and other locally owned (printing) businesses. We always say, "The blacksmith didn't do anything wrong, someone else just invented the car," so he wasn't shoeing any horses.

Technology has disrupted retail in general. Sometimes, we wish people would go back to a nostalgic mood and do things like in the old days. For example, coming into a brick and mortar print shop where you could talk to someone and get a design that was made on fifty-year-old equipment that looks better than digital.

What are some of the biggest lessons you've learned in owning a small business?

Cash flow is like a roller coaster. You can't let it make you nervous. There are ups and downs, and peaks and valleys. Small businesses are the first to feel any economic impact We know people that work in Nashville with bigger printers with equipment as big as our entire work room. When a recession hits, they start letting people go. Some of those presses cost over a million dollars. We were able to stick it out through the hard times and are proud of that part of our history.

If we'd had any debt during the pandemic or the great snow week (February 2021) where everything was shut down, we would have been in trouble. We put a sign on the front door saying we were still printing during the pandemic. We let all our industrial accounts know, but they were all shut down and not printing.

What has been your biggest business milestone to date that you are most proud of?

Being in business for forty years and counting.

What makes the experience of designing print jobs at Smyrna Printing & Design so unique and special?

Everything we do is custom-made for clients. They get a lot of advice that's backed with knowledge of design and the printing business. You get to come inside a storefront and talk to a real person. We have customers that come in with their sketched-out designs and ask us what they should name their business. You won't get that type of customer service or attention from an online retailer.

A lot of people don't understand the difference between traditional offset and digital. We can generally spot digital printing that is low quality as opposed to our offset. Our printing will be finer, sharper, nicer.

What does supporting local mean to you?

It means supporting other local businesses. I go down to Lube-Shop to get my oil changed, H.G. Cole has been here forever.

We have a lot of transplants moving here to save on taxes, and they oftentimes only look at price. They may not have the same hometown feeling and pride we have. They just moved in and are going to go to the big box store and the small businesses may get shoved to the side. Times have changed. Sometimes, people go online to various printing services and look at the price for the volume. We have a hard time competing when people make decisions that are purely price conscious.

We've seen people order their printing online then bring their business cards to us. They aren't happy and tell us they wish they came to us first.

You can go look at a public bulletin board and you will see fifteen business cards that came from a major online retailer that all have the same 'cookie-cutter' artwork. We do custom artwork for every customer. We don't use pre-designed templates.

We pay local taxes. That money circles back into the community and we donate to many local charities.

People tell us, "I was buying my printing somewhere else, but Smyrna Printing & Design sponsors my son's team, so I'm going to get my printing done here." We love when people tell us that. Your online retailers often don't do this. Supporting local is so important. Your local businesses are tied back to the community.

The Town of Smyrna has been very loyal to us. Years ago, Town Manager Harry Gill instructed the departments to use us for printing since we are local. That meant a lot.

How big of an impact has social media had on your small business?

We've gotten more business through word-of-mouth and referrals. We've never made a sales call in our over forty years of business. There has been loyalty from old Smyrna.

. . .

What do you enjoy doing in your spare time?

Mike: I collect antique motorcycles, radio control boats and airplanes.

We are both avid fishermen and even tournament fished for years at the lake. We both have boats and enjoy water skiing.

We love supporting Rotary and the Fish Fry. We aren't in Rotary, but we've supported them for nineteen years. We've supported the YMCA, the Smyrna Public Library, and Senior Activity Center, we've been donating printing for years. We don't want anything in return. We have tried to be active in the community over the last forty years. We have stacks of plaques that have been given to us. We've had a good run.

Is there anything else you would like people to know about you or your small business?

We are 1 N. Lowry, the epicenter of Smyrna. If you put Smyrna, TN into a GPS, it will take you to our building in downtown Smyrna.

ZACH BOHANNON, AUTHOR
AS TOLD BY ZACH BOHANNON

What inspired you to become an author?

I skipped out on college and spent most my twenties trying to make it as a drummer in a heavy metal band. Since I was a kid, I'd always thought about writing. I wrote lyrics for one band I was in, and they were always very story-driven. I thought about writing stories then and tried to, but never finished anything. What's funny is that I was a late bloomer to reading. I enjoyed it when I was a child, but when I got into music in my early teens, my desire to read faded.

But I became an avid reader when I was around twenty-seven, which also was around the time my aspiring music career was winding down. Fast forward to 2014, and I finally sat down to write something, and finished my first novel which became *Empty Bodies*.

You recently celebrated your five-year anniversary as a full-time author publishing thirty-three books to date. What inspired you to quit your day job to transition into being a full-time career author? What advice would you give to aspiring authors or creatives wanting to take the leap?

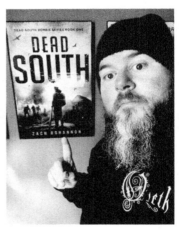

It's probably the scariest thing I've ever done! It took my friend Joanna Penn telling me after a few drinks at a bar in New Orleans that I need to quit being scared and just take the leap. Joanna has been doing this full-time for over a decade and has the most popular podcast for self-publishing (The Creative Penn) so her words carried a lot of weight. I feel like, as with so many things in life, we often wait for that "perfect" time to do things. But there's no such thing, and if you wait around for that, then you're going to be stuck in an endless loop. Few people who do tremendous things do so without risk and discomfort. The truth is that I had put myself in a great financial position and had enough income coming in from the books to quit, and I should've quit sooner. Having a track record of writing and publishing for a couple of years as a side hustle and seeing what I could make, and more importantly, not having any debt made the jump a lot easier. But the security I had, and especially health insurance, kept me at my old job.

It's possible, but difficult, to make a living doing this. You can also do it as a hobby or side hustle and make decent money if you get lucky without making it your full-time gig. I had circumstances that made it imperative for me to go full-time, but that might not be the case for everybody.

In 2017, you collaborated with author-publisher and podcast host J. Thorn to launch Authors on a Train, a four-day creative writing immersion that starts on an Amtrak where you lead a select group of authors through various writing workshops and seminars and you ultimately collaborate to publish an anthology all while exploring a new city. What inspired you to start Authors on a Train?

Because J. hates flying, he takes Amtrak every chance he gets. In 2017, he made an offhand comment on Twitter about how he'd written most of a novel on a train and would love to do that with other authors. Our friend and fantasy and science fiction author, Lindsay Buroker, commented and said she'd love to do that. So, a couple of DMs later, J. came to me with the idea of taking a train from Chicago to New Orleans and staying there a week and writing an entire book with Lindsay, and also Joanna Penn. It seemed crazy, but it was the type of opportunity I couldn't say no to. I'm glad I didn't because that trip changed my life. But near the end of that week, J. and I were sitting at a restaurant and came up with the idea of repeating the experience we had but by bringing a larger group of authors with us and making it a paid experience.

Since then, we have taken two groups from Chicago to New Orleans, and in January 2020, we did an Authors on a Train from Los Angeles to San Francisco. Additionally, we do events we call world building weekends which are one-of-a-kind experiences, each taking place in unique cities. We have done those in Pittsburgh, Cleveland, Seattle, New Orleans, and Salem, Massachusetts, each with their own unique genre and theme attached. Not only have these events given me the opportunity to travel the country and hang out with other amazing creatives, but they have also created a lucrative revenue stream for me. And especially as a full-time creative where royalties can go up and down, it's essential to have multiple sources of income.

What role does podcasting play in your business, and what have you learned from recording over three hundred podcast episodes?

I love podcasting! On the nonfiction side of my business, it plays a major role. Over one hundred episodes of The Career Author Podcast, J. and I built an amazing community, many of whom we have had the joy of not only meeting at our various events and retreats, but also becoming friends with.

We are now doing the same with Writers, Ink. (along with international bestseller J.D. Barker) while also getting to talk to some of the biggest names in literature, from Seth Godin to Matthew McConaughey to James Patterson. And considering the running gag is that J. starts a new podcast every week (which isn't far from true) you never know what the future might hold for me and podcasting!

How did publishing your first book change your writing process?

I feel like my process changes a little bit with each book. It has certainly evolved since writing that first novel. I learned so much publishing that first book. I got really lucky with how well my books began selling from the beginning, but made some mistakes along the way as well. Of course, we all make mistakes, especially as entrepreneurs. But you have to learn from those mistakes and iterate your process. I would also say it's common to view and treat your first book like a baby. It's very precious, but the further along you get and the more you publish, the more each book just becomes a product. Don't get me wrong, it's still my art, but I don't treat it so dearly. That allows me to keep moving forward and to make less emotional business decisions in regard to marketing and branding those titles.

What role does community play in your creative process and industry?

Community is huge, especially in the nonfiction part of my business. Through our podcast and events, J. and I have built a loyal and thriving community, who all help each other. Now, most of that community is online and involves people from all over the world. But I'd love to see the writing community grow more on a local level here in Smyrna.

How big of an impact has social media had on your business?

For authors, word-of-mouth is by far the biggest generator of sales and exposure. Whether it's posting about an author's book on social media or telling the co-worker next to you about the great book you're reading, no advertising or marketing can trump word-of-mouth. Reviews on whatever retailer's website you bought the book are very helpful, too!

What does supporting local mean to you?

It's community. It means support. It means friendship. I feel a stronger bond with the business owners when I shop local, and I know I'm helping somebody out who has a similar mindset to myself in most cases. I shop local as much as possible. Local businesses are what make your community special.

Why go to some coffee shop you can visit on any street corner in the country when you can get a better tasting brew at Bella Vista, and you're being served by the owner herself? Or, why go through a drive-thru and grab an ice cream when you can take your son or daughter to Janarty's and give them a real experience, and create memories they'll cherish when they're older? Support local. Support Smyrna.

Are there any other ways people can support your small business?

If you like reading post-apocalyptic science fiction/horror, then check out one of my books. Also, if you're an aspiring writer, have a look at *Three Story Method: Foundations of Fiction*, or listen to The Career Author and Writers, Ink. Podcast on your favorite podcast app.

We've loved being a part of your journey. What's coming next that we can be a part of to support you?

More books. More author events. I could possibly get more involved locally in the future, so keep an eye out! And hey, hopefully there is a movie of one of my books one day, or I get to write a major video game like I dream of! But most of all, just read! Support the library and read more books!

To support Zach and learn more, visit:

www.zachbohannon.com
www.writersinkpodcast.com

HOW TO SUPPORT LOCAL

AS TOLD BY BRITTANY SCARLETT STEVENS

Budget for Local. Set aside a small amount of your budget each month for local shopping. The possibilities for how to specifically support local businesses are endless, depending upon your lifestyle —simply read over these Spotlights to see how you can support these businesses by engaging with their respective niches. For example, instead of purchasing hair products and tools online or at a major retailer, perhaps consider purchasing these items at your local hair salon. Maybe you have a birthday, wedding, or life milestone to celebrate and need a cake or catering. Look no further than one of our local caterers. Sure, it may be slightly more expensive than purchasing a basic sheet cake from a chain store, but you'll be supporting a local business that's in turn recycling revenue back into our local economy and community. Or, next time you need to restock on cleaning supplies, lightbulbs, tools, or DIY projects, consider your local hardware shop that already gives so much back to the community.

Support Local for Services. Choosing local service providers is a surefire way to support the shop-local movement, whether it be for personal, professional, health, home, or automotive services. Smyrna certainly has no shortage of high-quality service providers in nearly all industries. For example, we have local legal, accounting, automotive, cleaning, home, healthcare (including local pharmacies!), business and professional services...and the list goes on! For a directory of some of the local service providers in Smyrna, please be sure to check out the business directory at simatn.org.

Bank Locally. Another way to support the local economy and keep more money here at home is to bank locally. There are plenty of perks to using local banks. Often, local banks offer lower rates and fees compared to larger banks. Also, local banks generally have stellar customer service. As an added bonus, Smyrna's local banks often sponsor local nonprofits and events. *Cha-Ching.*

Shop Local for the Holidays and Other Special Occasions. Local gifts feel even more special and sentimental when they come from your hometown. As you can see from these Spotlights, we have some unique local gift options for everyone on your list—and for all occasions!

One way to support local businesses and spread a little cheer during the holiday season is to participate in Small Business Saturday. This is an annual event that takes place the Saturday after Thanksgiving, encouraging people to start their Christmas shopping at their favorite local businesses. Small Business Saturday is a great way to kick off the holiday season and support our local businesses, but part of the point of this  book is to remember that we must keep the momentum going year-round in order for our small businesses to not just survive, but thrive.

. . .

Our Farmers Market. The Smyrna Depot Farmers Market is a community-supported event (hosted by Carpe Artista) where local farmers, small businesses, and local artisans come together to sell goods directly to consumers at the Train Depot. The Farmers Market takes place on Saturdays from May through September. There are several major benefits to shopping at the Farmers Market. Not only is locally grown produce more fresh since it's picked at its peak ripeness, it's also generally safer to consume, as local farmers often use fewer pesticides and other chemicals when compared to larger producers. Additionally, it's more eco-friendly to shop local at the Farmers Market because doing so drastically reduces costs associated with food transportation across the country. In the end, you can help a small business as you stock up on your groceries! For more information, you can visit Carpeartista.com or the Smyrna Depot Farmers Market Facebook page.

Leave Online Reviews and Share Your Experiences on Social Media.

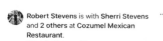

As you can see from the stories of many of the business owners throughout this book, online reviews and sharing of their social media posts has a tremendous impact on their businesses' digital reach and distribution, and helps potential customers discover them. So, after you shop, remember to review and share!

ACKNOWLEDGMENTS

What an honor it has been to publish this book. I want to begin by thanking our amazing business owners for believing in this project, and also for their willingness to share their stories. This is *our* book. *We did this together.* I hope you are just as proud as I am. Thank you for taking the time to answer my questions. Some were tough, some provoked deep thought and raw introspection, some brought back wonderful memories, and indeed, some were time-consuming. Thanks to you, we now have these incredible stories to preserve and pass down for generations to come.

As I stated in the Introduction, my wish is that these Spotlights educate and inspire each of us to be more intentional with our spending habits and to support our local businesses as much as possible, all in order to preserve our small (but growing!) town's uniqueness. This is a movement, and we are just getting started.

I would also like to thank my dear friend, mentor, and fellow author, Zach Bohannon (p. 333), for his guidance throughout this amazing journey. I first met Zach at the Bella Vista Coffee Shop in November of 2020. He was writing his thirty-second book, and I couldn't believe I'd met a top-100 Amazon bestselling author and respected podcaster in my own hometown! We became instant friends after sharing a deep love for books and reading. Zach was one of my biggest cheerleaders from day one, and he pushed me to pursue publishing this book after listening to me share my ideas. Zach helped me tremendously and answered so many questions regarding the self-publishing process. He shared his contacts in the publishing industry and his immense wisdom. To put it simply, Zach believed in this project from the beginning, and he believed in me. This would not have been possible without Zach. Thank you for everything, Zach. On a side note, I cannot recommend his book *Three Story Method* enough.

Thank you to Mayor Mary Esther Reed for your support and willingness to write the Foreword.

Thank you to Barbara Potter of Barbara Potter Photography for some of the beautiful imagery featured throughout this book, including all author photos, and for your love, dedication and enthusiasm for local creatives. "Hehehe."

Thank you to Marty Luffman for always sharing your love of local history and interesting stories of 'old Smyrna', as well as engaging some of the local legacies to make sure their stories could be shared.

They say to save the best for last, so lastly, I'd like to thank my wonderful family for their support and encouragement. Our conversations around the family dinner table have often surrounded this project. The idea behind *Smyrna Spotlights* came to me in January of 2021, and I began working on this book during the week of the great 'Snowpocalypse' that February while I was snowed in at my house. From that moment on, this book wasn't just at the center of my life, but theirs, as well.

On April 8, 2021, my family and I were blindsided with the tragic news that our beloved Granny had a massive brain tumor and only three to six months to live. I often worked on this book in various health care facilities while sitting with Granny when she'd dozed off. Granny was my book buddy and a voracious reader like me. She loved my idea for *Smyrna Spotlights*. Sadly, Granny left us for Heaven on June 21, 2021, surrounded by family who loved her dearly.

A little over two weeks later, tragedy struck again. Our sweet little thirteen-year-old family rescue Yorkie, Baby, very suddenly and unexpectedly left us to cross over the Rainbow Bridge for Heaven on July 10, 2021. We were heartbroken, and miss our little girl so much.

Even though this was a stressful and devastating time, this book gave me something meaningful to focus my attention towards. In some ways, *Smyrna Spotlights* gave me life in the inevitable and tragic face of death. I was reminded over and over again about the challenges these small business owners have had to overcome on a regular basis, and I knew that if, like them, I could just keep persevering and pushing forward, things would all work out in the end. This lesson seems quite fitting because that is what Granny used to always tell me. I'd like to think she (and, of course, Baby) would have been proud. At least, I certainly hope so.

Thank you again, very kindly. #SupportLocal

With appreciation, and every good wish,

Brittany Scarlett Stevens

ABOUT THE AUTHOR

Brittany Scarlett Stevens is a public official and an attorney. Her writing has landed her on national stages as a keynote speaker presenting on legal topics for small business owners including: Federal Trade Commission Guidelines, contract law, website terms of service, and data privacy. Brittany is passionate about supporting and educating small business owners and watching them succeed, which is why she wanted to shift her focus back to her hometown of Smyrna.

For more information visit www.brittanyscarlettwrites.com.

instagram.com/brittanyscarlett

Made in the USA
Monee, IL
28 September 2021